Praise for *Graduate Debt Free*

"*Graduate Debt Free* is a must-read for college-bound high school students and their parents. Over the past 20 years, as the owner of a private College Counseling and Educational Consulting firm, I have advised thousands of high school students on the sensitive issue of financing college. Shutler's book answers hard questions about college costs that people want and need to know but are often afraid to ask. I wholeheartedly recommend it for families diving into both the college application process and the daunting task of determining how to pay for their child's college years."

—**Casey Gendason**, College Guidance Counselor, Dallas, TX

"Students who are willing to chart their own path should put *Graduate Debt Free* at the top of their summer reading list. I've used many of the ideas discussed in the book since graduating from high school in 2018 and community college in 2020. My parents didn't have a lot of money, so I have paid my own college costs by alternating between studying full time at Florida State University and working full time. Shutler's recommendation of community college plus state university worked well for me. It allowed me to gain real-life work experience while building connections for my future career. This route took me a little longer, but I am now on track to finish my bachelor's degree in accounting next year without any debt. Get this book and make a plan to graduate without a boatload of debt."

—**O'Neil Finley**, Florida State University student, Tallahassee, FL

"For years I've searched for a guide to help students and their parents figure out how to finance a college education without sinking into debt. *Graduate Debt Free: Escaping the Student Loan Matrix* is exactly the guide I've been looking for. By first identifying the 12 common assumptions about college that form a "matrix" in people's minds and then exposing the factual weaknesses in those assumptions, Shutler has made a genuine contribution to both the college selection process and the college financing discussion that both high schoolers and their parents can relate to. This book is an absolute must-read for high school students who aspire to become college educated while minimizing debt."

—**Veronica Guzman Pulido**, Director of College Counseling,
St. Mark's School of Texas

"Every once in a while, a book reframes the discussion in a new light. *Graduate Debt Free* reframes the discussion of student debt in the same way Malcolm Gladwell's books reframe the discussion of social psychology. Applying a business owner's practicality, a lawyer's insight, and a parent's sensitivity, Shutler deconstructs college finance decisions to help students attain a degree without crushing debt. As a person who accelerated student loan payments to retire my graduate debt in eight years, I wish I'd had this book back then to help me avoid that eight-year suspension of normal life experiences. Don't read this book—drink it. Uncover the reasons behind student debt and protect yourself from it."

—**AmiLynne Carroll**, MPA, Denver, CO, author of
Conversations of Consequence: Lessons from the Still Small Voice

"As a parent with two daughters in high school and a son not far behind, I was thrilled to read *Graduate Debt Free: Escaping the Student Loan Matrix.* Before reading it, I had been deeply concerned about college debt and its impact on my children's futures. After reading it, my thinking has been rearranged about the entire college process. It presents a strong argument for students working backwards in the college selection process by first selecting their college major and then identifying the college that can deliver that major without a lot of debt. My children now have a summer reading assignment that will help them think through strategies to avoid college debt. *Graduate Debt Free* is an education in itself."

—**Thomas Browning**, PhD, Co-Founder and former COO of Foot Cardigan, Dallas, TX

"*Graduate Debt Free: Escaping the Student Loan Matrix* is essential reading for parents and their high school age students. Comprehensive, intelligent, reader-friendly, and thoroughly abreast of the times, it unveils surprising facts behind widely held misconceptions about college. At a time when the discussion of every national-level issue seems to be hyper-politicized, Shutler's well-researched book is refreshingly apolitical. A whole world of college guidance counselors and community college administrators will welcome the book as a trusted resource for themselves and their students. Read it with your college-bound high schoolers and watch old assumptions evaporate."

—**Eric Georgatos**, JD, Venture Capital/Startup Investor, Celina, TX

"After 20 years of counseling high school students and their parents in the college selection process, I found Shutler's book compelling. *Graduate Debt Free: Escaping the Student Loan Matrix* is a comprehensive guide to obtaining a fine education while avoiding burdensome student debt. With a lawyer's precision and attention to detail, Shutler explains the bewildering array of issues that confront 17-year-olds and their parents when they apply for college. His research is thorough: he buttresses his arguments with copious footnotes. This book will help facilitate the sometimes-difficult discussion between high school students and their parents about how to pay for college. This book is now mandatory reading for all my clients. Read it and discover a whole new outlook on college."

—**Rebecca Larkin**, EdD, College Guidance Counsellor, Greenville, TX

"As a financial planning practitioner with over 34 years' experience, I have seen the devastating burden of student debt on people and how it can derail their financial success. *Graduate Debt Free: Escaping the Student Loan Matrix* should be read by all high school students and their parents before their first college visit. Shutler debunks the myth that everyone needs a college education in order to be financially secure. Read this book as your defense against the groupthink that encourages people to blindly follow like lemmings into the crippling abyss of debt."

—**Brian M. Ursu**, CFP, President, Intentional Wealth Advisors, LLC, and author of *NOW WHAT? A Practical Guide to Figuring Out Your Financial Future*

"I've followed Dave Shutler's career since we were US Air Force ROTC cadets together at Duke. After he retired from the Air Force, I watched him grow a construction business from start-up to entrepreneurial success and launch several other ventures. With everything on his plate, I was curious why he would spend several years researching and writing this book, mostly at night. Get a copy of *Graduate Debt Free* and read it to find out the captivating answer. On every page you'll find useful tools to unmask the reality behind student debt and to help students graduate from college without a huge debt burden."

—**Bruce Luehrs**, MBA, Managing Partner, Rittenhouse Ventures, Philadelphia, PA

"*Graduate Debt Free* helped my high school age son make a workable plan to pay for college rather than relying on his prowess in sports to land an athletic scholarship. It laid out information on colleges in a simple and clear way, allowing our family to have a realistic conversation about ways to complete college without overwhelming debt. Thank you forever for researching and writing this guide to life after high school!"

—**Becky Neale**, Parent of High School Athlete, St Louis, MO

"As a professor of English at a private university, I've taught hundreds of incoming freshmen from all socioeconomic backgrounds. They need this book! *Graduate Debt Free* fills a gap in the college finance literature by identifying 12 faulty assumptions that can lead students and their parents into college debt. Shutler deconstructs the assumptions in a way that an English professor—and her students—can truly appreciate! This book should be required reading for aspiring (and current) college students. Grab a copy and let it recalibrate your thinking about the problem of student debt."

—**Heidi Barker**, MA, English Professor, BYU-Idaho, Rexburg, Idaho

"I have 16- and 17-year-old children thinking about college, so *Graduate Debt Free* is a very relevant topic for my family. The book challenges the status quo in a thorough and thought-provoking manner, giving insights and practical advice. My high schoolers enjoyed reading it because it addresses the choices they have to make head on and walks them through the thought process to help them reach their own conclusions. As a parent I found the detailed footnotes helpful to explain the legal background and the reasoning behind education policies. I highly recommend this book, especially for parents and students who are puzzling over the college decision."

—**Matthew Schwerin**, Advanced Medical Support Assistant, Dallas, TX

"As a high school student, I found the discussion of education à la carte in *Graduate Debt Free* very interesting. It showed how students can take advantage of the competitive pay at fast food restaurants as well as earn partial scholarships. I also liked the idea that students can pay for college by working at family dine-in restaurants. Besides getting inexpensive meals, they can make money through tips, learn how to give quality service, develop social skills with customers, and qualify for scholarships. The book gives a deeper view of college than just academic studies and shows a path for students to minimize college debt."

—**Kavish Patel**, Hebron High School Student, Lewisville, TX

"As the parent of elementary-school children, I have dual concerns always looming in the back of my mind: finding the right college for them and figuring out how to pay for it. Shutler's book, *Graduate Debt Free*, put my mind at ease by addressing the prevailing wisdom about college debt and debunking the myths that surround it with clear data and cogent analysis. I recommend this book to any parent looking for a more thoughtful and informed path forward for their children."

—**Jennifer Rowe**, MPA, Rowe and Company, Steamboat Springs, CO

"As a former Principal in California Public Schools, I've observed that students considering college after high school often feel overwhelmed. This book, *Graduate Debt Free*, will allay their concerns. Each chapter shines a light on specific assumptions that contribute to that feeling and then challenges those assumptions with factual analysis to help students address their concerns. If you decide to go to college, Shutler's book is your new best friend. It will help you deal with college anxiety and reach the goal of graduating debt free."

—**Robert G. Storm**, MA, former Principal,
California Public Schools, Wylie, Texas

"I am a homeschooling mom with a daughter in middle school and a son in high school. I have committed the past 10 years to my children's education. I want them to continue with college, but I don't want them to be saddled with debt. Shutler's book *Graduate Debt Free* was an answered prayer. It allowed our family to have a thoughtful conversation about college choices and how those choices can lead to burdensome student debt. Our decisions about college education will now be much more informed and intentional. I highly recommend this book for homeschooling parents and their college-bound children."

—**Wendie Hosmer**, Homeschooling Parent, Godfrey, IL

"As Head of a private school in Houston for almost two decades, I have made education my life's work. As a woman of color, education has been my lifeline. My grandmother had to drop out of college because she couldn't afford to finish, but my mother got her bachelor's degree, and I got my master's degree. More recently, my daughter earned her PhD and is now a university professor. In four generations, education has lifted up my family. But it has taken a great deal of debt to reach this goal. So when I saw Shutler's book *Graduate Debt Free: Escaping the Student Loan Matrix*, I was intrigued, to say the least, and read it right away. It offered ways for all people to overcome hidden assumptions that lead to college debt. I highly recommend this book to all students, but particularly to students of color, who aspire to earn an education to improve their lives, generation after generation."

—**Emily Smith**, MA, Retired Head of School,
The Branch School, Houston, TX

"As disabled veterans who utilized our GI Bills for college expenses, we have not personally experienced the reality of student debt, so we are learning the process in real time with our three sons. Because one son is in community college, one is preparing for an out of state university, and one is still in middle school, navigating college applications, scholarships, and student loans is at the forefront of our minds. It is a constant struggle to balance our excitement and our worry about their financial futures. *Graduate Debt Free* has proven to be the perfect tool to facilitate a meaningful conversation with our sons. It offers factual guidance in an unbiased manner by breaking down 12 common assumptions from the student's perspective. Being able to easily open that door to communication is just the beginning of the benefits this book offers. Graduating debt free IS a real possibility, and Dave Shutler has laid out the path to get there. I highly recommend all high school students and parents read this book . . . the sooner the better!"

—**Kelly & Brett Olson**, USAF Veterans, Fredericksburg, VA

"It could be a tall order to ask your high schooler to read this book, but do it anyway! Before they head off to college, read it with them and discuss every chapter. Student debt will be one of the biggest challenges facing our next generation—unless they protect themselves by reading *Graduate Debt Free* and putting these principles to work."

—**Tom Bronson,** founder of Mastery Partners, Inc. and author of *Maximize Business Value: Begin with the Exit in Mind*, Southlake, TX

"As the former General Director of the National Institute for the Evaluation of Education in Mexico and author of three books on youth counseling, I consider *Graduate Debt Free* essential reading for parents and high school students who plan to attend college, particularly Hispanic students. Shutler's book is a nuts-and-bolts guide to help them navigate the entire journey of deciding where to go and what to do after high school. It unmasks 12 false assumptions about college that can lead families into long-term debt and then offers resources to avoid that debt. For families trying to make wise decisions about colleges and careers, this book offers data-backed tools to help them tackle the decision process. Get this book and open up a healthy family discussion about avoiding student debt."

—**Estela Rodriguez,** MA Ed., former professor and author of *Youth and Professional Counseling,* Aubrey, TX

ESCAPING THE
STUDENT LOAN MATRIX

GRADUATE DEBT FREE

DAVID F. SHUTLER

JD, MBA

GREENLEAF
BOOK GROUP PRESS

Published by Greenleaf Book Group Press
Austin, Texas
www.gbgpress.com

Continued on page "Credits" on page 247, which is a continuation of the copyright page

Distributed by Greenleaf Book Group

For ordering information or special discounts for bulk purchases, please contact Greenleaf Book Group at PO Box 91869, Austin, TX 78709, 512.891.6100.

Design and composition by Greenleaf Book Group
Cover design by Greenleaf Book Group

Publisher's Cataloging-in-Publication data is available.

Print ISBN: 979-8-88645-070-5

eBook ISBN: 979-8-88645-071-2

To offset the number of trees consumed in the printing of our books, Greenleaf donates a portion of the proceeds from each printing to the Arbor Day Foundation. Greenleaf Book Group has replaced over 50,000 trees since 2007.

Printed in the United States of America on acid-free paper

23 24 25 26 27 28 29 30 31 10 9 8 7 6 5 4 3 2 1

First Edition

Photo Credit: Reed Sullivan

To Anika, Zephyr, and You.

Contents

Foreword

FOR OVER 30 YEARS, I've developed practical information, advice, and tools to help families and policymakers make smarter, more informed decisions about planning and paying for college. In that time, I've published several books, written thousands of articles, been quoted in more than 10,000 newspaper and magazine articles, and testified frequently on financial aid, scholarships, student loans, college savings plans, and education tax benefits.

At this point in my career, I am intimately familiar with the policies, procedures, and practices of student financial aid in higher education as well as the statutes, rules, and regulations behind them. So, it has been a great sadness for me to watch the burgeoning growth of student debt and its effects on students and their families. Due to a lack of transparency, more and more students are borrowing more in student loans each year than they can reasonably afford to repay.

We need new approaches about how to sensitize students and parents to college costs and education debt so that they don't fall into a student debt trap. Dave Shutler presents just such an approach to helping students and parents avoid education debt in his book, *Graduate Debt Free: Escaping the Student Loan Matrix.* This book shines a bright light on the mental assumptions that students and their families operate from, and it shows how those assumptions can lead them astray. It does this in a most disarming manner. It is, at the same time, a breezy read for high school students, a sobering guide for their parents, and a well-researched brief for education professionals.

As such, it makes a genuine contribution toward unraveling the dilemma of student debt. It starts with 12 assumptions about the college experience that form a bounding box that constrains and controls the thought processes of students and their parents. It dissects these assumptions, helping you to escape the box and think outside of its confines. When these assumptions operate without being questioned, they can contribute to financial pain. But when they are challenged, they lose their hold on your thinking. You can then escape the matrix that lures you into taking on too much student loan debt.

Dave Shutler is a lawyer by training, an entrepreneur by choice, and a writer by design. He was motivated to write this book because of his experience as a parent of three college graduates who struggled with debt. After that experience, he became intrigued by the puzzle it presented. To solve the puzzle, he spent many years researching why student debt is overwhelming students and their families.

Perhaps it was Shutler's outsider status that allowed him to discover this new approach to presenting the dangerous assumptions that lead to excessive debt. Or perhaps it is the fact that he has gained insights from so many careers. He practiced federal law for over 20 years as a JAG in the military before retiring as a colonel. Since then he has worked for a large corporation, founded and run a construction company, and developed several other business enterprises. He brings the practicality gained from these business endeavors and his life experience to the book.

When Shutler approached me about his book, I agreed to fact-check it. He incorporated my suggestions in the final manuscript. That's why you will find a number of references to me in the endnotes. Although he is a newcomer to the field, I am confident that his arguments are well supported by the evidence.

Who should read this book? I recommend it to high school students and their parents as an inoculation against the assumptions that generate student debt. They should read it before they choose a college. I also recommend it to high school teachers and school counselors, as well as college educators, because it presents fresh thinking about the whys and hows of college. This book will help you restructure your thinking about student debt.

—Mark Kantrowitz, Chicago, Illinois

Preface

AS OF SEPTEMBER 30, 2022, the *federal* student loan balance was $1.6345 trillion, with some 43.5 million borrowers owing an average of $37,575.[1] Those figures represent a sobering number of college students who are struggling to pay off burdensome student loans. And that's just federal debt. After adding *private* student loan debt to the federal debt, the outstanding balance rose to $1.768 trillion as of September 30, 2022.[2]

That trillion-dollar debt figure is hard to grasp, so let's visualize what a million, a billion, and a trillion dollars look like. Picture a million dollars as 10 piles of $100 bills, each stacked 4.3 inches high.[3] A million dollars will fit in a standard briefcase.

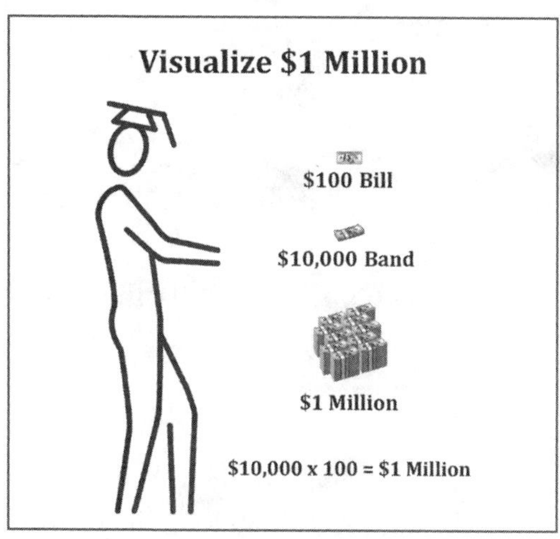

Figure 1.[4]

Now picture a row of four-by-four-foot pallets of $100 bills sitting side by side, stacked about five feet high. That's $1 Billion.

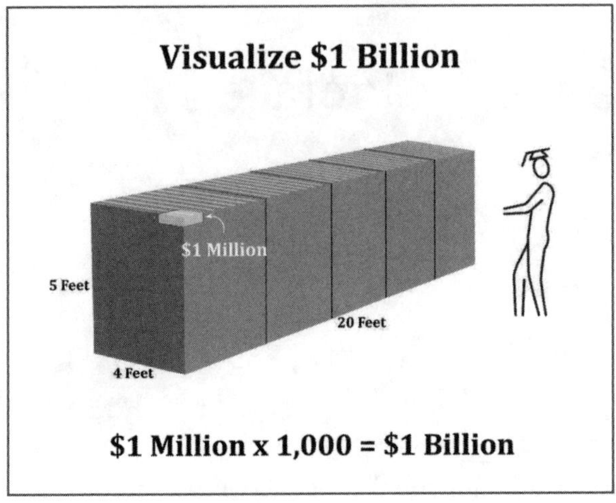

Figure 2.[5]

Now picture a football field measuring 100 by 70 yards covered with $100 bills stacked about 6.3 feet high. That's $1 trillion.

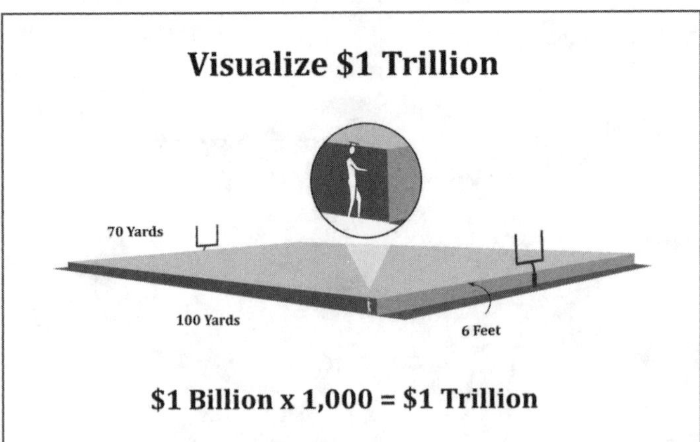

Figure 3.[6]

Total student loan debt exceeding $1.768 trillion is breathtaking. That figure raises the height of the stacked $100 bills on the football field from about 6.3 feet to 10.6 feet tall. Student loan debt at $1.768 trillion surpasses auto loan debt at $1.397 trillion, eclipses credit card debt at $925 billion, and is second only to home mortgage debt at $11.669 trillion.[7] How did the national student loan debt grow to be this large? This book reveals several reasons for this growth and the assumptions behind the student loan problem.

Burgeoning Debt Problem

We refer to it as a student loan problem,[8] but sadly, it's not just students who are caught in this net. Parents who supported their child's academic dreams are often trapped in a similar financial bind. After assisting with their children's education, roughly 10 percent of undergraduate parents now face the burden of their own onerous loans, with recent estimates indicating Parent PLUS loans exceed an average of $30,000.[9]

Combining student loans and parent loans into household debt gives a fuller picture of the problem a family can experience. According to the Federal Reserve Board's Survey of Consumer Finances (SCF), which measures household debt, the average household education loan debt was $40,549.84 in 2019, and it was held by 21.4% of households.[10] That's a lot of folks owing a whole lot of money.

What is going on here? Why is there so much student (and parent) debt? High school students who aspire to a college education generally do so to improve their lot in life. They want to obtain a better-paying job and a more rewarding career. They see a college education as their ticket to that end. Yet, many who start college are not aware of the risk that their hopes could get derailed before they even attain a degree. Although there may be a vague awareness of a debt problem, often students don't connect it with themselves.

Many students aren't aware of the high risk of failing to graduate with the degree they need to pay off their loans. They don't realize that only 66 percent of the students who started public colleges in 2014 actually graduated six years later in 2020.[11] The percentage of college students who graduated from public colleges in the general course of *four* years is even lower at 35 percent.[12] Even worse, students at "for-profit, private universities" attained a comparable six-year graduation rate of only 25 percent.[13] In other words, three-quarters of students who matriculate at for-profit universities don't graduate.

In short, many aspiring college students seem to discount the possibility of failure when embarking on their academic journeys. Without thinking through the problem, they can find themselves wearing a virtual ball and chain around their leg when they realize they don't have the financial resources to cover their newly acquired debt burden.[14]

A high school student's risk of not graduating from college with the degree they need to pay off their student debt is alarmingly high. This means their risk of being saddled with debilitating debt for decades is also very high. A recurring theme emerges in college debt literature of college students accumulating debt while simply being unaware of the danger.

One reason for this lack of awareness is the confusing language in college financial aid award letters. According to a recent GAO report, financial aid award letters blur the distinction between grants and loans and sometimes treat loans as if they cut college costs, rather than add to them, which increases the risk that students will graduate (or drop out) with unaffordable student loan debt.[15]

Federal law does not require colleges to provide standardized information in their financial aid letters. Although public universities comply, private institutions are not required to do so, which has been a source of the problem. The GAO recommends that Congress pass legislation to compel colleges to provide standardized information. We recommend you read the GAO's 10 best practices to protect yourself.[16]

This book grew out of a concern that college-bound students and their parents lacked the information and tools to conduct a practical risk analysis of college debt. In the construction business, I've learned that an accurate risk assessment is essential for my company's survival. The same holds true for education debt survival. In both instances, a fact-based risk assessment leads to better, more informed choices and less life disruption. After reading many accounts of soul-crushing student debt, I began to apply a business-based risk assessment to analyze the financial risks facing a 17-year-old high school student applying for college. In today's high-tuition environment, there are many risks because there are many unknowns.

In addition to the students who didn't finish their academic careers, I wondered about those students who *did successfully finish* a degree but had assumed their starting salary would cover their debt payment. What was the risk that, even if they graduated after four or six years, their starting salary would not meet their monthly debt payment and leave enough to live on afterward?

Those who completed college in 2021 faced a job market with an average starting salary of about $58,000.[17] But these past couple of years haven't been that easy for graduates to find work. Unemployment from the COVID-constricted job market spiked in early 2020 and was a bumpy ride until 2022 when it normalized to pre-pandemic levels.[18] The question to be addressed is whether the starting salary will cover the debt.

One would naturally assume that the average starting salary for college graduates today would have increased substantially in the last 50 years. Not so much. During that time period, in real terms, salaries have been fairly level.[19] Although starting salaries have not improved substantially over the past 50 years, the student debt for college graduates has mushroomed as a percentage of starting salary.[20]

Fifty years ago, when I was in college in 1972, the average salary upon graduation was $10,000[21] while the average debt at graduation has been estimated at about $1,200,[22] which would equate to about 12 percent of the average salary. The comparison of average student debt to average salary at graduation is a useful metric for our discussion because it measures how much effort will be needed to pay off the debt. In 1972, student debt was estimated at about 12 percent of salary.

Now 50 years later, in 2022, as the next generation begins college, the average starting salary upon graduation has reached $58,862.[23] Sounds impressive! But here's the catch—the average student debt has climbed to $30,000,[24] which means that average student debt has swollen to over 50 percent of average starting salary.

When we adjust for inflation to compare relative buying power, we see that a $10,000 salary in 1972 equates to $54,898 today.[25] This reveals that over the elapsed 50 years there has been only a modest increase in real buying power to cover the large increase in debt. Thus, in the span of a single lifetime, while the inflation-adjusted salary has stayed relatively level, the student debt as a percentage of that adjusted salary has jumped from about 12 percent to over 50 percent.[26] The starting salary is the platform from which recent college graduates pay off their student debt, so the rise in debt to over

50 percent means a greater share of that salary must be committed to pay off student debt.

This rise in student debt as a percent of salary is corroborated by relating it to college affordability, which is the cost to attend a year of college. Affordability is a helpful tool to understand student debt because greater college costs are correlated to greater college debt. For the affordability calculation, we have robust College Board reporting of college costs from 1972, so we don't have to estimate.[27] In 1972, the average cost to attend one year of a four-year college, including tuition, fees, room and board, totaled $3,090 ($21,690 adjusted to today's dollars). By 2022, that adjusted $21,690 cost had risen to $53,430.[28] Like student debt growth, the average cost to attend college has ballooned[29] while the average salary upon graduation has stayed relatively flat in real terms.[30]

In short, even though the average starting salary for college graduates has been relatively level over the past 50 years, the cost of college as a percentage of that salary has spiraled. Consequently, even when a student completes their degree and qualifies for a job in their chosen field, their salary often does not cover the debt they have incurred to get the degree. Why is that?

College graduation should be a time of celebration, when newly minted graduates congratulate themselves and each other on landing a good job and earning an improved outlook on life. Instead, after graduation, many college graduates find themselves swimming in debt at age 22, struggling to make ends meet and lacking the means to pay off their student debt.

I wondered how many graduates were affected by burdensome college debt. The answer is—a lot. One recent estimate indicated that 70 percent of students graduate owing an average of $30,000 in student debt.[31] Another estimate found that 65 percent graduate with student debt, and among those graduates, the average student loan debt ranges from $30,030 to $43,900.[32] So we can be certain that there are a substantial number of students in this predicament. Even though this part of the student debt story is receiving more public attention, there is very little guidance pointing out the pitfalls of the various assumptions about college costs and how to escape them.

What about the President's Student Debt Forgiveness?

Now hold on there with all this talk about a student debt crisis. Didn't I read in the papers that the president had forgiven student debt? Why are we even talking about this? Great question. On August 24, 2022, the president announced that "[t]he Department of Education will provide up to $20,000 in debt cancellation to Pell Grant recipients with loans held by the Department of Education, and up to $10,000 in debt cancellation to non–Pell Grant recipients. Borrowers are eligible for this relief if their individual income is less than $125,000 ($250,000 for married couples)."[33]

If this announced policy survives judicial review,[34] it will be good news for many college graduates who are holding student debt, and maybe not such good news for taxpayers. But even if the president's announced policy does survive legal challenges, it will not fix the student loan problem facing high school students today for three reasons.

First, the proposed one-time student loan forgiveness will not apply to prospective college students because the program will not be retroactive, and they don't currently have any college debt to forgive. The president's proposed student loan forgiveness plan applies only to federal student loans made before June 30, 2022, with an exception for consolidation loans for which an application was submitted prior to September 29, 2022. Unless a new policy is implemented, current and future college-bound high schoolers must still contend with college debt.

Second, many forms of student debt are excluded from the president's forgiveness plan. For example, privately held debt, which amounts to roughly 8 percent of the total student debt pie, is not included. "Borrowers with private student loans—loans given by banks, credit unions, and online lenders—are still on the hook for their payments."[35] Nor is the amount of current student debt that lies outside the declared ceilings of $10,000 and $20,000 being forgiven. Consequently, about three-quarters of the $1.7 trillion student debt load will continue to burden college graduates if and when the president's announced debt forgiveness plan is implemented.

The third reason high schoolers today may not benefit from the announced forgiveness plan is that it does not address underlying systemic problems with the incentives of lenders or colleges in student loan programs. Ironically, it may in fact exacerbate the issue for current high schoolers if it serves to "encourage students to take out more loans."[36] That is because the incentives of colleges and universities are not particularly affected by the student loan forgiveness proposal. Their concern is about the availability of student loans to cover the costs of running their institutions, not the availability of loan forgiveness. Consequently, regardless of the ultimate outcome of the proposed debt cancellation plan,[37] high school students are well advised to study the various student loan options at the outset of their college careers and chart a course to minimize their student debt.

Why I Wrote the Book

I am not a banker or an educator by profession, and I don't have any formal training or certification in the field of financial aid. But as a lawyer and a parent, I am deeply concerned that the college financial arena is not offering a level playing field to students. Incoming students with limited life experience and economic awareness are at a decided disadvantage to colleges and lenders with professionally trained staffs. An inexperienced high school junior and their unsuspecting parents must master a dizzying array of programs, laws, and rules to have any hope of analyzing the risk of college debt. The terminology alone is bewildering.

Since I'm not formally trained in the financial aid field, a reader might wonder how I came to write the book. Our family experienced college cost escalation firsthand during the past 24 years. Our first son attended St. John's College in Santa Fe, a private school, from 1998 to 2002. This was before the steep escalation of tuition costs, and his total costs averaged about $35,000 per year. Our second son attended Brown University between 2002 and 2006, another private school. His total costs averaged about $45,000 per year. Our third son went to New York University from 2006 to 2010 and paid an average of $55,000 a year. So in the space of 12 years, we saw the costs of similar-tier private universities escalate from $35,000 to $55,000. Although this escalation was only anecdotal in my personal experience, it turned my attention to the student loan issue.

Sparked by this experience, I became fascinated with the issue of the rising costs of higher education and began to collect newspaper articles and other media about student debt that caught my eye. I was curious to find the reasons behind the ballooning college costs. After a while, I had collected a trove of articles, books, magazines, editorials, and websites. As I read these materials, patterns began to emerge. The patterns evolved into recurring themes, and I began to notice that the themes all originated in a set of student assumptions about college. Each of the assumptions was flawed in some way, but if acted upon, could turn out to be costly to the student.

It then occurred to me to analyze the college debt problem from the perspective of a high schooler about to embark on the college adventure. Rather than look at it from the perspective of the college institutions, the lenders, or the legislators, I would examine the assumptions behind this rising debt through the eyes of a high school student and the thoughts in their mind. That examination would also include the assumptions of parents, educators, bankers, legislators, and taxpayers, who are all stakeholders in the student debt enterprise. It would analyze the underlying assumptions we all commonly hold about college to see why they are leading students into financial harm and how we can gain clarity to avoid that harm.

When my three sons graduated from private colleges around the early 2000s, I observed that the college costs they faced were much higher than what I had encountered a generation before. In round numbers, my private college in 1972 cost around $7,000 a year, while my sons' private colleges jumped from $35,000 to $55,000 annually during the span of 12 years. Now in 2022, 12 years after my third son graduated, similar tier private colleges cost as much as $75,000 to $80,000 a year.[38] That's a big leap in a relatively short period. What was behind that leap in undergraduate costs?

Attending graduate school after college can add yet another dimension of debt. After college, one of my sons went on to law school for a juris doctor (JD) degree and later earned a master of laws degree (LLM) in taxation. His five years of graduate school generated over $150,000 of graduate student debt, in addition to what he still owed from undergraduate education. This debt has been difficult to deal with, and his insights have been informative.

One might think that as a lawyer and a business owner, I would have assessed the risk of student debt for my own children and helped them avoid it. Nope. I was completely unaware of the risks they faced. Even as a "certified smart guy" with two professional degrees, I did not notice that student debt had been weaving a web around my family until after our third son was out of college. Frankly, I felt like a fool for having missed the signals.

From this personal experience, I extrapolated that people of any educational level and socioeconomic status can get tangled up in student debt. When I thought of other families who might be less fortunate than ours, I realized that although the debt problem was hard for me to deal with, it would be devastating to those who already operate at a socioeconomic disadvantage.

These families' lives can be upended by student debt and the wreckage it leaves. Seventeen-year-old students in general, and those in straitened circumstances in particular, may be unaware of the risks their assumptions about college pose to them. And unprotected in that ignorance, they are in danger of being laid low by circumstances outside their understanding.

Reflecting further on the experience of financing college, I realized that I had got into the problem because I personally held a number of assumptions that turned out to be both incorrect and costly. In writing this book, I wanted to identify those faulty assumptions about college costs that I had labored under and subject them to the analysis that I had failed to perform back when the college decisions were upon me. Researching this book was a voyage of discovery. It revealed a treasure trove of information I had failed to access or consider when my sons were attending college. The book is intended to help the next generation of high schoolers and parents access that treasure trove and navigate the waters of college debt on their own voyage of discovery.

In sum, this book is designed to alert high schoolers and their parents to several flawed assumptions surrounding student debt, help them discern the reality behind the assumptions, and offer preventive measures to avoid the consequences of those assumptions. Such actions taken at the outset of their college careers can minimize student debt at graduation time.

Since this book is being published in the middle of a rapidly changing college debt environment, cited facts may be overcome by events by the time you read them. The best we can do is put a marker in the shifting sands as a guidepost to move forward. The book does that. To account for the changing environment, numerous websites and references are included throughout the book and in the endnotes so readers can obtain real-time data in areas of interest and tailor their research to individual circumstances.

Acknowledgments

SEVERAL ACCOMPLISHED PROFESSIONALS contributed directly and indirectly to this book through friendly suggestions and support. Sarah Hoagland Hunter, an accomplished author of children's books, offered practical tips on the publishing process and enthusiastic encouragement along the way. A business associate, Gary Robertson, read the manuscript from the perspective of both a parent and an employer and offered insightful advice in both areas. Over several years, Sanford C. Wilder of the Unlearning Institute has provided sound advice regarding listening techniques and useful pointers to clarify the purpose of the book.

Field-level insights into college athletics programs were offered by John Brodhead Jr., MD, executive vice chairman, Department of Medicine, at the Keck School of Medicine of the University of Southern California (USC), former team physician for USC Athletics and director of Athletic Medicine. Dr. Brodhead's intimate knowledge of college athletic programs proved invaluable.

Several college counselors offered insights regarding how this work might be more relevant to college-bound high schoolers. Having guided our sons in their college journeys, Veronica Pulido at St. Mark's School of Texas and Casey Gendason, who now offers private college guidance services in Dallas, both provided practical advice to address the concerns of the current generation of aspiring students. Rebecca Larkin, EdD, a private school educator for 40 years, reviewed the book from a professional educator's perspective and offered insights from her extensive experience.

Throughout the writing of the book, I had superb research and editorial assistance. When I started on the project, I was fortunate to work with Dan Ayagh, JD, a tech-savvy lawyer with excellent analytical skills and a practical outlook. I am indebted to Dan for researching several chapters of the manuscript with painstaking care and persistence and for his insightful work concerning Community College options. Likewise, Ms. Mary Magouirk, SHRM-SCP, provided streetwise insights on numerous issues involving Human Resources from both personal experience and professional research.

Two outstanding graphic designers, Reed Sullivan and Russell Brown, helped me visualize and translate complex concepts into relatable graphics. I am indebted to both for the depiction of college debt as a hole being dug and for the depiction of the overall cost of accumulated interest from college debt. When one looks at a finished graphic design, it doesn't generally occur to them how much creative work is involved in developing the design. Having worked through the process with Reed and Russ, I know the level of creative energy involved and have deep appreciation for their commitment to the craft.

Over many years I have benefited from the sound financial advice of Richard Craft, AIF, ChFC, CPFA, CLU, at the Wealth Advisory Group. His financial insights helped structure chapter three and the data depicted on the debt graphics. Mr. Craft's unfailing encouragement and sound business advice also provided incentive to complete this project.

Starting with an abecedarian manuscript, my freelance editor, Ms. Hallie Raymond, chiseled her way through uncounted early iterations to sculpt a well-balanced document. I am also indebted to the professionals at the Greenleaf Book Group for guiding my first-time writing efforts. Justin Branch launched the overall effort. Lindsey Clark, Matthew Baganz, and Jeanette Smith each performed superb editorial services, Sally Garland provided outstanding permissions support, and Jared Dorsey created the eye-catching cover graphic and book design. Brian Welch provided invaluable production advice and piloted a polished printed publication to completion. Many thanks to the Greenleaf Book Group team for their sound professional guidance.

When the manuscript was nearing completion, I submitted it to Mark Kantrowitz, a nationally renowned subject matter expert in financial aid and student loan programs. To my great delight, he accepted my invitation to fact-check the work, and his extensive observations enriched it substantially. He also graced me with a foreword to the book, which is most appreciated. Mr. Kantrowitz's encyclopedic knowledge of the financial aid field and his willingness to share that knowledge added immeasurably to the completed work.

The book exists in no small measure because of the efforts of my dad, Lt General Philip D. Shutler, USMC (Retired). His sage counsel for many decades has been to "find a need and fill it," which I have tried to follow in writing this book. More recently, he gave me hope during some decidedly dark days and offered crucial assistance at a time when it was sorely needed. As the book was nearing completion, he wisely advised on ways to simplify the message. Thanks, Pop.

A special thanks to my three grown sons, Nathan, Nolan, and Neale, who had to experience many of the problems that are addressed in this book. Working through multiple issues that arose during their combined 12 years of undergraduate education, I discovered a wide range of questions I had failed to consider when they were in school. After graduating and starting to pay down their college debts, they also shared insights and concerns about the student debt dilemma, which were invaluable. My grandchildren, Anika, Zephyr, and "players to be named," motivated me to help the rising generation face the college conundrum with eyes wide open and a full tool kit. Thanks to each of you.

Finally, I could not have written the book without the selflessness, perseverance, and wisdom of my wife, Katie, whose unflagging support and love were and are a constant source of inspiration.

Introduction

STUDENT DEBT CAN REARRANGE your life. In an article by M. H. Miller titled "Been Down So Long It Looks Like Debt to Me: An American Family's Struggle for Student Loan Redemption," Mr. Miller describes his struggle with "never-ending student debt."[1] The article gives an arresting look at how high school assumptions can lead to unwieldy college debt. It recounts several assumptions Mr. Miller held at age 17 when he decided to attend New York University (a top-tier private university in Manhattan) and illustrates the process by which assumptions first take hold in thought and later impact life choices.

After graduating with student debt of $100,000 and struggling to pay the monthly bill of $1,100 on his teacher's salary,[2] Mr. Miller reflected on assumptions that contributed to his difficult financial circumstances. These simple assumptions about college illustrate how an idea can take hold and impact the college debt obligation.[3]

1. "Money doesn't matter." Although Mr. Miller knew his college education would cost some $50,000 a year, his family decided the cost didn't matter because a good education was important.

2. "We'll find a way to pay." Even though the cost of Mr. Miller's education was beyond his parents' economic means, and they had no plan to finance it, they assumed they could work this out later and hoped for the best.

3. "The value of education is priceless." Mr. Miller and his parents treated his college experience as though it was "beyond cost,"[4] but his bitter experience with student debt discredited that assumption. He realized his education had a price, and he would be 44 when he finally paid it off with interest at $182,000.[5]

Mr. Miller's intention when he started at NYU was to pave the way to a meaningful adulthood through a college education, but his life experience was turned around by his assumptions. As he put it: "What an irony that the decisions I made about college when I was 17 have derailed such a goal."[6] This is the crux of the dilemma facing today's high school students. The assumptions they hold as 17-year-olds in late adolescence can determine their life experience as emerging adults. Those assumptions, therefore, must be scrutinized. This book addresses 12 assumptions similar to the three that drove Mr. Miller. The 12 assumptions create a mode of thinking that can lead to financial suffering.

The Student Loan Matrix Analogy

The first movie of *The Matrix* franchise, a 1999 science fiction film depicting a dystopian future, begins with the protagonist, Neo, unknowingly trapped in a simulated reality.[7] Through the help of the guide Morpheus (played by Laurence Fishburne), Neo (played by Keanu Reeves) observes that *inside* the simulated reality of the Matrix, people are being exploited for their resources by a life-depleting apparatus. When he escapes *outside* the Matrix, he can see that the people inside the Matrix are actually being lulled into surrendering their life force by a simulated reality being generated by computer images.[8]

In the movie, Morpheus gives Neo a choice between a blue and red pill to encourage him to choose his life's mission. The blue pill would allow Neo to remain in blissful ignorance of his surroundings, while the red pill will reveal to him an unsettling but life-changing truth. Neo decides to take the red pill and see the world as it is so he can deal with it in all its sobering reality.[9]

After taking the red pill, Neo is indeed able to observe two different realities. He becomes aware that the reality he experiences is determined by whether he is thinking inside the Matrix or outside of it. Neo sees that the computer-generated virtual reality in which he appears to reside does not, in fact, exist. He discovers that he can be freed of this virtual reality but that it will take a heroic effort to escape.

Taking the red pill enables Neo to think outside the Matrix and see the world as it actually exists. The movie beautifully captures this perception of reality in a fight scene in which the antagonist, Agent Smith, fires several shots at Neo, who is able to dodge each bullet by realizing it is actually a computer-generated image formed by a stream of harmless zeros and ones.[10]

Many students applying for college today operate inside a similar perceived reality. Unlike the computer-generated reality in *The Matrix*, this perceived reality is formed by a set of assumptions. These assumptions arise from a complicated, interlocking set of circumstances that this book will address, involving colleges, lenders, and the federal government. The policies enacted by these institutions, though well intentioned, have had the unintended effect of lulling students and parents into thinking they can borrow their way through college without economic consequences. This book is the red pill to that myth.

Graduate Debt Free gives you an unvarnished view of the economic reality surrounding student loan debt. It offers strategies for you and your parents to escape this debt by understanding the assumptions behind it. The book encourages you to make informed choices about your education and its costs.[11] But, as Neo discovered, taking the red pill will require determination on your part.

Throughout this book, we will refer to thinking *inside the Student Loan Matrix* as a shorthand for the perceived reality inside the box formed by the 12 assumptions. Thinking *outside the Student Loan Matrix* refers to using a fact-based analysis to deconstruct the assumptions. By taking the red pill and deciding to proceed, you are choosing to think outside the box and challenge the assumptions inside the Student Loan Matrix, rather than be held captive by them.

On that account, much of the book might seem a tad depressing. Remember as you soldier through that by doing so you will be able to navigate the financial decisions you face as a college student with an understanding of the consequences of your decisions. You will be able to chart a course that makes economic sense for you and your family.

Why Do I Care?

At 16 or 17 years of age, you may not be thinking much about how you're going to pay for college or how deep into debt you might go. You're a high school junior or senior, living the best year of your life so far. Ironically, you're also probably stressed out of your mind because you're trying to figure out which college to go to and what you want to major in. That's bad enough, but when you add in parental pressure, unwanted advice from friends, and an overall feeling of uncertainty, you might just want to chuck the whole college decision process out the window.

The reason you care is that you want to avoid costly debt in the future. This book offers a roadmap for you to navigate potential pitfalls based on hard data. As such, it builds some fact-based certainty around the many uncertain choices you're facing. It also relieves some of the stress and anxiety you are experiencing about college.

Having watched three generations of friends and family navigate the college experience, I believe that the dream of graduating in front of wildly cheering family and friends is still valid. But I believe the dream should be tweaked by adding two words. In the updated dream, you graduate *debt free* in front of wildly cheering family and friends. There is a place for the pride of accomplishment and the satisfaction of meeting a long-term goal. But those worthy outcomes should not be overshadowed by overwhelming debt.

How College Assumptions Begin

You're looking at your options, thinking about how your grades in high school might stack up against others, and judging what college you might qualify for. You're worried about SAT and ACT scores (if they are required at your target school), concerned about doing well on AP tests, and wondering if you have enough extracurricular activities, volunteer activities, and hobbies to list on your applications. Your parents, school counselors, and friends have all told you that these things can impact your ability to go to the school of your choice.

You're deciding where you want to go to college. Do you want to go where your parents went? Where your friends are going? To one of the top-rated party schools in the US? Somewhere with a particular fraternity or sorority chapter? Maybe you're thinking about a college's reputation or its career network or the scholarships it has available.

College websites might emphasize the school size, its location in vibrant cities or idyllic rural settings, and its national ranking in *US News & World Report.* They might highlight campus resources, the level of intercollegiate athletics and the quality of athletic facilities, the strength of academic departments, and the quality of their professors. You assume all these factors are important to consider, and you begin to feel overwhelmed. Into this stew of thoughts, several assumptions begin to take hold and dictate your actions around college choices. Now is the time to be alert to those assumptions and learn to spot them in your thinking.

For example, why do the criteria just mentioned arise when you think about choosing a college? Because students often possess a set of assumptions similar to the significant people influencing their lives—peers, social media, parents, teachers, and counselors. These assumptions evolve through interactions with these influencers. You may not even be aware you possess these assumptions or know when or where they first took hold. But these assumptions fail to address the critical point of how you will pay for college. Without figuring that out, students seeking a better life through college education can end up in an economic disaster.

So this book will lay aside the clatter of college criteria and focus on one simple question: How will you pay for college? It is important to consider financial fit along with the academic fit and the social fit in the college decision. To measure the financial fit, a good reference is the college affordability index. This is the ratio of the one-year net price to total annual family income. Under the college affordability index, if the net price is less than 25 percent of family income, then the college is affordable. Along with an academic safety school, consider choosing a "financial aid safety school" where you can afford to enroll even if you don't qualify for any need-based financial aid. Become price sensitive and make affordability a primary consideration.

Typically, at this point, young adults are planning to pay for school by:

- saving up money for college;
- applying for grants and scholarships;

- working during college to earn spending money; and
- applying for loans to cover unfunded college costs.

But you may have no particular organizing principle, and your thoughts could be scattered.

One good way to organize your thoughts is to apply a "past-present-future" approach for funding college. The past refers to your accumulated college savings and long-term programs such as 529 plans; the current refers to contributions from parent and student income, along with tax breaks and gift aid; and the future refers to student loans to meet the need that still remains after the past and present resources are depleted. Using this theme helps you to think about spreading out the costs over time and dealing with a complex issue on simple terms.

Wouldn't it be nice to be able to see how other students and families apply this past-present-future approach to financing college? In particular, wouldn't it be nice to see a template of how much money should come from which sources? Happily, there is a great resource for this. Take a look at Sallie Mae's *How America Pays for College 2022.*[12] It includes a table showing the various sources of funding for college. In the 2021–22 academic year, about 43 percent was funded from parent income and savings, 26 percent was from scholarships and grants, 11 percent was from student income and savings, 10 percent was from student borrowing, 8 percent was from parent borrowing, and 2 percent was from relatives and friends.[13] Armed with this information, you can begin building a plan to address how you will pay for college, rather than simply assuming that everything will be all right. You are about to enter complicated terrain, and you will need a solid plan to navigate through college debt. Consider the Sallie Mae percentages your working template.

Perhaps you are fortunate enough to have parents who can afford to write a check for your college costs without denting their portfolios. Even if your parents have the financial resources to support you in college, both you and your parents will want to spend those resources wisely. Preserving those resources could help you generate a solid nest egg to launch a career, take a trip to Europe after graduation, or buy a house. Consequently, whether from wisdom, necessity, or both, you will want to have a plan to pay for college and be aware of the assumptions laid out in this book to improve your financial picture after graduation.

How to Recognize the Student Loan Matrix

The Student Loan Matrix, as defined in this book, is a set of 12 assumptions about college. Imagine each assumption as represented by a single line with the 12 single lines combining to form a cube or box. That box represents a mental trap that can ensnare college-bound high school students. You can generally recognize a Student Loan Matrix assumption if it ends up costing you money. Escaping the Student Loan Matrix requires the same thought process that Neo employed to escape the simulated reality he experienced—seeing through the appearance to the underlying reality.

Once the 12 assumptions inside the Student Loan Matrix have been challenged, a student can operate free of illusions as they work toward a rewarding adult life. They can see the risks they're facing and navigate around them to find safe harbor, either in or outside of the college experience. Thinking outside the Student Loan Matrix, a student's assumptions about college can no longer trap them in a life of debilitating debt.

In this book, each chapter addresses one of the 12 assumptions that form the Student Loan Matrix. As you become familiar with them, you will begin to notice as the assumptions arise in your thought, and you will be prepared to challenge those assumptions. Like Neo, you will be able to discern if the bullet headed your way is only harmless zeroes and ones. The concluding chapter offers an additional look at some of the emerging alternatives to a high-debt college education. There are also resources presented throughout the book to help you plan your financial journey through college.

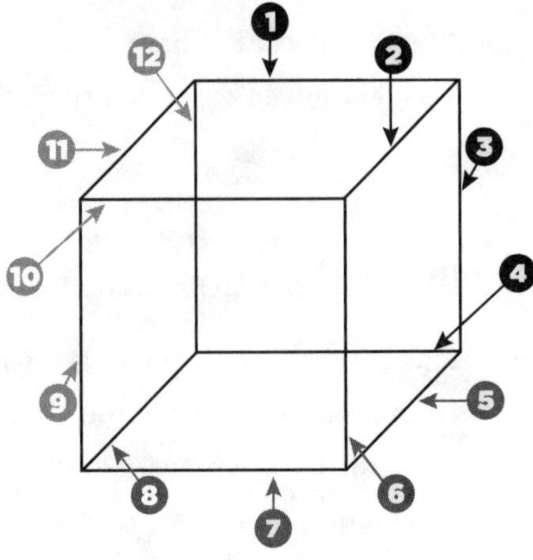

Figure 4.

Here are the 12 assumptions that form the Student Loan Matrix:

1. I gotta go to college.
2. I need a college degree to be successful.
3. Tuition is the total cost of college.
4. Community college is a step sideways.
5. I can live inexpensively on campus.
6. I could never qualify for grants or scholarships.
7. I can get an athletic scholarship.
8. I need networking in college for career success.
9. Going to college is a risk-free endeavor.
10. I'll get a job in my field that will cover my debt.
11. I can get a loan without collateral.
12. I can discharge my college debt in bankruptcy.

You're young. You're experiencing the best years of your life so far. You're excited about graduation from high school and moving into a better future—and you should be. Once you've escaped the Student Loan Matrix, you can be certain that the future you move into is no illusion, and you will be able to start building a foundation for success that is based in reality. Let's take that red pill and get started.

CHAPTER 1

I Gotta Go to College

THE MOST BASIC ASSUMPTION in the Student Loan Matrix is *I gotta go to college.* This assumption was satirized in the 1980 comedy classic *Caddyshack*[1] during a scene on the Bushwood golf course. Danny Noonan (the caddie played by Michael O'Keefe) confides to Ty Webb (the golf prodigy played by Chevy Chase) that he doesn't really want to go to college, even though he thinks he should and his family wants him to go.

On the fairway, Noonan declares, "I gotta go to college, I gotta."

Webb takes exception, then gets to the heart of the matter. "No, the thing is, Danny, do you wanna go to college?" The scene is a lot funnier than this retelling, but underneath this dialogue lies a true dilemma. The idea that you just "gotta" go to college is presented to American students at an early age and reinforced in countless ways.[2]

Right now, as you read this, you're probably wondering why this assumption is even here. As a high school junior or senior, you've probably attended school presentations and heard from guidance counselors, principals, librarians, and teachers in your school that the obvious next step for you is college. Maybe your parents have enrolled you in summer programs to get better grades and improve your standardized test scores. Maybe you've signed up for extracurricular activities to strengthen your application. After all this preparation, it has become abundantly clear: you have to go to college to be successful; you need a degree to have a fulfilling career.[3]

Many students even come to judge their prospects in life on their ability to get into a prestigious college. This message operates like a hard drive in the back of their minds, even though college may not be a good fit for them and even though they may not have the resources to go to college. Many high school students view college attendance as an inevitable rite of passage to adulthood, an unquestioned obligation—the thing to do. Let's take a moment to question this foundational assumption.

Do you *gotta go to college* to have a fulfilling career or a meaningful life?

You Don't Gotta Go to College

Nope. You don't gotta go to college to have a fulfilling career or a meaningful life. In fact, attending college might work against those long-term interests, particularly if you overextend financially or overlook other meaningful career prospects that suit you better.

It might lead you away from viable careers that require less preparation time and less money to get qualified than, say, an engineer or an educator. This could include careers with an entry point such as a license, a certificate, or an associate's degree, like an emergency medical tech or an electrician.

Many careers require no degree or postsecondary education. For example, you could be a fast-food manager. Does that sound a bit jarring? Being a fast-food manager doesn't sound like much of an aspiration for a crackerjack, college-bound student like you, does it? You gotta go to college.

However, outside of the Student Loan Matrix, being a fast-food manager is an honorable, useful, and necessary career that many Americans have come to rely on for their livelihood, not to mention their meals. A friend of mine confided that when her father was a single parent with three young children to feed on a teacher's salary, he relied on the McDonald's near their home. The manager there ran a Wednesday special that allowed her father to feed his three daughters cheaply and quickly at least one day a week, allowing him more time for grading homework and doing housework, giving him the chance to spend a little downtime with his children. The manager at that McDonald's fed this family and probably many other families in similar circumstances, providing hot food to those who needed it. Managers of fast-food franchises feed America and employ countless young adults, retirees, and other people in need of entry-level jobs.[4]

Inside the Student Loan Matrix, that may not seem so impressive. Outside the Matrix, there are many careers that do not require college degrees and that perform similar worthwhile community functions. Could our preconceptions about jobs that don't require a degree be a gauge of how blinded we are by the Matrix assumption that we gotta go to college?

A good place to analyze the validity of the predominant assumption *I gotta go to college* is a study popularly known as the Hamilton Project that was updated recently.[5] The study's full title is *Major Decisions: What Graduates Earn over Their Lifetimes*. It was originally published in 2014 by the Brookings Institute and updated in October 2020 by Dr. Kirsten Broady and Dr. Brad Hershbein as one in a series of Hamilton Project studies to address sound economic policy.

This informative study traces the lifetime salary of 98 college majors and provides a college debt calculator for each of those majors. The Hamilton Project study is often cited for the proposition that "college graduates make more money over their lifetime than nongraduates." The genesis of this proposition was an earlier study published by the US Census Bureau in 2002 that yielded an often cited $1 million difference between the lifetime earning power of college and noncollege graduates.[6] In this same vein, Georgetown University's Center on Education and the Workforce published an informative study that focuses on first-year earnings of 37,000 students and debt at 4,400 institutions.[7] The combined implication of these three studies is that you gotta go to college to make more money. While this premise is directionally correct, the key to determine its validity in your individual case is the college major.

The Hamilton Project and related studies merit a careful read, both for their treatment of the core premise regarding lifetime earnings and for their analysis of the earning power of various college majors. The validity of the proposition that college graduates make more money over a lifetime rests largely on the college major that a student selects in college. Different majors earn different salaries after graduation, so if the point is to make more money, be wise to the earning potential of your major selection.

What's the Value of a College Major?

The Hamilton Project and the cited studies[8] are particularly useful for college-bound students to help them grasp and compare the earning power of various college majors. This will help them better understand the economics of choosing their major as well as their college. Financial success need not be the sole motivator in choosing a college major, but it is a reasonable consideration in light of student debt. And it is important to use available data when making the choice between colleges and their departmental majors. Selecting a college major with eyes wide open about its future earning power is not mercenary, it's simply good practice. It can prevent sticker shock after college graduation, when you discover that your hard-won degree in your beloved major won't yield a job that can pay the freight on the student debt you just racked up.

Drilling down into the Hamilton Project reveals that its actual conclusion is that the *median* salary of college graduates is higher than the *median* salary of noncollege graduates. While that conclusion is an accurate depiction of the data analyzed, the study's findings are more nuanced than that statement sounds. Here's the actual language of Broady and Hershbein's analysis of the updated data: "At the *median*, career earnings for a bachelor's degree graduate are more than twice as high as for someone with only a high school diploma or GED, roughly 70 percent higher than for someone with some college but no degree, and more than 45 percent higher than for someone with an associate degree."[9]

On its face, that conclusion appears to be a worthwhile economic motivation for going to college. But take particular note of the term "median," which refers to the midpoint of observed values, when it is being used as a basis for the assumption of a higher salary and consider that the 98 various majors necessarily have 98 different salary results.

Granted, the median salary cited for college graduates indicates a substantial difference in earning power for college graduates and nongraduates. But, as statistics experts will tell you, the use of the median (the middle of a sorted list of numbers) to make the comparison often ignores the outliers in a data set. Let's return to the study to see what it says about the outliers.

The study makes two additional observations—both eroding the median salary conclusion. First, some workers without a bachelor's degree achieve higher career earnings than some workers with a bachelor's degree.[10] Interestingly, this includes some workers with bachelor's degrees in the highest-earning majors, which contradicts the notion that a college degree necessarily leads to higher lifetime earnings. That single observation is just one speed bump on the *I gotta go to college* road. But wait, there's another.

In addition to differences in lifetime earnings between workers with and without degrees, there is a wide variance in earnings between workers with different college majors. Specifically, "for the median bachelor's degree graduate, cumulative lifetime earnings for workers across majors range from $770,000 (early childhood education) to $2.28 million (aerospace engineering)."[11] This is a difference in lifetime earnings of over $1.5 million for college graduates with different specialties.

Because the median sits at the midpoint of a range of lifetime earnings (in this case between $770,000 and $2.28 million), the actual experience of an individual student in a given major could differ significantly from the median. What happens to the lifetime earnings of the students who get an expensive degree in a low-paying field? That is essentially what happened to Mr. Miller, the NYU graduate cited in the introduction, whose expensive degrees in English yielded a relatively lower-paying job in education.

Similarly, students who chose a career in a relatively high-paying field after attending an expensive private university may still struggle to make debt payments. A family member, for example, chose a career in law after graduating from an Ivy League university. He continues to make monthly payments on his debt burden 15 years after graduation. His lifetime earnings may be higher, but the monthly debt payment is reducing his current spending power.[12]

The point to ponder is that since the median is simply the midpoint in the scale, the premise that going to college will automatically improve your future earnings potential must be challenged before it can be relied upon to guide your choices. The assumption that *I gotta go to college* is not a bad assumption, just one that invites deep reflection in light of economic realities and your individual choice of majors. In some cases, it makes more sense to choose your major before you choose your college.

The premise could also be challenged on its underlying foundation—that higher pay is the result of higher education, sometimes referred to as a *wage premium.* That statement sounds logical and seems to make sense. But a strong case can be made that the higher pay earned by college graduates results not from what the academic experience brought to them, but from what they brought to the academic experience. A thought-provoking article by Josh Mitchell challenges the premise that a college wage premium that improves a student's economic future results from a college degree.[13] In "Rising Education Levels Provide Diminishing Economic Boost," Mr. Mitchell points out that the "wage premium argument" is an unprovable observation because many graduates arrived at college with inherent abilities that were simply honed during the four years they spent in college. Consequently, the degree itself just makes it easier for hiring managers to select worthy job candidates.[14]

The *nature versus nurture* debate is ongoing, but there is no debate on the need for highly skilled laborers outside of those holding bachelor's degrees. As we saw during the height of the COVID pandemic, critical trades such as plumbers, electricians, and heating, ventilation, and air-conditioning (HVAC) technicians are essential to home, office, and hospital operations. People can qualify for these trades with one or two years of college and an apprenticeship, rather than a four-year degree program. Even college campuses cannot operate very long without them.

The high demand has led to higher pay and more consistent employment for HVAC technicians than for some college graduates. In a noteworthy passage, the Hamilton Project itself acknowledges that "some workers without a bachelor's degree have higher career earnings than some workers with a bachelor's degree."[15]

Take stock of your beliefs and goals, and query what you've heard on the street. Are you under the impression that careers in the trades or in fields that don't require a degree are somehow second rate or less desirable? That's the impression some school counselors and college fair events—both pre- and post-COVID—may have created. Is it true?

It is curious that we don't often see career events at high schools sponsored by trade unions rather than colleges. Would such events encourage students to envision the trades like the college fairs encourage students to envision college? Where are the job fairs with manned booths touting the benefits of being a licensed EMT, medical nurse, baker, barber, chef, or real estate agent? Many high schools do offer vocational education as an integral part of the high school curriculum, but there is a perception that vocational positions may not pay as well as a plumber, electrician, or HVAC tech, which require at least a certificate and generally an apprenticeship, so vocational ed may get the short end of the stick. The general direction inside the Student Loan Matrix is toward academic achievement that will lead to matriculation at a four-year college or university.

Why don't we see events sponsored by the Small Business Administration (SBA) touting vocational technical skills like refrigeration services, insulation, pipe fitting, plumbing, or welding? Oh, wait. We do see these events. They are called career fairs or job fairs, and they promote a wide array of careers. In fact, the SBA hosts such events, often in conjunction with Small Business Development Centers (SBDCs). If SBDCs are unfamiliar to you, take some time to check them out. They are the engine behind the 27 million small businesses in America and are often located in local community colleges. Although career fairs may not be a big attraction for many college-bound high schoolers, you will want to know what resources are on offer so you can make an informed decision.

As a business owner, I have attended numerous training programs offered by the SBA at Dallas area SBDCs for two decades. Many of the people I have met in these programs are starting trade-related enterprises and working hard to offer worthwhile products and services. Perhaps college-bound students overlook these career choices because the trades exist as a culture outside the Matrix, which leads to reduced airtime in some high schools. Don't bite into the fallacy that trade schools and SBDCs have nothing to offer you.

The demand for skilled tradespeople is very high. People in Texas learned the value of a good plumber when water pipes froze during the mega ice storm (called the "Snowpocalypse") of 2021. Because of the freezing temperatures, water leaks occurred all over North Texas. With plumbers in short supply, demand skyrocketed. Since the demand for qualified tradespeople is high, their salaries are high, which gives a student cause to challenge the general premise that a college degree will lead to higher lifetime earnings.

Because technical skills are required in the construction industry, I am familiar with the lucrative pay available for tradespeople. The median pipefitter salary in New York City is $60,643 per year[16] as of this writing, not including bonuses. Similarly, the median police officer salary in New York City is $74,100.[17] Other cities have varying wage structures, but such compensation frequently compares favorably with college grads making $50,000 to $60,000 a year at roughly the same age.

This simple fact challenges the assumption that careers in the trades are less lucrative and, therefore, less desirable than other professions. The assumption can also be challenged on the basis of the underlying purpose of schooling—to find a good career fit for each individual student and prepare them for it. People who are interested in the humanities in college may not be well suited to become a pipefitter or electrician, and vice versa. The target for high schoolers should be to find a career that suits them and pays the freight on the student loan debt burden required to qualify them for that career.

Do I Gotta Go to a Four-Year College?

This brings us back to what you gotta do. If you do gotta go to college, do you gotta go to a four-year institution to get a degree?

Consider the life experience of an acquaintance in Dallas, Texas, whose educational experience is a model of practical thinking. This student had solid academics and a strong work ethic but limited family resources or financial support. He wanted to obtain an undergraduate degree, but neither he nor his family had the wherewithal to fund the traditional four-year, on-campus experience. So, he decided to attend a local community college while working part time and living at home. After completing community college, he transferred to a local state university, continued to live off campus with his parents, and graduated in four years. On graduation day, he and his parents were both debt free. Many students are pursuing this route to a degree.

In short, he didn't need to go to a four-year degree program or an expensive college to achieve a successful career. Rather, he found a practical way around the college debt dilemma. Sadly, this experience may be the exception rather than the rule. Of students who intend to obtain a bachelor's degree but start off at a two-year college, only about a fifth succeed in getting a bachelor's degree within six years.[18] That compares with two-thirds of students who succeed in obtaining a bachelor's degree when they start off at a four-year college. So students who intend to get a four-year bachelor's degree should be mindful of the possible detours that can occur if they start at community college.

We will return to the community college route in chapter four and consider the benefits of this route to avoid or minimize college debt. We also consider whether you need to attend college at all. That assumption should be challenged at the outset to determine what is best for you considering your economic circumstances.

But what if you still want to go to college? Great—go! There is certainly value in a college education, and there are certainly good reasons to pursue a degree. While college isn't for everyone, if you decide college is right for you, carefully select your major. The idea is to wisely choose your major to make sure going to college to gain a better future for yourself doesn't set that future back under the weight of crushing debt.

Go to a College You Can Afford

Many students, upon deciding to attend college, make two related assumptions. First, they assume that they must attend the best college they get admitted to. Second, they—and their parents—assume they can find a way to pay for it regardless of cost. In the introduction, Mr. Miller fell prey to both of these related assumptions. He chose NYU because he believed he should go to the best school he was admitted to. Then, his parents encouraged him to attend, saying they would find a way to pay the bill. You and your parents may hold similar thoughts as you contemplate that charming New England college with the leafy campus and the stratospheric price tag. Don't fall victim to the fallacy that you should go to the best school that accepts you. This assumption can be financially disastrous and can pile up a Mount Trashmore of college debt. Instead, plan to go to the best school that you can afford and that will allow you to graduate debt free or nearly so.

As a high school student in 1970, I was driven by both these assumptions when it came to my own college education. Back then, when I was 17, they made a lot of sense. But back then, the assumptions did not end up being a detriment because the cost for me to attend a private university like Duke in the 1970s was much less. The risk of accumulating a huge debt load at that time was relatively low. In fact, the notion of a huge college debt never even occurred to me. But times have changed, and those old assumptions must now give way to a new reality.

In the last 50 years, costs at that same university have increased more than tenfold, from about $7,000 to over $80,000 a year. According to Duke's published financial aid materials, the 2021–2022 estimated annual cost of attendance is $81,488, not including transportation. The financial aid materials indicate that more than 52 percent of Duke students do not pay the full cost, but that means 48 percent do so. Since only 12 percent of students at Duke University receive Federal Pell Grants, which is far below the national average, we can surmise that most of the 48 percent of the Duke student body who pay full fare are from families who can afford the cost.[19]

Given the escalating cost to attend college in general (and private institutions in particular), the assumption that *I should go to the best college I can get into* must be challenged. The hard experiences of numerous debt-shackled graduates illustrate how badly that assumption can play out in today's economic reality.

Similarly, when students or parents assume they can find a way to pay for college, the assumption warrants careful consideration. It can be problematic, particularly if the decision is left solely to the student. In a thought-provoking *Washington Post* article, columnist Michelle Singletary, a mother of three debt-free college graduates, offers profound insights to parents on this sensitive topic:

- "Don't leave the decision up to an 18-year-old.
- Don't let the ability to borrow a lot of money dictate your decision.
- Don't ignore the long-term drag of student-loan debt on your monthly budget.
- Don't assume you're only on the financial hook for four years.
- Don't believe the hype that it's the college that matters most."[20]

This sage advice merits a meaningful discussion between students and parents because it challenges the assumption that *we can find a way to pay for college.*

The ballooning cost of college is analogous to the ballooning cost of salaries in professional sports and should be analyzed carefully for the same reasons. Michael Lewis, in the book *Moneyball*,[21] noted that decades ago, when baseball players were earning about $100,000 a year, the overall cost of a complete team roster was relatively low, so a player's performance on the field did not need to be highly scrutinized through data analysis. The risk of hiring an underperforming player was modest compared with the overall cost of baseball team operations. However, in recent decades, with individual baseball players making millions of dollars a year, the cost of team rosters has exploded. It has now become critical for baseball managers to rely on detailed data analysis of a player's fielding and batting performance to determine the true worth of each player to the team effort.[22]

The same necessity for careful data analysis now applies to the process of college decision-making, and for the same reason—the stakes have grown too high to simply guess. While it may be true that your parents can find a way to pay for college, it could also be true that the only way is through Federal Direct Parent PLUS loans,[23] which can be devastating, as we will discuss later.

At this point, a word is in order about the quality of education and value for dollar at top-tier colleges. Generally speaking, the more one pays for anything, including the college experience, the better it will be. The value of an Ivy League education may be well beyond its price tag in terms of relationships formed, networks created, and exposure to top-flight professorial talent. Also, because of the extensive endowments of superlative colleges, the financial burden on any given student could turn out to be less than that of a counterpart at a less competitive and less costly college.

There is a reason Ivy League universities are so highly regarded. They have earned their reputations as selective proving grounds for developing talent over centuries, regardless of the *nature versus nurture* argument. Consequently, one can't criticize highly selective colleges or the students fortunate enough to attend them. (Besides, it would sound like sour grapes if I disparaged the Ivy Leagues, since I didn't make the Harvard cut in my high school years.) The schools are superb, and their students are top tier. But if we step outside the Student Loan Matrix, we can observe that the cost of attending them has escalated to a point that is out of reach without financial aid for the majority of families.

That said, if you determine that going to the best college you can gain admittance to is the right plan for your future, follow the *Moneyball* path of careful data analysis to find a way to pay for the privilege. Most students cannot afford to wait until later to *figure out a way to pay for it*. Save the *future* you some trouble by having the *present* you formulate a financial plan to address known costs from the start.

Consider Paying for College through Military Service

Many aspiring college students find they can fund their education through opportunities with the US Armed Forces. Service members can earn college credits through technical training courses and can also apply for tuition assistance that can vastly reduce (by 75 percent) their college price tag. College scholarships through the Reserve Officer Training Corps (ROTC) program offer full and partial coverage of college costs and can lead to a commission in the Armed Forces.[24] In ROTC, you will be required to take military science classes and physical training that may also qualify as elective hours at your school. Taking the first year of ROTC without a long-term active-duty service commitment is a way for you to learn whether a military career is right for you.

The four military academies located at West Point, Annapolis, Colorado Springs, and New London present an unmatched opportunity for a superb education, not to mention the prospect of guaranteed employment in a chosen field for several years after college graduation and a solid footing for a civilian career after that. But getting selected for a US military academy is extremely competitive, requiring a nomination from your congressman or senator, and requiring an academic, athletic, and extracurricular effort that some may find difficult to execute.

Funding your education through military service can occur beyond ROTC and the military academies. High school graduates can consider enlisting in the services and attending military technical schools that offer training in fields such as jet propulsion, information technology, and HVAC. These military fields are directly related to counterpart civilian careers.

Regular enlistees to the armed forces who serve continuously for 90 days may also be eligible for the Post-9/11 GI Bill, which covers the full cost of in-state tuition and fees at four-year public universities, as well as offers allowances for housing and book fees.[25] If you are considering this route, note that "the Yellow Ribbon Program can help you pay for higher out-of-state, private school, foreign school, or graduate school tuition and fees that the Post-9/11 GI Bill doesn't cover."[26] In addition to helping reduce the cost of college, military programs include training in management and leadership that can also be applied in civilian settings. During a 24-year US Air Force career, I benefited from several of these leadership training programs and can attest to the level of instruction and the value of the experience. In addition to building character, they instill a can-do attitude that is attractive to employers when you interview for a job after serving.

Education à la Carte

Not interested in military service? Still gotta go to college? Short on cash to pay for it? OK. There are numerous alternative routes to funding a debt-free university degree, even before we touch on the question of scholarships and grants in chapter six. Some of these alternative routes to paying for college are hidden in plain sight.

The first alternative route to paying for college is working at a fast-food franchise, where a student can take advantage of the competitive pay, the inexpensive food, the flexible hours, and the scholarships on offer. We call this opportunity *education à la carte* because (a) it sounds snappy, and (b) there is a wide menu of options available to an enterprising student. The opportunities a fast-food franchise may have on offer for their employees probably won't cover the whole cost of a student's degree. But even so, they can serve as building blocks toward the total package. Let's consider the pros and cons of the education à la carte scholarship programs available at several famous fast-food franchises in America.

McDonald's. Perhaps the most widely known fast-food restaurant in the world, they offer starting pay from $7.86 to $40.12, depending upon location. McDonald's offers a 20 percent tuition reimbursement of up to $3,000 a year at select colleges. They also offer a generous scholarship program for high school students who previously worked at McDonald's. On top of this, McDonald's offers a path to management by encouraging professional development and providing the means to achieve it.[27]

Taco Bell. Taco Bell offers a late-night drive-up window, with work hours that could fit nicely into a student's weekly class scheduling. (Their tacos aren't bad either.) Associates start at $7.79 to $14.04 per hour, and in so doing can also earn $5,250 a year in benefits toward college tuition. Additionally, as of January 2020, Taco Bell has begun a program of paying its restaurant managers $100,000 a year. That is roughly twice the average starting salary of a college graduate.[28]

In-N-Out. The starting pay at In-N-Out is about $13 per hour, which is a high entry point. But there is something far more rewarding about In-N-Out than its hourly pay scale. Working your way up the organization to be a restaurant manager can lead to financial rewards even greater than the Taco Bell franchise. Since 2018, In-N-Out managers have made a salary of $160,000 per year.[29] Let that sink in—$160,000 annually—and the Irvine, California-based franchise permits employees to work their way up to that $160,000 salary without a college degree. If your motivation to attend college was to better your economic lot in life, consider that the average In-N-Out restaurant manager likely has no student debt while making three times the average college graduate's salary. Says Bill Murphy Jr. in an *Inc.* magazine article, "This might be the surest (legal) path to a six-figure salary, regardless of whether you have a high school education."[30]

Chipotle. Returning from the In-N-Out stratosphere, the starting pay scale at Chipotle is $9 to $18 per hour, which is still a boost over competitors. In addition, Chipotle has a solid education program. Full-time and part-time Chipotle employees are eligible for the educational assistance program offered through Guild Education. The program provides up to $5,250 in tuition assistance per year. In addition, associates can earn one-third of their degree without going into a classroom and can earn credit toward the degree when they get a promotion. Any full-time employee who has worked at least 180 days is eligible for this program.[31]

Kentucky Fried Chicken. For decades, I've been a fan of the Colonel's finger-lickin' good chicken. More to the point, the Colonel's starting hourly wage is $7 to $13, and his educational program is superb. The Kentucky Fried Chicken REACH Educational Grant Program is focused on helping hourly employees and shift managers at participating KFC restaurants pursue their dreams of going to college. Under the REACH program, "Employees of any age, any position, pursuing any degree can receive money to help them attend the accredited four-year or two-year college of their choice."[32]

Chick-fil-A. Starting associates at Chick-fil-A earn an hourly wage that ranges from $8.03 to $17.55—very competitive. As part of their Remarkable Futures Scholarship Program, Chick-fil-A rewards over 6,000 team members every year with a "Leadership Scholarship." In 2019, 6,016 employees across the US received a scholarship for $2,500 each.[33] Again, not bad.

Papa John's. Starting associates at Papa John's make $6.84 to $13.44, which is, again, very competitive. But the more significant educational program is a partnership with Purdue University that Papa John's calls "Dough and Degrees." After working 90 days for 20 hours a week, an employee is eligible for this tuition reimbursement program that pays up to 100 percent of any employee's tuition. Papa John's will cover undergraduate and graduate courses in business, business administration, and information technology. Note that the program funds graduate work as well, including a master's in business administration.[34]

Starbucks. Who can resist Starbucks's Reserve Hazelnut Bianco Latte? Particularly during late-night studies. Starbucks's average starting hourly wage in 2021 was $11.64. And becoming a barista could qualify you for a unique scholarship through the Starbucks College Achievement Plan. The Starbucks website elaborates: "Every benefits-eligible US partner working part or full time receives 100 percent tuition coverage for a first-time bachelor's degree through Arizona State University's online program. Choose from over 100 diverse undergraduate degree programs, and have our support every step of the way."[35] If you are a student of modest means and are willing to work, you could be a barista part time and a student part time, and graduate from Arizona State University entirely debt free. Instead of accumulating college debt, you could graduate with money in the bank and with work experience to boot.

Burger King. Some aficionados in my neighborhood consider the Whopper to be the king of burgers. Likewise, the Burger King Scholars Program is a royal deal. It has awarded "nearly $55 million in scholarships to over 45,000 high school students, BK employees, and their families across North America since 2000." Scholarships range in value from $1,000 to $50,000. In 2022, for example, "the Foundation awarded over $4.6 million in scholarships to nearly 4,000 students."[36] There are threshold requirements for GPA, community involvement, and college enrollment, so check out the Burger King application.

While we're on the topic of education à la carte and restaurant scholarships, let's expand the menu from fast food to include family dine-in restaurants. These dine-in chains offer the opportunity to learn how to deliver quality service, earn tips for the effort, develop customer facing skills, and qualify for scholarships. The list includes famous family franchises such as Denny's, Bob Evans, Cracker Barrel, IHOP, Perkins Restaurants, and Shoney's.[37] Each restaurant program is unique and worthy of a closer look. For example, since 2011, Denny's "Hungry for Education Scholarship" program has awarded $1.8 million to 436 students who write a 300-word essay on how Denny's can "positively impact childhood hunger."[38] There are about 275 words on this page. It would not be overly hard to write a 300-word essay.

One of the best parts about making use of education à la carte to fund a college degree is that one or more of these restaurants is often located within easy access of the college campus, or in some cases, directly on campus. Consider this alternative to accumulating college debt, particularly if COVID continues, and fast-food pick-up windows continue doing a land-office business.

Escape the Matrix: Get a Big-Box Business Scholarship

Beyond fast-food franchise opportunities lies another major alternative for funding college—the big-box business scholarships. If you're not fundamentally a fan of fast-food franchises serving fried foods for many hours each week, consider getting a job at a big-box business with scholarship opportunities available to part-time and full-time employees.

Walmart and Target are big-box retail competitors who also compete in the college scholarship arena. On August 4, 2021, Target Corporation announced it now offers its 340,000 frontline workers debt-free assistance for select undergraduate degrees and certificates in some 250 business programs at over 40 institutions through its "upskilling partner" at Guild Education.[39]

Not to be outdone, Target's rival, Walmart Inc., has offered to pay the full cost of college tuition and books for its roughly 1.5 million full-time and part-time employees.[40] Walmart also offers the Sam Walton Community Scholarship, the Walmart Dependent Scholarship, and the Walmart Associate Scholarship, providing a wide array of college scholarship support.[41] Consequently, an aspiring student could work part time at either Target or Walmart, qualify for these remarkable scholarship opportunities, and, in doing so, earn a low-cost degree. Both of these programs are operated through Guild Education and are restricted to employees, so it is worth confirming eligibility if you intend to pursue one of these routes.

Beyond the notion of education à la carte through fast-food franchises, family dine-in restaurants, and big-box retail chains, a number of business scholarship programs are offered by other private enterprises. A useful Hip2Save website article lists over 40 companies ranging from restaurants and grocery stores to gas companies, banks, and airlines that all offer their employees some level of tuition reimbursement.[42] At job interviews, a forward-looking student might inquire if their prospective employer offers any Employer-Provided Education Assistance Benefits under Internal Revenue Code Section 127. That will impress the interviewer and will also inform the student whether they can take advantage of up to $5,250 annually in tax-free educational assistance for undergraduate or graduate work.[43] In sum, industrious students can fund their educational journey and begin earning valuable work experience by investing their time at these companies for a few years early on.

You don't gotta go to college after high school. You can choose to get a trade certification, begin an apprenticeship, secure a position at a store or a restaurant, or take a gap year. Some of these paths may lead to a prosperous economic future, same as the pursuit of some degrees. The education à la carte and big-box business routes can give you an opportunity to consider a major that works for you, such as business or marketing, while you work part time to reduce costs.

There are also many employers who offer *student loan repayment* assistance in addition to the previously described educational assistance. They typically provide $100 a month toward your student loans as a recruiting and retention tool. The money is tax-free through December 31, 2025, and is likely to be extended or made permanent. You might want to query if your employer offers a student loan repayment program.

If you decide you gotta go to college, there are many ways in which you can fund your education without sinking into debt. We examined some of them in this chapter, including education à la carte, big-box business scholarships, military service, and a variety of corporate scholarships. But before we dig into some of the more conventional ways for students to fund a college experience, let's examine a key assumption people make when they decide they want to attend college in the first place—*I need a college degree to be successful.*

CHAPTER 2

I Need a College Degree to Be Successful

ONE GREAT REASON to attend college is to enhance your economic future. But financial success isn't the only reason to attend school. Another, equally important reason is to develop your intellectual abilities—your tool kit of thinking skills to be successful in life.

In the most idealistic sense, one might go to college to pursue inquiry for the sake of inquiry, without regard for where that inquiry leads. But as Miles K. Davis, president of Linfield University, noted recently, colleges have "priced ourselves out of [the inquiry] market," and students now "want a return on their investment."[1] What does such a return on investment look like? We address the financial return on investment notion later, but for this chapter the question arises: What intellectual return on investment do college students hope to achieve to be successful?

As a business owner for the last 17 years, I have developed several ideas on what it takes for an employee to be successful in a work environment. Much of what employers look for in employees can be produced through completion of a college course. But it is not a foregone conclusion that college classes will make you a better or more competitive employee. To be that you must acquire critical thinking skills. As a student, wouldn't it be great if you could know in advance of the job interview what skills a prospective employer will be looking for? You'd have a leg up on the other competitors. So, what exactly is an employer looking for in a work environment? Here's my take on the question.

As an employer, I am looking for someone who has developed a tool kit of essential skills necessary to succeed in their chosen field. To me, that tool kit consists of three essential soft skills and two essential hard skills. These skills in some form are needed to be successful, and they can be gained either in or out of college.

Essential Skills from an HR Perspective

To introduce the essential skills, let's start with the viewpoint of the professionals responsible for hiring recommendations at most companies—managers of Human Resources (HR). These professionals have a bird's-eye view of critical skill sets needed by prospective employees. College students preparing for their careers would be wise to think deeply about the skills their future employers are seeking so they can develop those very skills in college. Hearing it straight from HR managers is like stealing the signs from the opposing baseball team. You know what to expect and how to prepare for it.

In a perceptive article from the Society for Human Resource Management (SHRM) titled "What Happened to the Promise of a 4-Year College Degree?"[2] Ms. Dana Wilkie shares insights about needed skills she gained over years as an HR professional. Wilkie highlights the "growing disconnect" between what the students will learn from professors and what their employers will expect from them. Because of this disconnect, new graduates "will be unemployed, underemployed, or struggling professionally," despite having applied themselves academically and despite having accumulated substantial student loan debt in the process.[3]

A leading disconnect between what colleges teach and what employers require is the absence of "soft skills" in recent college graduates. From a corporate hiring perspective, Ms. Wilkie identifies these skills as the ability to "write clearly, speak persuasively, think critically, work independently, and show initiative."[4] Take particular note of this list. These soft skills are critical in the workplace but may not be acquired during the standard college experience if a student isn't both aware of them and intentional about acquiring them through such activities as internships and summer jobs. Ms. Wilkie's article quotes Brenda Leadley, senior vice president and head of HR Americas at Allianz Global Corporate & Specialty in New York, regarding the level of preparedness attained by college graduates today. "They really haven't gotten to where I would expect people were 20 years ago."[5]

The skills employers look for can be acquired through a college education, but the student must focus on them. For example, a person who takes a college course in American history may acquire the soft skill of critical thinking and the hard skill of in-depth research. But if a student is unaware that they need to develop these essential skills, it is possible they might drift through classes without internalizing them. While it is true that a student may become well educated in college, simply going to college does not guarantee a quality education. A student must be mindful in this pursuit.

Essential Soft Skills

Three essential soft skills students should acquire—either inside or outside of a college education—include conversation, persuasion, and analysis. These skills enable an employee to effectively work with others, to be a good time manager, and to efficiently identify and prioritize tasks on the job, which are necessary at some level in every field.

1. CONVERSATIONAL SKILLS

Conversation is a useful skill to have in any social or business setting and is particularly critical in the fields of sales and marketing. The ability to engage in meaningful conversation is a cornerstone of those two fields, yet that ability receives little emphasis in college and can be weakened through lack of exercise. As Sherry Turkle has observed, "We live in a technological universe in which we are always communicating. And yet we have sacrificed conversation for mere connection."[6] Learning to converse well, in essence, gives you the ability to empathize with people, which is essential in the workplace.

When people fail to launch or move forward in their career, one can often trace the failure back to an inability to deal with people. They can't communicate comfortably. In her book *How to Talk to Anyone: 92 Little Tricks for Big Success in Relationships*, Leil Lowndes observes that the ability to converse meaningfully with others often starts with small talk because "small talk is about putting people at ease."[7]

Meaningful conversation starts with small talk? No way.

Yes way.

Small talk isn't a small thing. Small talk is an acknowledgment of the humanity of the person in front of you and a gateway into their thinking. Small talk is a stepping stone to improving how we deal with each other. It is also a skill you can learn and develop to deepen connections with other people.

Here's an example of small talk that led to a deeper connection. At a hotel in San Antonio, I met a Texan wearing a cowboy hat in the hotel spa and opened a conversation with small talk. "What do you think of this rain?"

He responded, "The fish hit better in the rain."

I then knew the man enjoyed fishing and inquired about this hobby. He explained how his father had taught him how to fish as a child, which led to his lifelong enjoyment of the sport. We talked amiably about fishing for another few minutes, and then he said to me, "I haven't shared this before, but my dad spent his last day fishing with me on a sandbar in the Brazos River." I nodded. He continued, "He was casting his line into the water and he suddenly had a heart attack. I rushed to his side. He told me he loved me and I told him I loved him too, and then he passed." Small talk had opened a path directly from the weather to this man's heart.

The foundation of the ability to deal with people is the capacity to communicate with them. If you decide to go to college, practice your conversational skills as you walk between classes or when going out for dinner. Don't coast through public speaking classes or presentational assignments, use them to develop your communication skills. Consider getting involved with debate. Recognize the conversational art as a worthy objective to pursue in school.

You can become a better conversationalist in college but doing so requires taking careful advantage of the communication opportunities available to you. Wherever you are, remember that educating yourself for future success requires an education in conversation, and only half of the conversation involves speaking well. The other half is active listening.

Most people I meet seem to think that "listening" is the time when they pretend to look interested while they formulate their next argument. You can tell when they're doing it, and it feels artificial. The listening skill that is truly attractive to others is "active listening," by which the listener discerns another person's true intent. There are four levels of this type of listening.

Before addressing the four levels of active listening, let's start with a bite-size chunk: listening to and remembering the name of the person to whom you are speaking. Sounds simple enough. But how many times have you been in conversations with another person and they forgot your name immediately after the introduction? One trick that often works, besides asking for their business card, is to ask them how to spell their name. Another is to use a mnemonic device linking their name with some feature of their face, like "Rose has rosy cheeks," or "Bill's eyes are blue." Then when you see the feature, you remember the name. In any case, figure out a way to listen for and remember people's names. Now let's dig deeper.

There are many courses in active listening available on the web. The best I've seen is offered by Mr. Sanford Wilder of the Educare Unlearning Institute in St. Louis. Mr. Wilder describes four progressive levels of listening as audible, visual, empathetic, and intuitive. Here is a summary of Mr. Wilder's Four Dimensions of Listening.

Think of how differently people might relate to you if, when they are speaking, you devoted your undivided attention to listening to what they were saying. It's simple in the saying, difficult in the doing. That type of listening engenders a trusting relationship. How refreshing! A good target for when you graduate from college would be to have mastered all four dimensions of listening. You can develop active listening in college even if your coursework doesn't include it. Nobody ever listened themselves out of college.

Effective conversation is a particularly tall order in modern times when we are accustomed to multitasking and scanning the small screen continuously. But in any business or employment setting after college, you'll be dealing with people and will need to connect with them. Being able to speak with others and relate to them under any circumstances ensures they will always take your call when that call matters.

FOUR DIMENSIONS OF LISTENING

Dimension	Attitude	Attention	Dialogue	Listening Activity
1	Interested	Audible	Chitchat—informational questions (who, what, when, where).	*Facts*: Focus on facts and details. Recognize what the person is saying. *Ideas*: Focus on concepts; understand the meaning.
2	Sincerely Creating a Connection	Visual	Gentle questions (why, how). Not probing to pry open or intrude. Ask the 2nd and 3rd questions. Self-disclosure—share common experiences, ideas, or feelings.	*Current Context:* Analyze meanings relevant to situation. *Understanding:* Synthesize meanings. Paraphrase to check for accuracy.
3	Empathetic, Curious	Mental, Physical, Emotional	Warm, perceptive, authentic questions and responses. Keep the focus on the other person and do not shift it to the listener. Do not judge—accept whatever is shared and let distractions fade.	*Motivation*: Recognize why the person is speaking. See and paraphrase the significance of the issue to the other person. This naturally increases your capacity for empathy. *Feelings*: Acknowledge how they are feeling and accept this as their truth. *Inspiration:* Allow them to breathe and pause between ideas and feelings.
4	Humble, Unselfed	Awareness, Intuitive, Being, Soul, Presence	No agenda or pre-determined outcomes. Lots of silence—patient, purposeful, appropriately timed questions and responses. The conversation feels ordered for and through you, not by you.	*Silent Surfing*: Ride the wave of the person's feelings to new shores. *Trusting*: Be willing to leave the known; open and reach to find the unknown. *Nurturing*: Promote the development of new ideas. *Discovering*: Explore new views together. Synergy.

Figure 5.[8]

To be successful in business and life means learning to both converse and listen. These soft skills connect you to people. Make learning to listen one of the stops in your educational journey.

2. PERSUASION SKILLS

Persuasion is the second essential soft skill in the workplace, and it flows right out of the first one. After you've established trust through conversation, you can use that trust to guide another person's thought toward an intended outcome through persuasion.

Managers value persuasive employees. These are the individuals who sell products, who make deals, and who establish beneficial connections with other companies and promote valuable services. These are the individuals trusted to manage others. Persuasive employees are the individuals who get promoted.

Unlike some other soft skills that are not part of the college curriculum, persuasion skills may be part of it. For example, you can acquire persuasive skills through debate programs and courses in logic that teach how to marshal facts. You can improve your skills through philosophy classes that teach the difference between inductive and deductive reasoning, *a priori* and *a posteriori* knowledge, *ad hominem* and *ad rem* arguments, and how to be intentional in your thinking. Those academic pursuits will enhance your ability to convince others and will help you master a complete tool kit of persuasion skills. You'll want that tool kit when you graduate and move into the workforce, so start now.

The basic persuasive skill allows you to marshal arguments in favor of positions you stand for and against ones you disagree with. Shape your arguments in a way that leads a listener to reach your conclusion. You can be persuasive by stacking fact upon fact, "line upon line, precept upon precept," as the Bible admonishes in Isaiah 28:10, until your conclusion is seen as indisputable.

You can learn logic and persuasive argument in college, but you can't learn when to persist in persuasion and when to give it up. That's something experience teaches you. But it's also an essential component of being well educated. Determining the point at which your persuasion is seen as overbearing and becomes counterproductive is a fine art. It takes time and practice to walk that line.

If you decide to attend college, use your elective courses in a productive manner and take courses in logic and philosophy, but also make good use of your extracurricular activities. Get involved with student organizations requiring good relations with others and participation even when you are not the designated leader of the activity. Develop your soft skills in conversation and persuasion and learn to relate to and manage others in the controlled environment that college provides.

If you have a part-time job or internship or choose to pursue full-time employment instead of attending college, take advantage of the opportunities your work affords you to become more accomplished in soft skills. Get experience in what it is like to build a connection with others and then persuade them to a certain course of action. As you practice your soft skills, you will become more adept, more confident, and a more valuable employee.

3. ANALYTICAL SKILLS

The third soft skill that I look for as an employer is the ability to analyze data. Analytical skills give you the capacity to think through problems based on data acquired in your research. The skill of analysis helps you assign proper weight to the various factors in a decision process so that the most important elements receive the strongest consideration. Analyzing problems in a business or organizational setting is not just the function of a data analyst. Every individual in a work setting is asked to analyze what's going on around them.

When I worked in the Pentagon for the Undersecretary for Personnel and Readiness, my boss was a career civil servant who had perfected her analytical ability to make sound policy decisions. How did she do it? For starters, she studied issues until she became the subject matter expert on all the major policies in her domain.

To our point, she had schooled herself in weighing competing aspects of a problem and assigning a value to each aspect. She analyzed issues without getting attached to any particular viewpoint or outcome. She sought counsel from subordinates and superiors in the organization. She knew the strengths and weaknesses of everyone in her sprawling organization, so she could identify and discard any bias that might color an argument from any individual.

Once she had gathered and weighed the information necessary to make a decision, she drew her own well-informed conclusion. Here was an analytical mind at work, sifting through reams of information to make sound policy decision after sound policy decision. Time and again, my Pentagon boss exemplified the ability to apply analytical skills to guide important policy positions for the Department of Defense.

Developing analytical skills requires an inquiring mind and a capacity for critical thinking. How does one acquire an inquiring mind?

Good question.

Ask questions.

My high school history teacher, Mr. Robert N. McKenney, taught the wisdom of the ages when he observed, "Education is not about getting the right answers to questions, it's about asking the right questions to answer." That, right there, is solid gold. To master the art of analysis, focus on unbridled inquiry. Asking the right question flows from a hunger to figure things out. Imagine a college experience that feeds that hunger.

You can develop the analytical habit of asking questions both in and out of college. Start researching things you're interested in. Make a point of finding answers for yourself instead of taking what you are told on faith. Once you've found your first answers, ask more questions. Ask, "What does this mean?" and "What can I do with this information?" Ask, "Is there any inconsistency here?" and "How can I apply what I know to be more efficient?"

When you develop and wield an inquiring mind correctly and when you have mastered the art of analysis, you will have increased your value to potential employers. You will be able to do your work, whatever it is, more effectively and use that efficacy to build a foundation for future success. And after all, isn't that the point of a good education?

Essential Hard Skills

In addition to developing essential soft skills, there are several hard skills that are critical for the workplace. Individuals hoping to be effective in their job can consider themselves well educated when they master these skills. Here, the disconnect between what colleges teach and what employers expect is even more apparent. For example, many business students lack skills in using spreadsheets.

The previously cited SHRM article references Martin Fiore, a managing partner in tax for a firm in New York City, on this point. Surprisingly, many college business graduates he hires lack basic spreadsheet skills in tools such as

Microsoft Excel, even though these skills are essential for "collecting, organizing, and analyzing data"[9] and would be expected of a college graduate.

This gap in hard skills between employer expectations and student competency raises broader concerns for the future. The SHRM article cites Sue Bhatia, founder of Rose International, a staffing agency based in Chesterfield, Missouri, who notes a lag between the old model of education and the new model of work. Many skills learned in college will be irrelevant soon after the graduating students begin their careers.[10]

This trend does not bode well for students who, while still in college, fail to focus on the hard skills that employers need. Employer investment in training new workers seems to be declining. In the SHRM article, Ms. Wilkie notes that in times past, business leaders would task their managers to teach new employees on the job. That provided a transition for new employees to gain needed skills. However, in today's environment, small and midsize businesses may not have the resources to train new employees on the job. The problem goes deeper, Wilkie explains, because even if businesses do train new employees, "the tendency for younger workers to job-hop and the rise of gig workers" may deter employers from expending their limited training budgets on new hires.[11] When you think about it from an employer's perspective, the employer spent resources to recruit you, on-board you, and equip you. Why should they spend more money to train you when you could be leaving in a few months? You need to show up on day one having trained yourself.

Wilkie raises useful questions for college students about what the focus of their education in college should be. If college is meant to prepare students for meaningful employment, students should spend their time in college making certain they acquire the hard and soft skills their prospective employers are looking for. If those skills are best developed through self-study, should students spend their money and accumulate debt to pursue college courses?

1. RESEARCH SKILLS

Research skills are critical in any professional setting. You can pick them up through college from the exercise of writing term papers, performing lab studies, participating in debate, taking prelaw classes, and completing related assignments. Or you can be an autodidact and teach them to yourself through online study. But the research skill that will catch an employer's interest is the capacity to maintain curiosity about a topic and dig beyond the initial Google search until you have found actionable data.

The keys here are inquisitiveness, curiosity, and the drive to understand the *why* behind the issue. The research skill that's needed for work is the ability to determine what's missing from the existing analysis and then research the solution until you find that missing element. In the military, this was sometimes called a "sanity check" or an "acid test" to distinguish it from a cursory review or a textual edit. The terms refer to a fresh look at a problem with inquisitiveness to identify any key elements that have been left out of the first analysis. This open-minded curiosity is the requisite mental outlook for research in a professional setting. This outlook can uncover the truth that applies to a problem at hand so that it can be acted on at work.

The outlook of inquiry requires that students pursue the question *Why?* until they find the answer, regardless of where the answer leads. This approach to research includes the requirement to lay aside one's preconceptions and biases in favor of pursuing the unvarnished truth. A person who does this consistently will be highly sought after by an employer.

On many college campuses today, the notion of unbridled inquiry may seem to be in decline, in favor of received wisdom. But that will be no concern to a person who is committed to the pursuit of analyzing issues to uncover truth. People are entitled to think what they want in college (and to pay as much as they want to think what they want). But in a business or work setting, believing what you're told simply because you haven't researched your own conclusion can be a recipe for disaster. That's how problems get missed. It's how mistakes get made. Sometimes, it's how people get fired. The better outlook is to pursue analysis through inquiry tethered to initiative.

For example, one of my employees in the construction business once researched Salesforce software as a means to improve our customer relationship management (CRM). He discovered the software could be expanded to include construction progress. He then set his mind to programming the available Salesforce software modules that our company had purchased to link construction progress to our reporting system. When he completed the programming, he could track the sales cycle from initial prospect all the way to project completion.

His insight saved our company time, money, and effort. He demonstrated initiative in the workplace that increased his value as an employee. Interestingly, this employee didn't have a college degree. But he did have an inquisitive mind and the initiative to first analyze the problem, then teach himself how to program Salesforce software, and lastly to institute the program upgrade.

2. COMPUTING SKILLS

Let's let the great Steve Jobs, the pioneer of the personal computer revolution, speak to us on computing skills. Some 30 years ago, Mr. Jobs included a Lip Service voice clip when sending out his NeXT Computer. There aren't many of the clips left, but Tim Berners-Lee recalls the Lip Service voice clip he received in September 1990 that captured Steve Jobs's vision, "It's not about personal computers, it's about interpersonal computing."[12] It's not about computers, it's about the skill of *computing.*

Steve Jobs's comment revealed he was focused on using the computer to perform computing functions needed in life and in the workplace. Computing is the destination, computers are the route. If that's good enough for the world-famous dropout from Reed College, it's good enough for me. I don't have any particular subject matter expertise in computing, but I'm a happy consumer of it.

Computing skills can include programming, networking, and data analysis. At a more basic level, they include the capacity to work within the Microsoft Office suite, Google Workspace, and the Apple universe to get things done effectively and efficiently. In my current business setting, Microsoft Outlook, Word, Excel, and PowerPoint seem to be a standard office software package. Google Workspace Mail, Docs, Sheets, and Slides offer another popular suite. A forward-looking student might want to learn them both, along with how to navigate the Mac world if, like me, that world is not familiar to you.

As a minimum, a well-educated person today must have basic office computing skills. At the entry level, this means the ability to create emails, documents, spreadsheets, tables, and presentations. In the construction world that my company inhabits, there is a need for office computing skills to create proposals, analyze data, perform construction, and a host of other sales, operations, and financial functions.

Interestingly, some recent college graduates that I've interviewed for job openings have had only the most rudimentary understanding of office computing skills. Does that describe you? If so, as a strategy to improve your competitive advantage, take some classes in each of the Microsoft and Google packages during a summer break. There are computer training schools in every town and city. These computing courses generally cost about $125 each, last about a day, and can seriously elevate your skills. Or get trained online. Check out www.onlc.com for Microsoft training or www.wyzant.com for a computer skills tutor. Then, after you graduate, when you're in a job interview, you can comfortably converse with your prospective boss about your office computer skills and convince them that you can make an immediate contribution to the enterprise. A few certifications here can go a long way.

To advance in the workplace today and make yourself indispensable, add network and programming skills to your basic computer skills. These additional skills will allow you to ask and answer your employer's question: "How can we do this task better, cheaper, smarter, faster, and more profitably?" The answer often lies in automating multiple tasks to eliminate repetitious, time-consuming work. I'm preaching to the choir for all the computer science majors, so you can skip over this next part.

You may not feel that you were cut out to do computer work, which may well be true. But you are certainly cut out to ask a question about how your organization could do a task more efficiently and effectively. And for that question, you need to acquire elemental office computing skills.

From an employer's perspective, the hard and soft skills discussed previously are essential to be successful in any work setting, whether those skills are developed inside or outside of college. If you have acquired these skills by the end of your college education, you will be well educated in the eyes of anyone who might want to employ you. As an added bonus, if they should ever decide to let you go, you will have a good start on the skills necessary to be your own boss.

Ultimately, the skills you acquire, rather than the sheepskin you display, could be your ticket to succuss. This is particularly true in light of an emerging trend among federal and state hiring authorities to replace the job requirement of a college degree with a more targeted requirement for a skills-based assessment. In the federal sector, the US House of Representatives recently passed a bill titled "The Chance to Compete Act" that would effectively put skills-based assessments above educational requirements for some federal hiring.[13] Championed by the Society for Human Resource Management (SHRM), "the bill would prioritize candidate evaluations based on knowledge, skills, abilities and competencies while limiting the use of education when determining if someone is qualified for a role."[14] To take effect as law, this bipartisan House bill will need to pass the Senate and be signed by the president, which has not occurred as of this writing. But a trend is clearly emerging toward skills-based assessments. The trend is gathering momentum on the strength of initiatives by several state governments including Maryland,[15] Utah,[16] and Pennsylvania,[17] which are discussed in more detail in the endnotes. As momentum builds, and as the workforce shrinks, skills-based governmental hiring is likely to expand into private sector hiring. The skills you acquire in your educational journey could be as valuable to you as your degree.

Escaping the Matrix: Get What You Want from Your Education

You can be successful with or without a college degree by developing your hard and soft skills to be effective in the workplace. There are ways to obtain those skills outside of academia, so if you don't feel you are developing the essential skills in college, look elsewhere. For example, students can self-educate through Khan Academy and other avenues that offer free online courses, sometimes called MOOCs, that are available for anyone interested.

The counterpoint argument is that these soft skills are obtainable in university by choosing the kind of institution you attend (say, a technical institute) or by curating your classes carefully (especially noncore courses) to include computing skills.

You might also be the sort of person who is able to teach yourself through personal study or YouTube videos. If so, you may well be able to acquire the essential skills needed for business and life without attending postsecondary schooling. If, however, self-study isn't your strength or you simply prefer the help and broader knowledge available through a college education, by all means, attend college.

But make sure you go into the experience with clarity on what skills an employer is seeking from you as a prospective hire. And either during or after your college experience, acquire those skills. If you decide to attend college, plan on being a good consumer of the education products on offer. Rather than drifting through the four years without a clear purpose, set some simple objectives.

As a well-informed investigator of education programs, you also might want to make good use of a gap year to hone your hard and soft skills. That honing work could facilitate your becoming a better consumer of your education while in college. As noted by Doug Belkin in a *Wall Street Journal* article, "Going to college to find yourself has become a luxury many Americans can no longer afford."[18] Mr. Belkin cites Brandon Busteed, executive director of Education and Global Workforce Development at Gallup, to emphasize that drifting through college is not a viable option. If a student can't really afford college, Mr. Busteed suggests a gap year. This way, students can identify areas of interest and develop a plan to acquire the skills needed to succeed in future employment. After the gap year, when the student matriculates into college, they can make a point of using the classwork to develop and exercise essential soft and hard skills for post-college employment.[19]

The counterpoint to this argument is that a gap year could derail your college experience. Citing student matriculation data to argue against taking a gap year in his book, *Who Graduates from College? Who Doesn't*, Mark Kantrowitz notes, "Students who take a gap year or delay their enrollment in college are almost half as likely to graduate with a bachelor's degree."[20] Only 90 percent of students who take a gap year return to college. At that point, they are about half as likely to graduate with a bachelor's degree within four years and a third less likely to graduate within six years.[21] So if you plan to take a gap year, be firm in your intention to return and enroll in college.

There are many ways for you to become well educated outside of the Student Loan Matrix thinking and outside of college itself. If you elect to attend college, you can apply these same means to become well educated in college to prepare for a successful career and life after school. The key is to set your sights on acquiring essential skills by the time you graduate so you can begin to build that successful career.

CHAPTER 3

Tuition Is the Total Cost of College

MANY PEOPLE MAKE THE MISTAKE of underestimating the total cost of college by looking only at the tuition price and concluding that is all they will need to cover. They confuse the college's tuition cost, which is simply the charge for teaching or instruction, with the total cost of attending college, which includes other costs such as housing, meals, transportation, entertainment, books, fees, and loan interest.

Generally speaking, the largest element of college cost will be tuition. However, in some states, where the public colleges do not control tuition rates, they compensate by increasing the fees. In this case, the cost of "fees" may approach the cost of tuition, so it is important to understand the school's cost of "tuition and fees" as well as its cost of "tuition." Tuition is the benchmark used in common parlance for comparison with other colleges. It is the variable that contributes most to student debt. But it is not the total cost of college. To get a clear idea of total college costs, let's be very precise in defining the various elements of cost and then tracking them through the four-year process to get the big picture.

Defining Terms to Understand College Debt

To better understand the various costs involved in obtaining a degree, let's begin by defining three key terms regarding college costs: the *total cost of college* (the basket of all expenses), the *total resources for college* (the student and family–combined resources available for college), and the *total spent for college* (the total amount spent, *past tense*, for college up to the point of graduation).

We define the term *total cost of college*, consistent with the federal definition, to mean the basket of all expenses required to complete college including tuition and fees, room and board, books, supplies, equipment, transportation and miscellaneous personal expenses, as well as the cost of a computer, software and peripherals (and Internet access), dependent care costs, and disability-related expenses. In individual circumstances, the total cost of college may also include student athletic event fees, entertainment, and unique expenses relating to specific majors. Although it is not included in the federal definition of total cost of college attendance, in this book we add the cost of *interest* on the loans because the majority of students will take on student loans. Pay particular attention to the cost of *interest incurred on debt* because over time this unheralded cost can have disproportionate consequences as we will discuss later. The emphasis on tuition in some college brochures may lead students to conclude that tuition is the only cost for students and their families to address. Not so.

This misconception can produce sticker shock when students learn the full cost of attendance and realize their savings and earnings won't cover the total cost.[1] Later on in their academic career, coming to the full realization of college costs can lead to the unfortunate outcome that a large percentage of students then drop out. Studies have shown most students who drop out of college choose to leave after their first year. Perhaps that is when economic reality hits and the total cost of college is fully understood.

The next term we need to define is *total resources for college*. This is the combination of cash, college savings, 529 plans, or other assets that a student and their family have set aside specifically to meet the demand of college costs. The resources may include:

1. a student savings account

2. a savings account created by the student's parents for college

3. earnings of both the student and their parents during college to make payments

4. long-term savings plans such as a tax-advantaged 529 college savings plan, a prepaid tuition plan, a Coverdell Education Savings Account (ESA), and a Roth IRA for education

Note that for our discussion here, the term "total resources" refers to internal family resources and does NOT include grants, scholarships, and other external funding sources. Those are included in the term *total spent for college* as discussed next. Note also that while a family can build their total resources in preparation for the economic impact of college costs, the total resources are generally less than what is required to pay the total cost of college, depending on a student's choices of college and other funding avenues they can use.

The final definition for our discussion is the *total spent for college*. The past tense of the word "spend" is used here because this amount is determined in retrospect after graduation. The total spent is the bucket of funds that was actually used to meet the total cost of college and includes the external financial resources used in addition to the family resources. Specifically, these external resources may include the following:

1. Scholarships

2. Grants

3. Loans

4. Gifts

5. Discounts

6. Trust funds

7. Specific federal program

This last category includes education tax breaks, like the American Opportunity Tax Credit, the Lifetime Learning Tax Credit and the Student Loan Interest Deduction, as well as the Student Loan Repayment Assistance Programs (LRAPs). This category also includes student employment, like Federal Work-Study and College Work-Study with part-time jobs on campus if federally funded. Other jobs on or near campus could fall into this category or be considered part of the total resources discussed previously.

All of these categories of funding, plus the family's total resources, may be tapped to cover the total costs of college—and some combination of them will add up to the total spent for college. We discuss the remaining debt and accumulated interest on that debt later.

One might ask, why go to the trouble to make these distinctions about funding and costs? Why use these specific terms? Answer: because the common usage of the words "student debt" can hide an important fact about actual college costs that needs to be carefully considered. Specifically, the term "student debt" commonly refers to the average loan amount remaining after college graduation, which we often hear is in the $30,000 range. We need to be clear that the student debt remaining after college costs does not represent the total amount spent for college. Recall that in the introduction, we noted that only 10 percent of the total college cost was covered by student borrowing while 8 percent was from parent borrowing. The rest of those costs sometimes get overlooked in the debt discussion.

What is commonly referred to as "student debt" is simply what remains to be paid after four (or more) years of expenses have already been shelled out as of graduation day. Those payments typically included expenditures over four years from many sources: parent savings, student savings, parent earnings, student earnings, gifts, college savings plans, loans, scholarships, and grants.

Consequently, the notion that the average student debt is $30,000 fails to account for the student and family resources already contributed prior to graduation day. When they review their student loan repayment plan after graduation, students may overlook what they have already spent on college. So we use the terms *total cost*, *total resources*, and *total spent* to focus on the larger financial picture.

At the conclusion of this chapter, we discuss an additional cost, the *lost opportunity cost*, which must be added to the total cost of college to get the complete financial picture. The *lost opportunity cost* arises from the inability to pursue income-producing work full time during your years of college attendance. It represents what a student could have earned if they had chosen to enter the job market or a trade immediately after high school graduation. When we add the lost opportunity cost to other college costs, we get a fuller picture of the dollars involved in the college decision. In short, there are numerous costs in addition to the cost of tuition. Before exploring those costs, let's quickly address "free college" programs that relate primarily to tuition.

IS FREE COLLEGE REALLY FREE?

Several states are now offering programs known as "free college" or "college promise" that sound like they cover the total costs of college. Not so. These worthwhile programs often provide free tuition to specific, usually low-income, students at community or state institutions, but they don't cover the total costs.[2] A good example is the New York Excelsior Scholarship program, which covers "public tuition not already paid for by other grants for students with a household income under $125,000."[3] In order to qualify, "recipients need to be state residents for a year before college, enroll as full-time undergraduates, and stay on track to finish on time."[4]

However, the author of an insightful *Christian Science Monitor* article titled "Is 'Free College' Really Free?"[5] notes that free college programs aren't "as simple as the hyperbolic label makes it sound," because the living expenses, textbooks, and other nontuition costs "are often higher than public tuition and aren't covered by most programs."[6] Consequently, "free college" programs, while helpful, useful, and worth pursuing to offset college costs, often only account for tuition,[7] rather than the total cost of college, which is our focus in this chapter.

Elements Composing the Total Cost of College

When students think inside the Student Loan Matrix and become trapped by the assumption that tuition is the total cost of college, they can severely underestimate their expenses over four to six years. Let's review some of the costs they may not have thought to include in their total cost for college.

Colleges and universities typically post costs of attendance on their websites but not necessarily on their financial aid award letters as noted by the GAO study discussed previously. Some don't list any costs on the award letters, while others list just direct costs (amounts for tuition and other expenses that are paid directly to the college). To their credit, they often include the estimated costs of the other factors in the figures they provide. However, read the qualifiers about those estimated costs carefully. Are they averages, medians, or estimates? Textbooks and transportation are often low-balled underestimates, intentionally understated to make the college look less expensive. Including PLUS loans in the package as if they operate as grants is another trick used to make the college look less expensive.[8] As a knowledgeable consumer of this information, be very wary and ask questions about the figures presented. What is the sample group, and how was the data developed? Does it include empirical studies on what students actually paid for food, rent, or transportation on campus? Or are they truly just estimates? How recently were these figures updated?

A college's reported average for estimated costs may not match up to your actual individual costs. Consider the travel costs for families from California whose children attend eastern universities. Consider the housing costs for students who live off campus in New York City or the utility costs for off-campus housing in northern Michigan. And consider the food costs for off-campus students in all locations. Your individual expenses could vary substantially from published data so you want to query the source of the information. Be aware that colleges are required to have four "student budgets," one for students living on campus in college-owned or operated housing, another for students living off campus in an apartment, and a third for students living off campus with their parents or other family. A fourth student budget for students who live in military housing zeroes out the housing cost since it is covered by the federal government.[9] The point is that these costs may not be personalized to your individual circumstances so it's useful to know the source of the reported costs to be able to compare those costs to your personal circumstances.

Several other costs may be unique to your experience. For example, entertainment costs for theater majors may not find their way into reported costs. If your off-campus housing is located a good distance from campus, your commuting costs may outstrip college averages, particularly if you choose to use Uber/Lyft over public transportation. Likewise, fees for laboratory use, computer time, and printing or copying that may be necessary to complete requirements for technical degrees may or may not show up in official cost estimates. Also be alert to the issue of "differential tuition," where tuition may be higher for specific academic majors or captured by a separate course fee.[10] As a shrewd consumer of the educational product, you will want to know if the average college costs reported include all the costs you might personally incur.

An important concept to understand in this regard is the term "net price," which describes the price after the college has lowered the estimated sticker price tag by including significant downward adjustments such as discounts, scholarships, or grants. Be alert to the use of the term net price—particularly if you don't qualify for those adjustments. The net price represents the average number of students who received scholarships, grants, and loans in previous years to determine how much the student body (as a whole) pays on average. The net price may not apply to your specific circumstances.

When discussing the actual cost of tuition with the financial aid officer, particularly at private colleges and universities, it is useful to know if the *published* tuition cost can be substantially discounted for the students. A 2019 study by the National Association of College and University Business Officers (NACUBO) revealed that new freshmen at private schools received an average discount of 53 percent in 2019.[11] According to the study, incoming first-year students were actually paying less than half of the published price. But this information is only applicable to the few hundred private colleges who participate in the NACUBO survey, and does not include figures for public colleges. For those figures refer to the book *How to Appeal for More College Financial Aid* by Mark Kantrowitz.[12] As this book title highlights, when you negotiate with the financial aid office, don't overlook the prospect of appealing your financial aid award to get a higher amount. Determining the actual cost for your circumstances and lowering that cost is critical.

Equally significant, the NACUBO study shows that about 89 percent of the incoming first-year class received aid from the institution they planned to attend. Among those, the average award equaled 60 percent of the published price.[13] These discount statistics merit an informed conversation with your financial aid officer[14] to determine where your particular package lands in the spectrum. The crucial question to ask the financial aid officer is "What is the net price after applying the gift aid?" This will reveal the difference between the total college costs and the grants and scholarships that do not need to be repaid. Then ask if the net price changes from the first year to subsequent years. In short, net price is the concept that matters to the family. It will give you a sense of the actual tuition expense that your family will have to cover.

Why Is Tuition Rising So Fast?

Even though tuition isn't the total cost of college, it is a big driver. Discounts and extras aside, you may well be wondering, "Why does tuition cost so much?" What are the factors that drive that number higher each year? An article by Amanda Ripley in *The Atlantic* noted that "the US would still spend more per college student than any other country (except . . . Luxembourg)," even if the fancy room and board were subtracted from the bill.[15]

According to Ms. Ripley, the root cause of rising tuition costs is the increase in normal institutional expenses. Says Ripley, "It turns out that the vast majority of American college spending goes to routine educational operations—like paying staff and faculty—not to dining halls. These costs add up to about $23,000 per student a year [in 2017]—more than twice what Finland, Sweden, or Germany spends on core services."[16] So one explanation for why tuition costs are astronomical is that colleges have to pay their faculty and staff and maintain the physical plant.

But looking beyond routine educational operations, college costs are also rising because faculty, administration, and staff have expanded in academia proportional to the increase in enrollment. Regarding this rising cost of overhead, Holman W. Jenkins Jr., a columnist in the *Wall Street Journal,* observed that "[t]he price of a college education is inflating out of sight . . . and meanwhile educational overhead is ballooning. America's four-year colleges spend less than 30 percent of their budgets on their actual mission, i.e., 'instruction.' "[17] A wise consumer of educational services would therefore want to know what percentage of the college budget goes toward overhead as opposed to instruction.

A noteworthy exception to the model of ballooning educational overhead costs is Purdue University in West Lafayette, Indiana. Purdue has not increased its overall costs for the past 10 years through a strategy of holding tuition level and actually lowering the cost of books, room, and board.[18] Purdue's President, Mitch Daniels, attributes this phenomenon to Purdue's unique budget approach: "We simply ask ourselves each year, 'Can we solve the equation for zero?'—meaning, What would it take to avoid the fee increase? This approach has had a favorable impact on the student population. Ten years on, more than 60 percent of our students graduate debt free."[19] The Purdue University strategy demonstrates that ballooning educational overhead costs can be controlled. Sometimes, this may mean larger class sizes, more adjunct and part-time faculty, and more cuts in services. But savvy students can look for colleges that model this kind of approach to costs and find one that is affordable in their particular financial circumstances.

Since tuition and other costs at the majority of universities have grown faster than an average college graduate's salary can cover—and the student is ultimately obliged to foot the bill—we need some tools to calculate the total cost of obtaining a college degree. The next three sections offer a methodology to make that calculation for a private university, a public university, or two years of community college plus two years at a public university.

CALCULATING THE TOTAL COST AT A PRIVATE UNIVERSITY

It is relatively easy to read college literature and spot the stated cost. But what you need to dig out is the actual total cost for you to attend that college or university as compared to the published cost. Since the school's published literature may not be sufficient for an individual student to determine their total cost, it's best to conduct some independent research.

There are several resources to make this independent research easier. The College Board website, www.collegeboard.org, offers a useful tool to begin to estimate the total cost of college attendance. Then investigate websites like www.smartasset.com and www.studentloanhero.com that offer financial calculators to help determine how much your student loans will ultimately cost you and what percent of your future paycheck that would be. For best result, these tools should be used together to project the total cost of attendance based on your unique situation.

For fun, let's work through an example using published data from a top-tier private college, Harvard University, to arrive at the total cost. Let's assume that in 2021–22, Harvard's website advertised the total cost of attendance at the university to be $78,028 per year. This figure includes tuition, room, board, fees, supplies, books, and transportation. But does it cover your personal costs? Hard to tell. To tailor the figure to your personal situation would require further inquiry. But we will use the $78,028 figure for this example of how to go about determining college costs at a private university for yourself.

Harvard's website also shows a net price calculator that asks for certain financial information and estimates the amount of financial assistance you may receive. That calculator is useful to you, but remember a couple of factors that influence the amount of financial aid. Harvard has no control over your FAFSA application or the number of grants or loans the FAFSA report may recommend for you. Since Harvard uses the CSS Profile for determining eligibility for its own grants, not only the FAFSA, Harvard's net price calculator is somewhat personalized to your situation and Harvard's financial aid packaging philosophy. The estimate, as stated before, is an excellent starting point, but may be slightly misleading if you fail to calculate your unique circumstances.

In addition to the Harvard tool, let's use the College Board estimator on the website at www.collegeboard.org, and for a level comparison, let's exclude any financial assistance. The College Board tool asks you to enter certain information, such as the total cost of attendance and the number of years you will attend. It also asks you to enter an inflation rate for the cost of attendance, which was estimated at 5 percent per year on average. This means your college tuition portion will increase by 5 percent every year you're in college.

Other estimates of college inflation range somewhat higher. With inflation in 2022 well above 5 percent, it should be carefully projected. For example, the financial aid website www.finaid.org has posted a rate as high as 8 percent.[20] Consider calculating the tuition inflation each year at various rates between 4 and 8 percent to arrive at a worst case, likely case, and best case scenario.

The other important factor to calculate is family contribution, which will be unique to you and your family. The FAFSA may estimate your family contribution to be 35 percent. But that may be a little high. Think about your costs and enter them accurately. For our Harvard example, let's assume the family will not be able to help at all. Multiplying the four years of annual cost and adding 5 percent inflation each year yields a total cost of $327,615 after four years. The amount that Harvard discounts, which can be 50 percent or higher, and the amount you contribute from savings, a summer job, scholarships, and grants will determine the remaining amount that could be covered by family loans.[21]

For a level comparison among the various routes to obtaining a degree, let's assume you had nothing to contribute and that you did not receive grants or scholarships. You can now calculate how much you would owe using www.smartasset.com. We recommend this website because it gives you a real-life estimate of your actual total costs. Applying the SmartAsset methodology, you would need to take out a loan of about $80,000 a year to pay for college according to the total cost after four years (including inflation).

If you plug that figure into the debt calculator, you will see a total cost at the end of four years approximating $400,000. Remember, that $400,000 figure assumes that you *contribute nothing*, so consider it only as an example and apply your own circumstances. Again, the $400,000 figure is NOT your student debt load upon graduation. Rather, it approximates the previously identified basket of total costs of college on the day you graduate. This exercise is only intended to introduce the thought process.

To determine the debt load, you would want to reduce that $400,000 total cost by your contribution from your total resources during each of the four years. But here we are only trying to calculate the total cost of a college education, rather than the debt burden you carry after graduation. We will show the debt burden calculation process in the following public university example.

We also want to know the total cost of a college education because that is the amount for which you surrender other opportunities, such as the opportunity to travel, work, play music, or write. Adding the total cost and the lost opportunity cost yields a combined overall cost of attending college.

CALCULATING THE TOTAL COST AT A PUBLIC UNIVERSITY

Since not every student plans to attend a private university, let's next calculate public university costs. To arrive at the annual public university tuition cost, we can average the College Board national 2022–23 in-state tuition of $10,950 with the out-of-state tuition of $28,240[22] to arrive at an average of $19,595. For example, Michigan State's published in-state tuition is $14,460, while its out-of-state tuition is $39,766. And Arizona State's in-state tuition is $11,338, while its out-of-state tuition is $29,428.

Note that this methodology would be meaningless to you as an individual student, since your total bill will differ depending on whether you pay in-state and out-of-state costs. In addition, the average is not weighted by the percentage of students who are in-state versus out-of-state. So averaging the in-state and out-of-state tuition on a national basis is an admittedly imperfect model. We use it in this exercise only to explain the process. You will note that in the detailed graphics that follow, the in-state and out-of-state costs are broken out separately to illustrate the cost comparison.

Applying the same parameters used for private universities to public universities, the average public undergraduate costs for four years would tally $97,061, while the total cost at graduation (including inflation) would reach $121,611. Compare this with Harvard's total cost at graduation of $327,615. Assuming that after graduation the $327,615 Harvard debt will be paid over 10 years at an average interest rate of 6 percent, the monthly payment would calculate to $3,637 per month. Now, assuming that after graduation the $121,611 public university debt will be paid over the same 10 years at the same interest rate of 6 percent, the monthly payment would calculate to $1,270 per month.

The monthly income generated by an annual salary of $58,000 would be $4,833, so the monthly Harvard debt repayment of $3,637 would leave only $1,196 per month, while the monthly public school debt repayment of $1,270 would leave $3,563 per month, which is a bit more feasible to live on. These examples are not definitive. They are intended to present a methodology to analyze the effect of student debt on monthly payments after graduation.

CALCULATING THE COST OF A 2+2 PLAN

For further comparison, we calculate the cost of two years of community college plus two years of in-state tuition (the 2+2 plan), which yields a national average total cost of $83,122.

To corroborate the national average, let's compare it with an example from a state. Specifically, let's calculate the published costs of the Northern Virginia Community College (NVCC) tuition in Virginia and its nearby public neighbor George Mason University. In-state NVCC students pay $5,610, while the out-of-state students pay $11,693. After two years, having paid out an average of $17,302, the NVCC student can then transfer to George Mason University (GMU), a state university located 17 minutes away. The GMU costs amount to $13,014 tuition for Virginia residents and $36,474 tuition for out-of-state residents, which averages out to $27,744 per year.

If a student took this route, the total cost for four years under the 2+2 plan would be calculated by adding $17,302 for two years at NVCC plus $49,488 for two years at GMU to get the four-year total of $66,790. Using the same methodology and parameters from our earlier analysis, the total costs paid over 10 years would be $88,980. Note that the Virginia 2+2 plan cost at $88,980 correlates with the national average estimated cost for the 2+2 plan at $83,122. At an interest rate of 6 percent, the monthly payment would be $741.51. Therefore, with an average starting salary of $58,000 and monthly income of $4,833, this Virginia 2+2 plan payment would leave $4,091.49 per month to live on.

In sum, what's left to live on each month from the private university debt is $1,196, from the public university debt is $3,563, and from the 2+2 debt is $4,091.49. Of the examples calculated here, which one looks most financially advantageous?

Steps to Paying Down College Debt

Even after exhausting all available total resources (savings, earnings, discounts, ESAs, grants, and scholarships), the usual undergraduate student loan debt averages $30,000 as noted previously. This debt must be tackled by each college graduate individually. Not everyone carries the same burden, but an alarming number of college graduates each year are being locked into debt traps with little hope of escape. Unlike you, they may not have been able to predict the costs to make a considered judgment.

Let's turn now from the affordability question to the debt question—from analyzing the total cost of college to addressing the expected payment for debt after graduation. Assuming you paid down some of your total costs of college as you went along, your debt remaining could be the frequently mentioned $30,000. Using the debt calculator at www.privatestudentloans.guru to determine the pay back amount and inserting payment terms of 10 years at 6 percent yields a total cost of $40,398, with monthly payments of $336.65. This calculation points to a good rule of thumb: assuming a 10-year repayment term, the monthly payment will be about 1 percent of debt at graduation. However, that rule may not work for you because research has shown the average repayment period stretches from the original 10 years to 21 years.[23] Therefore, another good rule of thumb to bear in mind is that every $1.00 of student debt requires $2.00 to repay.[24]

If your debt payment is too onerous, you could be delayed in your pursuit of other life events, such as starting a career, buying a house, finding a partner, or having a family—all because you would be underwater paying off student loans. Knowing how the scenario plays out can help you avoid it as you begin your college career. Even better than making all those loan calculations, try applying another useful rule of thumb: if your total student loan debt at graduation is less than your annual starting salary, you should be able to repay your student loans in 10 years or less. This rule only requires you to compare two numbers, instead of making a bunch of calculations.

As you compare your college options, make sure to compare the costs of each option. Use the calculators. Do the math. Your numbers will be different from the examples used in this book because you or your family might be able to contribute more toward your education. Perhaps you have been offered discount and scholarship packages at a university. Hopefully, you have won other scholarships and grants to help fund your education.

It is crucial that you approach higher education costs with your eyes wide open. Know how much tuition will cost you not only this year but throughout your tenure at the college of your choice. Know your estimated debt load. Only then will you be able to make an informed decision.

College Costs Include More than Tuition

As you do your expense calculations for your educational journey, remember that college costs include more than tuition. Tuition is likely the largest educational expense you will encounter upon the decision to attend college. But outside of tuition, you must also consider other variable costs, such as transportation.

How long will it take to commute from your dorm room or apartment to the classroom and back each day? Will you be taking a car? If so, how will you cover gas, maintenance, and parking, which can all add to the monthly tab? Could you take a bus? Could you commute by walking or biking? You will need to consider not only gas or public transportation expenses on a daily basis but also the amount that is needed to travel home for spring break, summer break, Thanksgiving break, and winter break. Of course, the farther you travel across campus and across state, the more cost you incur.

This presents the trade-off between living near classes on campus and living off campus with a significant commute. As is discussed in more detail in chapter five, the University of Texas in Austin has relatively high on-campus housing costs compared to living arrangements in the suburbs. However, the transportation via metro bus adds up in both time and money. The trade-off is between the higher-priced housing on campus with no commute and the lower-priced housing off campus with a lengthy commute. One costs less but also yields less time available for extracurricular activities. Interestingly, the off-campus living cost could be even greater than the out-of-pocket expense incurred because students who live off campus are often less likely to graduate. Be alert to dangers that could deter you from finishing college. Depending on where you reside, transportation costs can be significant.

Another way to determine the total cost of college is to compare the sticker price and the net price. In a groundbreaking 2016 study by Sara Goldrick-Rab and Nancy Kendall titled "The Real Price of College,"[25] the authors explain that the federal terminology of "sticker price" includes tuition and fees, along with costs such as textbooks and supplies, commutes, and room and board. According to Goldrick-Rab and Kendall's article, the average college sticker price had increased "approximately 10 to 25 percent (depending on sector and time period) every five years since 1995."[26] The information was sourced from the college institutions themselves and is reported to the federal government though the Integrated Postsecondary Education Data System (IPEDS)—so it can be considered reliable. And the sticker price increases have continued as their study projects.

The researchers explained the federal terminology of "net price" accounts for federal, state, and local financial aid that reduces the college sticker price. The net price is the sticker price, minus any gift aid that does not need to be paid back. But even the net price was high for most students. "About three in four Americans who attend a public university pay or borrow an amount equivalent to 20 percent or more of their annual family income to pay for a year of school," the study explained.[27]

Goldrick-Rab and Kendall found that at "the nation's community colleges, 80 percent of the average $16,833 sticker price comes from non-tuition expenses" while "at public four-year colleges and universities, non-tuition expenses make up 61 percent of the total costs" driven principally by room and board living expenses.[28]

A college's sticker price may be reduced by grants and scholarships. But for many students, aid from colleges themselves and the federal government varies depending on family income, which necessitates examining individual cases. Actual grant and scholarship amounts for each student are calculated using a complex formula to arrive at an "Expected Family Contribution" (EFC) using the Free Application for Federal Student Aid (FAFSA) application. Good news. Starting in 2024–25, the EFC will be replaced with the Student Aid Index (SAI) as part of a FAFSA simplification which will reduce the number of questions on the FAFSA by about two-thirds.[29]

The expected family contribution could well exceed the actual monies available because the FAFSA "does not collect many types of critical information affecting [a family's] financial strength."[30] Goldrick-Rab and Kendall's study found that, as a percentage of annual income, both the sticker and net prices of college are "quite substantial for all but the wealthiest families."[31] In addition, many students are not aware that failing to complete the FAFSA can terminate their student aid and, unfortunately, skip the FAFSA after the first year. That's why we give several warnings about skipping the FAFSA in the second year.

Grants and scholarships can substantially offset direct college costs. Harvard is a good example. An article by Abigail Hess on CNBC's Make It website cites Harvard statistics indicating "Harvard estimates total billed and unbilled costs of about $73,800–$78,200 per year to attend the prestigious school." Considering that "about 55 percent of Harvard students receive need-based scholarship aid with average grant totals around $53,000," the net amount students pay in direct financial costs is greatly reduced.[32]

But the indirect costs of attending college are also noteworthy, particularly considering the recent pandemic. Because of COVID, Harvard moved to online classes that did not require local attendance. Interestingly, Harvard did not decrease their cost of attendance during COVID because tuition and fees were paying for necessary upkeep of the buildings and facilities even though students could not use them. COVID revealed the indirect costs for services that a student would need to duplicate at home.

When you think about the cost of attending any college at home via Zoom, you may want to adjust your estimated total cost of college by any duplicate costs you might incur at home, such as paying for your own gym membership, your own rent and utilities, your own meals, and your own concerts and social events.

The Aggregated Cost of Student Loan Interest

The cost of interest is a frequently overlooked element of college debt, yet it might be one of the most burdensome for graduates. In a cautionary *New York Times* article, Molly Webster details the effect of aggregated interest on the total cost of college. The title of the article summarizes the dilemma: "I've Spent $60,000 to Pay Back Student Loans and Owe More Than Before I Began."[33] The author chronicles her "secret shame" that she still carries "enormous federal student loan debt" 14 years after completing graduate school.[34] At 38 years old, she finds herself struggling financially because the cost of her loan interest is rising beyond her ability to pay. Ms. Webster's story is a wakeup call for prospective students and their parents. We recount it in some detail here to underscore the necessity to be alert to the effects of student loan interest and to describe debt accumulation.

After graduation in 2007, with a master's in science journalism, Ms. Webster owed $78,060 in federal loans.[35] For the next three years, she deferred payments on that loan (as the loan terms allowed) to get started in her career. Then she began making monthly payments on some of the 16 federal loans she had acquired, while simultaneously paying off some of the private loans. Although she lived frugally and worked full time as a journalist, she didn't see much progress because the interest rates some of her federal (Grad PLUS) loans were as high as 8.5 percent.[36]

At the suggestion of counselors at Sallie Mae, she temporarily suspended loan payments through a program known as *forbearance* to avoid going into default. However, under the forbearance program, interest continued to accrue and be added to the principal. Although it sounded like a good idea at the time, forbearance exacerbated her problem. As her principal grew, so did the corresponding minimum monthly payment. So when she could make a loan payment, it largely went to pay down the interest rather than the original principal of the loan. In fact, when she logged into her student loan account on April 1, 2020, she noted that $731.36 in interest was due. But when the interest payment was deducted from her account, her "principal didn't budge."[37]

Ms. Webster tried several strategies to get control of the debt. She searched for higher-paying jobs but couldn't find one. She became thrifty, borrowing instead of buying a laptop and looking for free furniture. She took on more work to earn extra cash. All to no avail. Despite her efforts, because of mounting interest costs, she found herself going deeper in debt in 2021: "I've paid $60,000 toward $78,000 of loans. Somehow, I am now $100,000 in debt."[38] A good lesson for other borrowers to learn from this unfortunate situation is to avoid paying less than the new interest that accrues, which is called getting negatively amortized. Based on her account, she may have paid only 60 percent of the new interest. Being negatively amortized can produce an extremely difficult situation.

After all this, Ms. Webster does not qualify for the CARES Act that might have alleviated this problem.[39] One would hope Ms. Webster could resolve this debt dilemma under some federal program. So it is useful to briefly explain the legal conundrum surrounding the CARES Act. Ms. Webster and some six million of her contemporaries are not eligible for the CARES Act because in 2010, Congress determined it would cost the federal government more to make loans through the FFEL Program than through the Direct Loan Program and decided to end FFEL.

At that point, Congress determined private banks should no longer operate in the federal student loan business and they terminated the FFEL Program on June 30, 2010. So for all *new* loan applicants after 2010, federal student loans would be held only by the federal government, and private student loans would be held only by private lenders. However, for all *existing* loans that were held by private lenders and guaranteed by the US Department of Education, the path forward became murky—the federal government decided to buy some but not all of these loans from commercial lenders.[40]

That 2010 decision by Congress left some six million college debt holders in an ugly catch-22. Their student loans were categorized as federal, so Congress set the interest rate, but the loans were actually held by private lenders, so the borrowers did not qualify for the CARES Act.[41] Consequently, for many borrowers the interest costs set by Congress continue to accumulate while the principal amount continues unabated.[42]

Beyond the conundrum involving the CARES Act, Ms. Webster's vexing experience with runaway debt highlights the insidious nature of debt interest facing many current student loan holders, and serves as a cautionary tale for prospective college students. Interest payments can be as onerous as the principal payment itself.

If that weren't bad enough, there is one more cost of college that needs to be addressed to reveal the full financial picture of the college experience.

The Lost Opportunity Cost of College

The last college cost to consider is the *lost opportunity cost*.[43] It is not listed in any of the other categories of cost because it operates differently. The *lost opportunity cost* is the opportunity to earn an income that you surrender while attending college. It is a cost related to time that you cannot replace. Going to college means giving up four (or more) years of income generation, while also accruing debt during the entire period.

In the vintage college-themed comedy *Animal House*,[44] when Dean Wormer (played by John Vernon) informs "Bluto" Blutarsky (played by John Belushi) that he's being expelled, Bluto laments, "Seven years of college down the drain!" Hopefully you won't take seven years, but however long you take, the opportunity costs accrue until you complete your degree, and that is time for income generation that you can't get back.

Consider that if you chose to pursue a trade or enter the workforce instead of attending college, you would begin earning a paycheck that generates positive cash flow while *not* incurring college costs that generate negative cash flow that leads to student debt. Instead of incurring debt without earning income, you could earn income without incurring debt. Over four years, these diverging paths can create a significant difference in financial standing.

Let's look at an example using the minimum wage. Assume a recent high school graduate decides to take a job at the current national minimum wage. According to the Department of Labor website, the federal minimum wage for covered, nonexempt employees is $7.25 per hour under the Fair Labor Standards Act (FLSA).[45] Figuring roughly 2,000 working hours per year, the lost opportunity cost would be $14,500 per year or $58,000 for the four years the high school graduate would have been attending college. However, when the minimum wage is calculated at $15 per hour, as is mandated in several localities, that figure rises to $30,000 per year, with the four-year total reaching $120,000. After subtracting the cost of housing, food, health care, etc., the net opportunity cost would be considerably lower, but the fact remains that more money is coming in from a job than is going out for college costs.

Here's an illustration. After graduating high school, Sam Student worked at Papa John's in Dallas, Texas, at an hourly rate of about $9, which would yield a lost opportunity cost of $18,000 per year. Then during the pandemic, when some nine million jobs went unfilled, many business owners increased their starting salaries to attract workers. Under these circumstances, Sam earned an average hourly rate of $12.50, multiplied by the 2,000 hours a year to yield a salary of $25,000 per year. If Sam had decided to attend college, over the same four years he would have surrendered the opportunity cost of $100,000 by not working at Papa John's. The demand for workers has risen after COVID, and unemployment has fallen. This workforce demand will fluctuate, but over time the workforce is shrinking, so salaries, and attendant opportunity costs, are likely to be rising.

To be evenhanded, let's work through the example to see what actually happens to the $100,000 generated by taking this route. The average rent in Dallas, Texas, is about $1,500 per month, which totals $72,000 over four years. Groceries cost about $275 a month, which totals $13,200 over four years. Bus fare is $2.50 per ride, yielding $5,000 over four years. And health care costs another $250 a month for a total of $12,000 over the four years. So, that $100,000 generated by working instead of attending college is reduced nearly to zero when you subtract expenses. That's because the salary he earns does not exist separate from normal living expenses. Rather, the salary pays his living expenses. In short, taking this route doesn't make you rich, it simply avoids the prospect of adding student debt to ongoing living expenses.

What if, instead of working at a fast-food franchise, however, Sam decided to apprentice in a trade? His hourly rate could then be substantially higher. Using ZipRecruiter as a guide, we discover that "[a]s of June 12, 2022, the average annual pay for a trade apprentice in the United States is $43,567 a year," which equates to $20.95 an hour, and "the majority of trade apprentice salaries currently range between $33,000 (25th percentile) to $46,000 (75th percentile), with top earners (90th percentile) making $62,500 annually across the United States."[46] In this case, Sam's total opportunity cost for choosing to attend college instead of working as an apprentice in a trade could range between $58,000 and $160,000 for the four years enrolled.

Bottom line: If you decide to go to college there is an opportunity cost, so make the most of the time spent in college. This isn't a time to float through classes. That approach could lead to some hard times ahead. Instead, focus on gaining an education that will be useful to you after graduation. Think about it beforehand, not afterward. Otherwise, you may waste prime years of your life doing something that isn't going to pay you back, either monetarily or experientially. As you think about it, try to find the right balance of work and school for your individual circumstances. Keep in mind that a student who works 40 or more hours a week is only half as likely to graduate with a bachelor's degree within six years.[47] So in order to graduate debt free, you first need to graduate. That said, without examining why you want to go to college and what you want to do with your degree, the greatest cost of attending college could well be the lost opportunity cost.

College Debt Illustrated

Take a look at the following four graphics depicting the depth of the financial hole a student digs when pursuing college. We've used national averages because they are easily researched, verified, and compared. Our average college cost data has been compiled from the US Department of Education, National Center for Education Statistics, National Association of Colleges and Employers, and the College Board. The graphics compare costs for four commonly chosen routes to a bachelor's degree:

1. Average Cost of 2 Years of Community College
   Plus 2 Years of Public University In State (the 2+2 plan)

2. Average Cost of Public University In State (4 Years)

3. Average Cost of Public University Out of State (4 Years)

4. Average Cost of Private University In State or Out of State (4 Years)

Note that routes 2 and 3 specifically depict the in-state and out-of-state costs separately to show how greatly these two routes differ in cost.

The graphics can help you visualize and compare the average depth of the financial hole you are digging while pursuing one of these four principal routes to obtain an bachelor's degree. As you will see, tuition and housing are the key drivers. The other recurring costs, such as books and fees, would be largely the same regardless of the chosen college degree route, so they are held constant across all four routes in the graphics.

The graphics incorporate four basic assumptions:

First, they assume the student completes the college degree in four years. While some students can finish in three years and a substantial portion take six years, we normalize at four years for comparison.

Second, they assume the student pays the "national average" cost for each identified element of the college student debt (e.g., books and fees).

Third, they assume that while a student is attending community college in the 2+2 plan, they incur no room or board expenses because they are living at home. This comports with common life experience and is built into the graphic for that route.

Last, they assume all the students pursuing any of these four college routes receive the same national average of grants and scholarships. Likewise, the students have *no* savings to apply to college costs, have *no* parental support, ESAs, or 529 savings plan, make *no* contribution from summer earnings to offset college costs, and engage in *no* work-study programs during the four years.

Of course, this last assumption does not reflect common experience. But we exclude these contributions in the graphics to achieve a level comparison between the four college degree routes. Many students will actually work their way through college using several of the identified means to earn funds and thereby reduce their student debt at graduation. Under those circumstances, the total debt would decrease by that same amount regardless of which college route the individual chose. So, for the sake of a level comparison of costs among the four routes, we assume the national average of grants and scholarships is awarded, but no student or family contributions are made.

As you consider the costs for your own college education, make sure to figure in your individual circumstances. For example, the average scholarship award per student is $4,202, but your award could vary significantly from that, particularly if you apply yourself to scholarship applications.[48]

Begin with these illustrations. But don't stop there. Each student's college costs are different.

Community College Plus Public University Average Cost 2 Yrs Ea

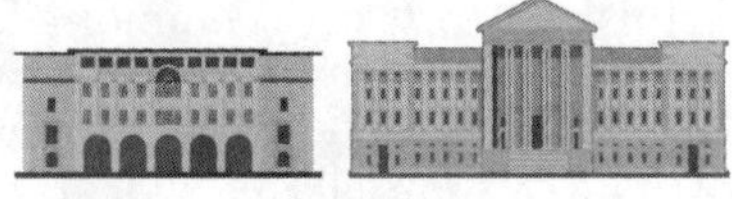

Cost of the Degree	
$28,196	Tuition & Fees
$18,588	Housing
$4,083	Interest
$8,366	Miscellaneous
$4,525	Transportation
$5,020	Books
$68,778	Total cost of Degree
- $16,114	Scholarships
- $21,666	Grants
$30,998	Student Debt at Graduation

What You Owe at Graduation

– 0
– $10,000
– $20,000
– $30,000
– $40,000
– **$50,000**
– $60,000
– $70,000
– $80,000
– $90,000
– **$100,000**
– $110,000
– $120,000
– $130,000
– $140,000
– **$150,000**
– $160,000
– $170,000
– $180,000
– $190,000
– **$200,000**
– $210,000

$30,998 Student Debt at Graduation

Figure 6.[49]

Public University In-State Average Cost 4 Years

Cost of the Degree	
$45,585	Tuition & Fees
$37,177	Housing
$6,327	Interest
$8,366	Miscellaneous
$4,525	Transportation
$5,020	Books
$107,000	Total cost of Degree
- $16,114	Scholarships
- $21,666	Grants
$69,220	Student Debt at Graduation

What You Owe at Graduation

$69,220 Student Debt at Graduation

Figure 7.[50]

Public University Out-of-State Average Cost 4 Years

Cost of the Degree	
$101,733	Tuition & Fees
$37,177	Housing
$11,909	Interest
$8,366	Miscellaneous
$4,525	Transportation
$5,020	Books
$168,730	Total cost of Degree
- $16,114	Scholarships
- $21,666	Grants
$130,950	Student Debt at Graduation

What You Owe at Graduation

$130,950 Student Debt at Graduation

Figure 8.[51]

Private University In-State / Out-of-State Average Cost 4 Years

Cost of the Degree	
$165,827	Tuition & Fees
$42,207	Housing
$18,858	Interest
$8,366	Miscellaneous
$4,525	Transportation
$5,020	Books
$244,803	Total cost of Degree
- $16,114	Scholarships
- $21,666	Grants
$207,023	Student Debt at Graduation

What You Owe at Graduation

$207,023 Student Debt at Graduation

Figure 9.[52]

Now let's apply the interest rate of 6 percent over 10 years for two routes.

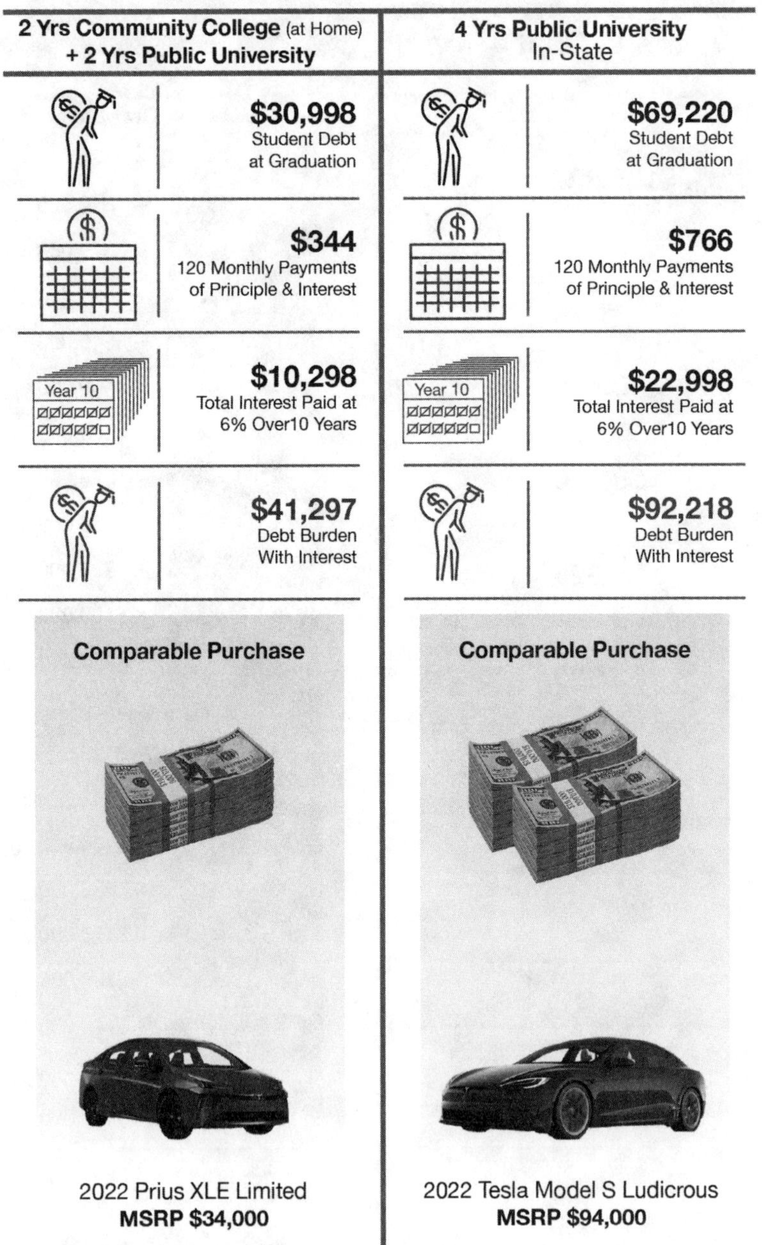

Figure 10.[53]

This chart shows the 6 percent interest rate over 10 years for two other routes.

4 Yrs Public University Out-of-State	**4 Yrs Private University** In- or Out-of-State
$130,950 Student Debt at Graduation	**$207,023** Student Debt at Graduation
$1,453 120 Monthly Payments of Principle & Interest	**$2,298** 120 Monthly Payments of Principle & Interest
$45,508 Total Interest Paid at 6% Over10 Years	**$68,783** Total Interest Paid at 6% Over10 Years
$174,458 Debt Burden With Interest	**$275,806** Debt Burden With Interest

2022 Rekon Mercedes-Benz Van
MSRP $175,500

2060 Sq. Ft. House in Midwest
MLS Listed Price $285,000

Figure 11.[54]

These graphic illustrations of debt may prompt you to consider how much you should expect to borrow for college. The statistics published by the National Postsecondary Student Aid Study (NPSAS) can give you a preview of what you may need to borrow. Based on the 2015–16 NPSAS, some 39 percent of undergraduate students in certificate programs, associate's degree programs, and bachelor's degree programs receive an average of $9,174 including Parent PLUS loans. That number falls to $7,639 without Parent PLUS loans. For just bachelor's degree programs, the figures show $10,459 with Parent PLUS loans and $8,349 without them.[55] According to the federal budget, the average Pell Grant was $4,325 in 2021 and $4,353 in 2022.[56] These figures give you a preview of what amount of federal aid might be available for you.

Escaping the Matrix: How Deep Do You Want to Go into Debt?

Students spend a great deal more for college than just tuition. The total spent includes a range of expenses such as housing, books, transportation, and loan interest. These costs are outside of posted tuition and are sometimes overlooked when thinking inside the Student Loan Matrix. As you can see, when you calculate the total cost of college, even after expending your resources, the total spent can leave you with a mountain of debt.

When you consider your future, think about what level of debt is sustainable for you. With that in mind, consider how to avoid or mitigate the costs of a college education. Have that hard conversation with your parents before you march off to college in the thrall of the Student Loan Matrix. Remember that parents can also find themselves drowning in student debt from attempting to help their children. This often occurs through the Parent PLUS program. Once you and your family understand what is workable within your family finances, it's time to meet with the financial aid officers at prospective universities to finalize a game plan. When you visit with the financial aid officer consider asking the following questions:

1. What is their net price and their sticker price?

2. What is the average family contribution toward these two prices?

3. Does the college practice front-loading of grants in the first year?

4. What kind of aid, outside of federal loans, does the college itself offer students?

5. How much will the total cost increase year over year, for planning purposes?

6. Are there any plans to reduce the cost of tuition if COVID reemerges?

7. What online options are available to reduce the total cost of obtaining a degree?

8. After the first year, how many students still live on campus?

9. How many students use the available meal plans? Which is most popular?

10. How many students work on campus, and what do campus jobs pay?

11. How would a scholarship displacement policy affect your private scholarships?

12. What is their outside scholarship policy and how will it affect you?

When you have a better idea of the costs of attending the college of your choice, use a debt calculator to estimate your particular projected loan costs—before those costs hit your bottom line. An example of this tool is located at https://smartasset.com/student-loans/student-loan-calculator. Parents can use the Parent Debt Calculator at bigfuture.collegeboard.org to fill in the picture of total debt burden on the family.

After completing college, if you have incurred debt, it is also useful to be able to calculate your loan repayment schedules. Since much of student debt (about 92 percent) is now in the federal arena, check out the federal calculator at https://studentaid.gov/loan-simulator. This tool also gives useful guidance on how payments may be adjusted to fit current needs. Additionally, you can use a private loan calculator to determine the payback amount at http://www.privatestudentloans.guru/loan-calculator.html.

In sum, if you decide to attend college, don't get blindsided by the costs and don't mistake tuition for the total cost of college. You're going to be paying more than tuition. Figure out how much. Once you and your parents know how to calculate the basket of total costs of college and determine the total resources available to cover that basket, you are well on your way to minimizing the total amount spent. You've decisively stepped outside of the Student Loan Matrix box, and you're now ready to take charge of your own financial future.

CHAPTER 4

Community College Is a Step Sideways

ONE EXCELLENT WAY for hopeful college students to minimize their costs is to begin their education at a community college. But here, many of them run into another one of the faulty assumptions locking students inside the Student Loan Matrix: after graduating from high school, *community college is a step sideways.*

This misconception may be fostered by a belief among some students that community college is a backwater for noncompetitive students who couldn't make it in regular college. The 2+2 scenario challenges the economic validity of that "sideways" assumption, but it is worth exploring the assumption's origins in more detail.

Across the nation, each fall there are high school juniors sitting in library presentations given by their school guidance counselors. These counselors tell them that pursuing an associate's degree at their local community college is an affordable way to begin an education. But then these students watch TV shows full of protagonists who get accepted into Ivy League universities. When students rank in the top 10 percent of their classes without much effort, and when they attend graduation ceremonies where students are highly recognized when they are accepted into a prestigious university—why would they want to attend community college? The guidance counselors' recommendations are wise and practical, but they can be a hard sell to students in this environment.

To a precocious 17-year-old, getting into that prestigious university doesn't seem particularly difficult. Nor does paying for that university. The guidance counselors' sage advice can seem like an insult to that cherished dream of getting away from home and making your own way in the world. Many students and their parents see a four-year university, particularly a private university, as the most respectable option. It's another assumption within the Student Loan Matrix that needs to be scrutinized in light of costs.

What about the Costs Involved?

Tuition for a typical community college semester hour of instruction costs under $250. Compare this to the cost of a typical private four-year college semester hour, which averages 10 times that at $2,500. The hourly requirement to complete a single year of college is 30 hours of instruction. At a community college, those 30 hours would cost an average of under $7,500. Compare that figure to the average cost of those same 30 hours at a private university, about $75,000 annually. Let that 10-fold difference sink in.

To unpack this cost difference, the next table compares the actual costs of community colleges in five different cities across the nation. Depending on the course and major, most public universities will accept the transfer of credits taken at community college, though this assumption should be confirmed for your specific institution. Planning to obtain a four-year degree on the 2+2 plan at the outset of your college career is wise.

Compare four-year community college costs to those of private universities located in those same five cities—$70,000 per year for a total of roughly $280,000. Then ask yourself if it is more uncool to have $40,000 of student debt or $20,000 of student debt or zero student debt when you graduate from college.

The practical aspects of living at home, working part time, and taking courses on a less-pressured schedule are additional benefits that could be as valuable as the reduced tuition costs. But it is very enlightening to compare the substantial difference in costs.

TABLE OF COST PER COURSE AND TOTAL COST AT FIVE COMMUNITY COLLEGES

Community College	Cost per Course	Total Cost	Online Courses
Dallas County Community College	$237 for in-county residents, $405 for noncounty residents, $600 for out-of-state residents	Roughly $58,000 for a 4-year degree living off campus as a county resident	Yes
Seattle Central College	$339 for in-county residents, $384 for noncounty/out-of-state residents	Roughly $60,000 for a 4-year degree living off campus as a county resident	Yes
City Colleges of Chicago	$438 for in-county residents, $1,152 for noncounty residents, $1,443 for out-of-state residents	Roughly $70,000 for a 4-year degree living off campus as a county resident	Yes
The City College of New York	$250 for in-state residents, $620 for out-of-state residents	Roughly $30,000 for a 4-year degree living off campus as a county resident	Yes
Community College of Philadelphia	$477 for in-county residents, $1,431 for out-of-state residents	Roughly $41,000 for a 4-year degree living off campus as a county resident	Yes

Figure 12.[1]

Isn't that an eye opener? The City College of New York costs $30,000 for a four-year degree. Note that the tuition cost for the two-year associate's degree at community college would be about half that amount. The economics of attending community college are persuasive, even if the coolness factor may not be.

Community college allows a practical work-life balance that affords greater flexibility in housing, meals, and transportation—particularly if you can live at home and save on room and board. Lower community college costs can facilitate earlier access to economic independence as an adult.

Students in community colleges are not in a cocoon. They share their experience with people who are working in similar situations. Students at community colleges can operate independently and navigate college on their own terms. Many courses at community college are customizable to an individual's personal pace and pocketbook. For students zeroed in on what it truly means to be well educated and acquire the essential skills they need to succeed in life, the goal can be achieved in a community college setting.

Almost every city or county has some sort of community college. These colleges are typically funded by taxpayers, which allows the tuition to be substantially lower than other state colleges and universities. For example, in Collin County, Texas, a four-year degree would cost about the same amount as one year at a private college. Students who choose to attend community college can take out fewer loans and therefore can experience an earlier release from long-term debt.

Community college also presents the possibility of transferring courses to a four-year institution over time. A student can begin their educational career at a community college and then transfer those credits to a university to graduate in four years or take longer if needed. On this path of two years at community college plus two years at public university (the 2+2 route), they would only pay the higher costs of a university for two years, rather than four. The savings can be substantial. An article by Abigail Endsley at Pearson Accelerated titled "How to Transfer Community College Credits to University" offers several helpful tips that are worth knowing beforehand.[2]

Let's consider the experience of an actual student at Collin County Community College from 2011 to 2013.[3] In that time, he accumulated 60 credit hours toward the undergraduate degree requirement of 120 hours. These credits were transferred to the University of Texas at Dallas (UTD), and he graduated in 2015 after a total of four years.

He tallied his costs incurred in five categories: tuition, books, rent, food, and transportation. The total costs in each of those categories were as follows:

Tuition	$164 per credit hour x 60 hours	$9,840
Books	$50 a book x 20 classes	$1,000
Rent	$300 a month x 24 months	$7,200
Food	$20 a day x 512 days	$10,240
Transportation	$30 a week on gas x 73 weeks	$2,190
	Total	$30,470

Figure 13. Community college costs incurred

The student spent approximately $15,000 per year for the two years totaling just over $30,000. In those years, his costs for food and rent were almost twice his tuition. Because he lived at home, his parents generously refunded him the rent payment of $7,200 for his use at college when he matriculated at UTD. Additionally, he ate several meals at home, which often reduced his actual food costs to $5 a day.

This student was able to work part time and cover all his costs for community college with a job as a seasonal store associate earning $10 an hour. When he completed his two-year community college curriculum, he had accumulated zero debt. That cut two years off his debt load after he graduated from UTD. In this case, the student did indeed take a step sideways with his decision to attend community college—he effectively sidestepped the debt and interest for those two years.

Many community colleges also offer online courses at a comparatively low price point that offer the flexibility students need to study remotely while integrating a work schedule or familial obligations. An online-only course of study may require more discipline from the student, but the flexibility available may be worth it. In addition to online courses and transfer opportunities available at community colleges, many community colleges offer certification programs for easy entry into the workforce without obtaining an associate's degree.

These certification programs present another inexpensive route to obtaining marketable credentials. Melissa Korn, an expert in higher education, observes that "[c]ertificates, offered mainly by community colleges and for-profit schools, generally take one to two years to complete and can prepare individuals for work in fields including cosmetology and medical office billing. They tend to be far less expensive than a bachelor's degree."[4]

Even though certificate programs are less expensive, Ms. Korn warns that certification students must still be mindful of incurring debt. In a *Wall Street Journal* article titled "Default Rates for Certificate Program Graduates on Par with College Dropouts, New Data Show,"[5] she looked at graduates of certification programs over 10 years, as compared with other undergraduate programs. As the article title implies, certificate students have a high default rate.[6] Citing data from a multiyear study, Ms. Korn reported, "Undergraduate certificate program graduates who started their programs in the 2003–04 year owed a median $3,700 in student debt, including principal and interest, a dozen years after starting the programs, the new data showed. That is substantially less than the $13,800 median sum that those who graduated with associate's degrees owed."[7] The key point for our purposes is the relatively lower amount of debt accumulated by certificate students.

On the downside, despite the lower amount of debt, some "44 percent of undergraduate certificate program graduates who borrowed in the 2003–2004 year had defaulted by 2015," as reported by the National Center for Education Statistics of the US Department of Education.[8] If you decide to pursue a certificate program at community college, be aware of the pitfall so you can avoid it.

The takeaway for our discussion is the need to match the certificate program at a community college with employment prospects so students obtain a certificate that leads to financially and professionally rewarding work. Students seeking a professional certification at a community college should look to industries such as manufacturing that "have strong outcomes as measured by their graduates' ability to land jobs."[9] In addition to manufacturing, these jobs include construction managers, veterinary technicians, electricians, and welders. According to a National Public Radio (NPR) report published in February 2023, "some 30 million jobs in the United States that pay an average of $55,000 don't require a bachelor's degree" and instead require certificates, associate's degrees, or other credentials.[10]

Ms. Korn's research reinforces the idea that the available job market and the average annual pay for certificate holders are worthy of careful consideration. It is fascinating to note that the annual salary of $55,000 for two-year community college graduates in 2015 was $5,000 higher than the average annual salary for four-year college graduates at the time. Who knew?

Consider the Costs

All in all, community colleges offer impressive incentives for savvy students looking to pursue both higher education and earlier economic stability. But let's consider a counterpoint argument regarding going to the best college you get admitted to. On the one hand, community college is often the more affordable option for the average student trying to be mindful of their finances. On the other hand, reputations of prestigious college institutions are earned over centuries, and they count for something in the job market.

If a workplace is looking at two applicants, one with a degree from a nationally known private university and the other with a degree from a state school preceded by an associate's degree from their local community college, the private university grad is very likely to get that job. Well-established, highly regarded four-year universities carry a hard-earned prestige, as do universities known for specific programs, such as the Wharton Business School at the University of Pennsylvania.

In that specific sense, the idea that students should go to the best college they can get admitted to does hold some water. But here is where careful analysis will serve you well. Students must balance the merit of a prestigious degree and its enhanced employability against the merit of a 2+2 state degree that has left its holder in a debt-free financial position. The two competing interests can sometimes be reconciled if, for example, the big-name school offers a full ride. Think it through.

Initially in their career, a graduate of a state school with a two-year community college background may not be offered the same kinds of opportunities as the graduate of a prestigious private university. The state school graduate may have to work harder to compete and be noticed. But at a certain point, work experience and work ethic will matter more than education to the hiring official, and at that point the debt load of the prestigious school might begin to irritate the debt holder.

Regarding the work ethic factor, there is convincing research that suggests that earning capacity later in life is not dictated so much by an individual's degree as by their capacity. A study by Stacey Berg Dale and Allen B. Krueger reviewed the earnings of 14,239 graduates at 30 colleges and concluded that economic success correlated with the selectivity of the colleges which admitted them, rather than with the college that they chose to attend. Specifically, Dale and Krueger found that "students who attended more selective colleges do not earn more than other students who were accepted and rejected by comparable schools but attended less selective colleges."[11]

This finding is consistent with research presented earlier indicating that success in life may be determined by the individual's native wit and industriousness, rather than the name of the institution on their college diploma. Interestingly, Dale and Krueger's study also found a correlation between the average tuition cost at selective universities and a graduate's later economic success.[12]

The common perceptions of community college as a backwater are changing. Let's hear from a practicing college counselor on how community colleges are currently perceived. Casey Gendason, a professional guidance counselor in Dallas, observes that "[i]n Texas, we've seen a sharp change in how community colleges are viewed and their purpose. In the past, community colleges were viewed as the place 'the unsuccessful students go' because they could not hack it in high school. But this is no longer the case. In many states, the community colleges are THE pipeline to fantastic four-year state institions."[13] Could that apply to college prep schools as well as public high schools? It could. Every year, St. Mark's School of Texas, a highly competitive prep school in Dallas, "sees a handful of students head to Austin Community College as a pathway to UT Austin."[14] Rather than being a step sideways, community college could be a measured step forward to a reasonable cost education.

However, a word of caution is in order here. Community colleges are great if your goal is to obtain a two-year associate's degree or a one-year certificate. But be wary of this route if your goal is a four-year bachelor's degree because you may miss your destination. Data published by the US Department of Education shows that of the students who start at a four-year private nonprofit college, 75 percent graduate with a bachelor's degree within six years,[15] while only *15 percent* of students who started at a community college went on to obtain their bachelor's degree within six years.[16] The point to digest is that students who undertake the 2+2 route must stay focused on achieving the goal of a bachelor's degree to avoid a detour that could derail their plans.

Escaping the Matrix: Community College Can Be a Step Up and Out of Debt

Choosing the community college 2+2 route could be a low-cost alternative to the four-year route. For many high school graduates, the guidance counselor could well be right: community college is emerging as a favored route to a four-year degree and the financial benefits outweigh the possible perception of reduced prestige.

Furthermore, community college graduates can gain a financial step up on four-year college attendees through hard work at their studies, taking advantage of education à la carte opportunities and making use of flexible class schedules while minimizing costs. Community college gives students an opportunity to test their aptitude for college-level studies without betting the farm on it at a high-cost university.

The Association of Community Colleges provides information on more than 1,200 community colleges and two-year colleges in the US through its website at www.aacc.nche.edu. The Association also offers a Community College Finder with a mapping feature at www.aacc.nche.edu/college-finder/ to help you identify community colleges available in your local area. Students interested in keeping costs down by attending courses near their home will find this tool particularly helpful.

Community colleges are likely to expand or become more widespread (or free) in the future because of their flexible delivery systems and integration in the local community. Therefore, their availability is likely to expand. If these arguments appeal to you, do some research and find a community college near you. Obtain an associate's degree or a work certification while taking advantage of the flexible hours and low-cost tuition to work part time and gain experience. Get a head start on your savings. If it makes sense for you, plan to transfer to a four-year college in two years' time. At community college you can step up to a more secure and prosperous economic future and sidestep costly student debt.

CHAPTER 5

I Can Live Inexpensively on Campus

POP QUIZ: Please put away your books and take out a #2 pencil and a clean sheet of paper.

Question: How much will you pay for housing costs each month when you go to college?

Any idea? No? Nothing? Bueller? Bueller? Well, it's kind of an unfair question. How could you possibly determine the cost of room and board without knowing the details of your living arrangements at college? For example, will you pay for housing as part of your college package, pay rent outside that package, team up with several roommates, or live at home? Is the college located in a large city, suburb, or small town? Without knowing a lot of particulars, the question is unsolvable. This chapter will help you think through housing and meal costs so you know the answer to the pop quiz before you arrive on campus.

In addition to being hard to determine without knowing all the living arrangements, the cost of housing on campus can be hard to calculate because, unless you watch living costs closely, the actual total amount may not hit you until after those four idyllic years have faded in the six-month rearview mirror. At that point, you open your first college debt notice and exclaim, "How come this college debt is so high? I thought tuition was only $10,000! Why do I owe so much? Wasn't housing included?"

We discussed the idea that tuition is not the only cost of college in chapter three. Since housing is often the single largest college cost outside of tuition, let's examine in detail the assumption that you can live inexpensively in campus housing. Just like the mistaken notion that tuition is the full cost of college, the assumption that college students can live inexpensively on campus can be a misconception inside the Student Loan Matrix. Your mind wants to believe it. The assumption makes sense when you explore the campus living arrangements. Because you are living in relatively tight quarters with relatively spartan amenities, the housing costs should be modest. You could also reasonably assume that the college would be looking out for your financial interests. Ergo you would assume that housing on campus would be less expensive than living off campus.

So what makes this cinderblock cave so expensive? You'd think that colleges would want students to live on campus to make it easier to attend classes, right? The Jeffersonian ideal of an "academical village"[1] envisions students and faculty interspersed around a central gathering point like the "lawn" at the University of Virginia in order to promote a holistic learning environment. When we think of the college experience, we usually imagine on-campus housing provided at a low enough cost to make that experience affordable. But don't bet your lifelong debt on it. In this chapter, we address costs of both housing and meals (i.e., room and board) as the combined living costs.

Housing Costs

The cost of on-campus housing has increased dramatically in the past decade. In addition to the effects of inflation, at many universities, on-campus dormitories and nearby apartments are being torn down to make room for higher-end, higher-cost housing that reflects the rising cost of real estate.

Consequently, the housing experience is quite different for the haves and the have-nots. For wealthy families, this may be a good solution to their concerns for security and safety on campus. Housing that is well situated, well appointed, well protected, and safe may be ideal for wealthier families, but for families of more moderate means, this housing is likely out of reach. Students who might have lived in the now demolished dorms on campus or apartments nearby are pushed into living in outlying housing with a longer commute. As a wise consumer of housing services analyzes the private college housing figure, they might pose the following questions:

1. What amenities are included in my university housing costs?
2. Are there any surcharges outside the stated housing costs?
3. How many incoming students qualify to live on campus?
4. How many students in the upper classes live on campus?
5. How do fraternity/sorority housing options compare in cost?
6. How do on-campus costs compare with off-campus rentals?
7. Do off-campus rentals include utilities, insurance, furniture?
8. Must I pay a full 12 month lease if I'm only there 9 months?
9. Can I sub-lease for 3 months if the rental is for 12 months?
10. What public transportation is available if I live off campus?
11. How does having a roommate impact these arrangements?
12. What are my total costs for on- and off-campus housing?

Let's work through an example to illustrate how to analyze housing costs. For this analysis example we'll look at a private college of high reputation. The IPEDS empirical data lists room and board at Harvard as $17,682 in 2019–20 and $18,941 in 2021–22.[2] That sounds high, but we need to investigate to determine if it is indeed high.

A quick Internet check of apartment costs in Cambridge, Massachusetts near the Harvard campus in 2021 yielded an average $2,885 rent for an 800-square-foot apartment with one bedroom. Another search found the average studio rental goes for $1,900. Heat and water are extra. Remember that this hypothetical Harvard student must also calculate their commuting costs for athorough comparison of whether it is cheaper living on or off campus.

Let's put some numbers down on paper. This hypothetical Harvard student living off campus in Cambridge, Massachusetts, might expect to pay $1,500 a month for housing and utilities with a roommate. Alone, their costs may come out to $2,000 or more. Multiplied by the nine months of the academic year, an off-campus student living with a roommate might pay upward of $13,500 per academic year.

By this analysis, Harvard students could potentially live less expensively off campus than on campus. However, depending on the rental market, the $18,941 on-campus cost might be low compared to the local alternatives. Using this example, you can do the analysis for your own housing circumstances. The key is to determine the housing cost beforehand so the ending price tag does not surprise you.

As you project what your own housing expenses in college are likely to be, consider whether you will be able to live on campus throughout your four-year to six-year college career. This is a foundational question since your estimate of college costs will have to be adjusted if you had counted on lower on-campus housing costs and later had to move off campus.

Another way to analyze the housing question is to determine the number of beds available on campus. For example, let's say there are 4,000 undergraduates at a hypothetical college, with a class of 1,000 first-year students. Does the college require its first-year students to live on campus? Assume the answer is yes. Then, how many undergraduate beds (rather than dorm rooms) are on campus? Say 1,000. In this scenario, we can surmise that upperclassmen must live off campus. The school's published housing policy may also make that clear.

Students facing such circumstances at their chosen colleges must project their off-campus living costs for every year they attend the university after their first year. This is an important exercise because many students are forced to leave college after their first year when they discover how much more costly college turned out to be compared to their expectations. The difficulties of continuing to pay for college in the face of escalating costs could be a contributing factor of why only 35 percent of public university students complete college in four years.[3]

For a more in-depth look at living costs both on and off campus, we turn again to Goldrick-Rab and Kendall's 2016 study for its noteworthy analysis of federal data. It presents research that can arm you to speak with your financial aid counselor at college and to prepare your own housing financial plan. The study points out that the estimated costs and the actual costs of living on campus can vary widely by institution depending on how costs are attributed for living at home.

The critical question is "To what extent does official data on the costs of living in college reflect the true costs that students face?" The federal government requires colleges to report estimated "living cost allowances" in the sticker price. "Unsurprisingly, there is a great deal of variation and inconsistency in living cost allowances across colleges and universities in the same region," explain Goldrick-Rab and Kendall.[4]

The underlying reason for the variance of living cost allowances among institutions is an assumption that students who live at home incur no costs for room and board. Since the data shows that "37 percent of undergraduates live at home with their parents while in college," that assumption can have a profound impact on the reported living cost allowance.[5]

The reason given for living at home by nearly half of those who elect to do so is, predictably, to save money. But here's the rub: according to the Century Foundation study, "when reporting the sticker price (and the net price), colleges and universities are not required to include any living costs for these [live at home] students."[6]

Colleges are allowed to assume that because a student lives at home, they accrue NO costs for living expenses of room and board. How are colleges permitted to make such an assumption? The operative guidance for financial aid administrators in the *Federal Student Aid Handbook* states, "For students without dependents living at home with their parents, this will be an allowance that you determine."[7] Naturally, many financial aid administrators choose to set this allowance at zero. With 37 percent of students living at home and colleges reporting zero living costs for those students, how should you interpret the published data?

In the good news category, this zero-allowance rule is changing. Starting with the 2024–25 FAFSA, as enacted by the Consolidated Appropriations Act of 2021, colleges will no longer be permitted to zero out room and board for students who live with their parents.[8] But that time frame is still a ways off, so in the meantime be alert to this practice.

As you calculate the housing cost options of your undergraduate institution, be alert to the rationale behind the reported costs of living at your intended institution. Does your intended college attribute zero costs to students living at home? If so, how closely will the college's published estimated living costs reflect your actual out-of-pocket living costs?

Goldrick-Rab and Kendall report some fascinating facts from four representative colleges revealing the assumptions about the costs of living at home:

> [A]t Miami Dade College in Florida, the sticker price includes an estimated $8,455 expense for room and board for students living off campus, but estimates that expense at just $2,345 for students living at home. At the City University of New York, a student living off campus faces estimated room and board costs of $10,386, while a student living at home is expected to face just $1,918 in living costs over nine months. The University of California at San Diego budgets $9,650 for housing and meals if a student is living off campus, but just $4,643 if they are living with parents. Further north, the University of California–Berkeley budgets $7,184 for housing and utilities for a student "living in an apartment" versus $2,616 for one "living with relatives," and also assumes the latter student saves 47 percent on their food costs.[9]

As the study makes clear, the costs of college living can vary significantly between on-campus and off-campus arrangements as well as between colleges in relative proximity to each other. Consequently, you won't be trapped into relying solely on an estimate posted on a college website. Wise prospective college students will investigate the origins of these estimates and do their homework to determine if they can indeed live inexpensively on campus.

Talk to the housing office at your college of choice. Ask them if they have empirical studies showing actual housing costs for the four years of college attendance. In regard to the cost of college housing, forewarned is definitely forearmed.

College Housing Availability Is Shrinking

Outside of the difficulty of accurately estimating the true cost of living arrangements, either on or off campus, another problem may await incoming college students. The stock of affordable on-campus dormitories is shrinking year over year from natural wear and tear and from the influx of high-dollar, high-rise condos.

The increasing presence on campus of expensive condo-type living arrangements accommodates affluent families and ensures security for their children on college campuses today. But it is driving the cost of living on campus out of reach for many. In an article titled "If the Tuition Doesn't Get You, the Cost of Student Housing Will" in *Bloomberg Businessweek*,[10] Ali Breland offers several sobering insights worth factoring into the projected cost of living during college. First, the cost of rent off campus may actually exceed the cost of tuition. Not only is tuition not the only cost of college, it may not be the biggest cost. "At UT Austin, the median annual rent in the neighborhoods closest to campus exceeds the annual in-state tuition . . . without including other costs such as utilities and groceries," says Breland.[11]

Also, because the number of students exceeds the number of beds on campus, students can be forced to live off campus. For example, at UT Austin the majority of students move off campus after their first year.[12] That's an important consideration when determining the total cost of the college experience over your four to six years of enrollment.

Finally, with the destruction of old or inexpensive dormitory options on campus in favor of new luxury condos and apartments, lower-income students are being forced away from many college campuses. Breland warns that the on-campus luxury housing phenomenon is gathering steam, with high-end options growing and affordable ones shrinking around such college towns as "the University of Michigan in Ann Arbor, the University of Minnesota, Twin Cities, and Colorado State University at Fort Collins."[13]

Moving farther away from campus affects both the amount of money these students must spend on commutes and the time they have available for studying. Neither the middle seat of a crowded bus nor the front seat of a car locked in a traffic jam is the most desirable of study venues, and over time, this can hurt a student's prospects for getting educated and reaching graduation.

As a prospective college student, after you have researched the housing costs involved with living in dorms on campus compared to living off campus, you are invited to decide for yourself whether students can live inexpensively on campus. You can also determine whether off-campus options, including a commute, are ultimately more or less expensive. In either case, you will be making a fact-based decision on housing.

One professional college counselor has challenged the premise that on-campus housing will be more expensive than off campus. Casey Gendason, based in Dallas, offers this contrarian view: "I feel strongly that living on campus in standard housing is doable and affordable. I think students get caught up in living off campus or in the fancier apartments and newer housing. I understand why, but as someone who lived in the typical college housing or residence hall–style arrangements while in college, I do not think it's vital to live in the more expensive housing."[14] As a knowledgeable consumer of campus housing options, you will want to weigh your choices and decide what works best for you and at what cost. The key is to research those options at the outset.

It may well turn out that you can secure an on-campus dormitory room for the entire four- to six-year stay at the college of your choice at a reasonable cost. But if not, it is important to consider how the cost of housing could add to your debt in the end. Otherwise, you face the prospect of being stuck inside the Matrix and owing a ton of money.

When you inquire about housing, nail down precisely what is involved in the offering and how that offering compares with living in an apartment, condo, sorority, fraternity, or private home nearby. As a free agent, you can determine what is best for you and your situation as you steer toward graduating without debt. Also, after a year you'll have a better idea of what inexpensive living arrangements are available.

Meal Plan Costs

On-campus living arrangements often entail mandatory food services. Like other areas of campus life, it may be difficult to ascertain specific detailed costs in this area. Goldrick-Rab and Kendall's research reveals several ways in which costs can be hidden in meal plans. The study found that "[o]n-campus food costs exceeded the sticker price estimates because food plans often included large administrative fees (often over $700) that were deducted from students' food purchasing power, students were often unable to claim all of their meal plan dollars, and students had to spend more than expected to get a full meal."[15]

It can be difficult to calculate from a given college meal plan exactly what the actual cost of a given meal is. Meal plans may also specify mealtimes that are unworkable with a student's work or class schedule. One plan in Goldrick-Rab and Kendall's study "provide[d] a specific number of meals per week that must be used during set times of the day. Students must show up to consume the meal during the designated time, or they lose the funds allocated for that meal. Those who miss meals because of work, family, or other obligations simply forfeit those funds."[16] Shrewd students will want to inquire of administrators whether they follow this *use or lose* practice.

Another frequently used type of plan offers meal points rather than actual meals. The Century Foundation study highlighted the problem with this plan: "Although students pay $8.46 for each meal point, the points have a different cash equivalency during different hours of the day. For example, at breakfast, a meal point can buy a student only $3.75 worth of food, while at dinner, it can buy a student $5.50 worth of food."[17] In short: 100 meal points did not provide students with 100 equal meals.

More troublesome are meal plans that include undisclosed administrative fees. Goldrick-Rab and Kendall explain that "students at one university did not realize that almost one-fifth of the money ($771) they paid for their meal plan was an administrative fee and would not be available to them for food purchases."[18] An additional trap is that some meal plans are not based on three meals a day, but two. This practice will be changing in 2023–24.[19] In the meantime, inquire about the meal plan coverage at your school.

This section has highlighted a number of meal plan features to alert you to meal expenses that can add to your total cost of college. About now, you might be wondering whether a meal plan might actually be a wise idea in college, despite the drawbacks. The campus dining hall offers convenience, easy social gathering, and access to balanced meals. If you are asking that question, well done! You are in the process of analyzing the available information and balancing the costs and benefits of various meal plans to find a solution that fits your personal circumstances.

When contemplating the cost of living on campus, think about your meal costs as well as housing costs. Discover what the meal plans on offer will provide you and choose the most economical option. Also, if economics are the biggest consideration, consider whether you could eat less expensively by purchasing groceries and living off campus.

Escaping the Matrix: Examine the Housing Alternatives at Your College

To escape the Student Loan Matrix and not get blindsided by the cost of housing (on or off campus), students can investigate the room and board situation in the environs and be prepared to minimize the costs of residing at college before they arrive at the college of their choice.

You may well find that living on campus is the cheapest option for you. If it's not, try to balance the costs for lodging off campus and the cost of required meal plans with the costs of transportation to get you back on campus. Recall chapter four where we discussed how living at home while attending community college can cut living costs for two years. Give that idea due consideration.

Published college estimates of living costs on and off campus should be given due consideration and subjected to Reagan's *trust but verify* analysis. How much housing is available at the college of your choice? Is it more or less expensive than the rental options off campus? What about when you figure in your commute? Are the college's meal plans truly a bargain, or do they offer less food for more money than options you could find elsewhere? And—if living on campus and purchasing a meal plan is mandatory at the college of your choice for at least a certain period of time—would you be better advised to look somewhere else for your education? Do the work and dodge the bullet. Be prepared for all the costs of housing and meals at college so you can live as inexpensively as the circumstances permit.

CHAPTER 6

I Could Never Qualify for Grants or Scholarships

WOULD YOU EVER imagine that billions in available federal grants *go unawarded* annually?[1] Would you be surprised to learn that a recent high school graduate was awarded $1 million in scholarship funds?[2] The two statements sound unbelievable, but they are true. Believing the assumption that you could never qualify for grants or scholarships is discouraging and might dissuade you from applying for winnable scholarships. This chapter will disarm that depressing assumption and arm you with tools to claim a healthy share of grants and scholarships to help you reach the target of graduating debt free.

Let's work through this assumption with Taylor Roberts, a high school senior. Taylor is minimally involved at her high school and its extracurricular activities. She makes Bs and Cs. Taylor is more interested in Pokémon Go and Fortnite than in academics. She's a lot like a lot of high school students. Maybe a little like you?

Despite a lack of engagement in high school, Taylor genuinely wants to earn a bachelor's degree in social sciences. But now the time has come to apply for college scholarships to help pay for college, and Taylor is depressed. She has succumbed to the assumption and is convinced she could never qualify for a grant or scholarship.

Does this scenario sound familiar? Perhaps you, too, are convinced that without extraordinary grades and extracurricular achievements on your high school résumé, you could never qualify for scholarships and graduating college debt free would be impossible for you. But this thinking could be stuck inside the Student Loan Matrix assumption of limitation. You may think there is no money available to you because you're average in your classes or in other areas of school. If so, here's some good news—with some targeted research and reasonable effort, you can obtain substantial grants and scholarships.

Throughout this book, we question the assumptions inside the Student Loan Matrix to help students escape from college debt before it takes hold. One of the most pervasive assumptions is that an average student cannot qualify for a package of grants and scholarships that will help them graduate without significant debt. When grants and scholarships are on offer, consider what they cover and, when you win one, what you need to submit each year to renew the package and ensure it takes you all the way to graduation. Handled correctly, grants and scholarships can help you pay for college in ways other than using your savings, your earnings during school, or taking out student loans.

Grants, Need-Based and Otherwise

We start with grants because grants operate like gifts and equal free money. The primary avenue to obtain grants is through the federal government. The same government website on which you record your financial assistance needs contains the Free Application for Student Aid (FAFSA).[3] The FAFSA form is used by many colleges to determine how to allocate their funds on a need basis, so this is a critical document to apply for grants. In addition, some 188 colleges use a supplemental form, the CSS Profile, to award their own institutional grants to students. So to cover those schools, both forms should be completed. Start with the FAFSA. After you complete the FAFSA, the US Department of Education processes the form and sends your information to the list of schools you provided.

Depending on your income and your family's income, you may be eligible for a grant. If you don't come from a traditional two-parent family, you may find some hurdles in fitting your situation into the FAFSA application. But if you qualify, the government may give you grant money that does not need to be returned to pay for college expenses. Take it.

If you do not qualify for grants through the FAFSA, there are other options because there are other organizations besides the government that award grants. These options may not be as abundant as scholarships, but they still exist, and it is important to note that some grants are *need based*. This means that you as the student do not have adequate access to finances to pay for school. We include numerous website resources in this book for students to research and apply for these grants.

In your search for college funding, you may also find grants for individual ethnic, religious, or career choices. There may be a grant that fits perfectly for each college applicant in terms of personal qualifications. There are grants for those who want to be entrepreneurs or those who want to go into agriculture, grants for science, and even grants for those interested in Christian Science.[4] The point is to conduct a broad-based search. Don't rule out grants that only apply to a current interest or hobby of yours.

Keep in mind that many college students change majors, sometimes several times over the course of their education. Your grant search may introduce you to a promising new field of study that you have never seriously considered. If you have a talent or an interest and can gain funding for it, why not consider taking a new path?

As you apply for grants, give special consideration to sources that might have more funding than applicants for that funding, such as religious organizations. Church attendance is down these days. But there are church grants available for students of faith. Similarly, long-established civic organizations such as Kiwanis[5] or Rotary International[6] have robust funding for academic or citizenship scholarships. Time spent researching grant-awarding organizations could pay off handsomely.

Just to be clear, we don't recommend sacrificing your principles to apply for a grant if you have no intention of living up to the requirements of the grant. However, we do recommend you apply for all grants that fit your principles and then plan to live up to the requirements of the grant.

Scholarships: Research and Apply!

Scholarships are the next and equally important avenue for funding your education with other people's money. Unlike grants, scholarships are generally merit-based rather than need-based, though that line gets blurred.

Typically, we think of scholarships as being awarded to those who have shown excellent academic performance in a particular subject in high school. However, scholarships are also awarded to students who meet other specific criteria. For instance, some scholarships are awarded only to students of color with excellent academic performance.

In your research of scholarships, don't be discouraged that some prestigious scholarships are extremely competitive. Take the National Merit Scholarship. The recipient must be a top academic achiever. The competition to be a National Merit Scholar is rigorous, and there are multiple phases with increasing levels of competition. Winning that competition is very satisfying and gives you and your parents significant bragging rights. But not necessarily a lot of cash.

Also, since very few students can qualify for such highly competitive awards, don't be discouraged if you fail to win one. Highly competitive awards aren't the only scholarships to target. Rather, go after as many scholarships as you can find. Put together a solid application essay that can be repurposed for a wide range of applications and use it unsparingly. The objective is to minimize your student debt load by maximizing the number and amount of scholarship awards. Be ambitious in the number of scholarships you pursue and streamline the time required to apply.

As you consider scholarships to pursue, have a look at merit scholarships offered by the college to its own student body and by outside organizations. These scholarships are "awarded to students who have a record of achievement in academics (including grades and test scores), extracurricular activities, and leadership in their community."[7] If you have strong qualifications in these areas, merit scholarships offered by the college could be your golden ticket. "Unlike need-based financial aid, merit scholarships do not take into account a student's financial need as assessed through the FAFSA or CSS Profile. Instead, they are solely determined by a student's academic achievement."[8] They can also be renewed annually, which could help get you through all four years.

One college counselor advises, "the most money a student will ever receive for merit is directly through the university. Many colleges use merit scholarships as a recruitment tool. If the student is willing to cast a wide net and has an academic profile that is at or above what the college typically admits, then significant merit money can come their way."[9] To take advantage of the merit scholarship opportunities, think more in terms of your finances than the prestige of the college.[10] "The key is to cast a wide enough net and look beyond highly and most selective colleges. There are so many wonderful colleges out there—the challenge is that everyone wants to attend the same 50 colleges! When students can 'come down' a notch or two in prestige, then the merit scholarships can be plentiful."[11]

Outside of merit-based scholarships, some colleges and universities offer grants and scholarships for unique abilities, for overcoming hardships, and for an individual's specific circumstances. These scholarships are often created by alumni of your chosen college who are now successful and want to give an opportunity to go to college to someone with a similar outlook or life experience. If you're willing to spend some time researching scholarship opportunities, there are some great possibilities out there. Many are overlooked by students who simply don't spend time doing the research and filling out applications. With your eye on the prize of graduating debt free, that won't be you.

To give you a leg up on the competition, there are website resources throughout this chapter to help you identify available scholarships. We encourage you to consider all grants and scholarships applicable to you and apply for all you can. After you matriculate in college, maintain the requirements for the ones you are awarded so you can continue to receive the grant or scholarship money throughout your college education.

Let's return to Taylor, who is still depressed about her chances of receiving a scholarship award, and give her a pep talk. "Taylor, did you know you can find which colleges are the best value for you based upon the financial aid packages on offer?" Even if the price tag of a private college is high, that cost can be offset by a financial aid package that zeroes it out. Then we point out that there are several scholarship databases showing colleges with beefy financial aid packages.[12] Many private universities have hefty endowments and offer generous financial aid packages to attract students from all economic backgrounds.

Taylor is interested in this. She was unaware of these possibilities. But after a moment, Taylor looks away. "Big deal. Those fancy private schools—they don't want a student like me! They'd never give me a package."

"Taylor—some school *will.* Did you know that there are many states that provide tuition-free aid programs for students at eligible community colleges?"[13] You can google the Promise Program in your state to figure out if you're eligible.

"But what if I want to go to a four-year school, like Mateo?" Taylor asks, gesturing to a fellow student in the high school courtyard. "I need a bunch of scholarships." We promise Taylor, "There are a ton of scholarships out there. The latest National Postsecondary Student Aid Study says there are approximately 1,581,000 scholarships available to students each year.[14] Surely one of those 1.5 million scholarships applies to you. Maybe even a couple of them."

Taylor has to think about that. "Well, maybe I could apply. But really, how much money are we talking about here?" We point at the figure on the page. When you put all the available grants and scholarships together, there's a boatload available to students. Taylor is intrigued. This is all new information, but Taylor's mind isn't out of the Student Loan Matrix yet. "Dude, have you seen my grades? How could I qualify for any of that money?"

"Well, the *average* scholarship award is $3,852 per student.[15] There's money out there for you, Taylor. You just have to go and get it." Taylor is very interested now. She realizes that $3,852 per academic school year would be very helpful, especially if she decides to attend a four-year public university within the state. "All right, so where can I find these scholarships?"

You've been listening in on this conversation for a while and you're starting to get antsy. Right at this point, you can't hold back any longer. You jump into the discussion with: "Taylor, just read this guy's book, *Graduate Debt Free: Escaping the Student Loan Matrix.* The book has a ton of links to scholarship sites." We modestly say thank you and then deflect from the obvious self-reference by pointing out that another great place to start is the College Board's Big Future website with 6,000 programs totaling $4 billion in scholarships.[16] Taylor stands up from the table. "Count me in!"

How about you? Still under the impression that there's nothing out there for you?

There's good news for highly motivated students who are willing to fill out and submit the needed paperwork, particularly the FAFSA. There is indeed grant money available. The *New York Times* recently reported that "roughly 1.7 million high school graduates didn't file the Free Application for Federal Student Aid in 2020–21" which "left an estimated $3.7 billion in available Pell Grants unclaimed."[17] This info is discouraging and also a bit saddening. Available federal grant money goes *unawarded* each year because eligible students neglect to submit the FAFSA. As a motivated student, be sure to fill out the FAFSA, discussed in more detail later, and take advantage of available funds.

One industrious student proved this point by obtaining over $1 million in scholarships to fund her college education. Shanya Robinson-Owens, a 17-year-old at George Washington Carver High School of Engineering and Science in Philadelphia, Pennsylvania, was accepted into 18 schools and was awarded $1,074,260 in total scholarships.[18]

Ted Domers, principal at George Washington Carver, observed that Shanya is a well-respected student. He noted, "In addition to being a part of a movement to bring more social action to our school, she's involved in a number of extracurricular activities that show the breadth of her skills, from robotics to journalism."[19] Those are very encouraging words, but how do they explain $1 million in scholarships? Was it her superlative academics or extracurricular activities? No. Shanya had a solid but unremarkable 3.2 grade point average. As far as extracurricular activities, she was involved in the yearbook committee. In short, her activities were about the same as many other high school seniors.

What set her apart? In a word—drive. Christine Owens, her aunt, described Shanya as "a leader and a hard worker."[20] To apply to 18 colleges and countless scholarships did indeed require a lot of hard work. This remarkable accomplishment is a testament to the work ethic that drives her, and her achievement stands as an example for other students to emulate. It proves that any student with sufficient determination and a commitment to perform the hard work of submitting applications can succeed in landing scholarships.

Research Data-Rich Website Listings

As noted previously, great place to conduct your research is the College Board's Big Future website with 6,000 programs totaling $4 billion in scholarships at https://bigfuture.collegeboard.org/pay-for-college/scholarship-search. Also, check out FastWeb.com at https://fastweb.com/ for a database of 1.5 million college scholarships that have been researched and vetted by a team of experts. Then expand the search criteria. Some scholarships are designed for those with special skills or talents, others are more generally accessible. A number of scholarships are based on characteristics unique to an individual. For instance, a scholarship may be designed for first-generation college students from a particular country who speak a language other than English.

For people of color, a superlative resource is the United Negro College Fund (UNCF) at https://scholarships.uncf.org/. The UNCF is a comprehensive clearinghouse for scholarships and grants created for students of color. It is also a superb source of scholarship information for students of all backgrounds. For Hispanic students, there is the Hispanic Scholarship Fund at https://www.hsf.net/ and the Hispanic Heritage Foundation at https://hispanicheritage.org/. Both sites offer broad opportunities for Hispanic students to find available scholarships.

The Federal Student Aid navigator at https://studentaid.gov/understand-aid/types gives a breakdown of types of financial aid a student can receive from federal, state, school, and private sources to help pay for college or career school. Besides financial aid, the website helps students see what they can do to lower costs when they go to college.

Lastly, there are a number of scholarships based on a student's state of residence. For example, the Vermont Student Assistance Corporation at www.vsac.org presents a wide array of offerings to students who live in the state of Vermont. If you are a resident of Vermont, this site could be a huge help because it uses a clearinghouse approach tailored to a particular population. This same type of clearinghouse is available in other states and is limited to each state's residents.

Forget the notion that a student of your particular achievements cannot obtain grant or scholarship funding for college. The money is there. The question is whether you have the persistence and dedication to find it and apply for it. One note of caution as you do so: watch out for scholarship scams. If you have to pay money to get money, it's probably a scam. Stick to the free sites. After you research the many sites listed in this chapter, go claim your scholarship money.

Get a Job!

In an earlier chapter, we outlined the opportunities for college grants offered by several major fast-food franchise chains in what we called the education à la carte program. Many fast-food franchises are located near college campuses, have flexible hours, give a solid paycheck, offer promotion opportunities, provide free food, and include the possibility of a grant. We called this financing option education à la carte because it gives you a menu of possibilities. Think of driving for Uber or Lyft in this same vein with flexible hours and the opportunity to work near campus.

Another useful form of financial assistance to pay for college is work-study. Work-study is a federally funded program that helps college students who have financial needs get part-time jobs. We cover it here because the work-study application process also requires filling out the FAFSA application.

There are several sound reasons for engaging in work-study programs in college. Aside from the obvious benefit of reducing college debt by earning money during college, you get to keep what you earn, your earnings won't affect your eligibility for financial aid, you can work on campus with convenient times and locations, and you can gain valuable work experience.

For a success story on how work-study could prove useful later in your career, let's review Steve Jobs's study of calligraphy at Reed College in Portland, Oregon, way before he thought about Apple. Even though he had to drop out of college for financial reasons at the time, he stayed on campus and sat in on classes. He became fascinated with the study of calligraphy and the art involved in forming letters. "Reed College at that time offered perhaps the best calligraphy instruction in the country," Jobs observed during a speech to Stanford's graduates in 2005.[21] "Throughout the campus, every poster, every label on every drawer, was beautifully hand calligraphed. . . . I learned about serif and sans serif typefaces, about varying the amount of space between different letter combinations, about what makes great typography great."[22]

Steve Jobs later applied that knowledge of calligraphy to the creation of Apple typeface fonts such as Helvetica Neue and Garamond that exploded past the then-standard IBM typewriter fonts of Times New Roman and Courier in 10 and 12 pitch. Although Mr. Jobs wasn't actually in a work-study program, wasn't actually receiving pay toward college, and wasn't even a registered student at the time, it's a great story about how work-study could prove useful later in your career. And we can extrapolate from this story to glean a useful lesson. Under slightly different circumstances, he could have been employed through the work-study program with a position in the college sign shop.

Now let's assess the value of a work-study program through the eyes of a prospective employer. If you were an employer looking for talent, would you rather hire a prospect with zero practical work experience or someone who had excelled in a work-study program? The answer is predictable. An employer has much less risk of making a hiring mistake if they see a prospect has already gained work-study experience. In an article titled "4 Ways a Work-Study Job Can Pay Off," Kathryn Flynn points out, "A work-study job in your academic field can offer valuable experience that may even guide your future career choices. Since many schools offer convenient ways to find jobs that are flexible and accommodating to class schedules, work-study can be a great way for students to earn extra money while building a résumé."[23] As an employer, I look for that type of experience.

When you apply for college, check with the financial aid office to see if they offer work-study. Before accepting a work-study program, compare it with the opportunity to work à la carte to ensure the most flexibility and best return on investment of your time. Even if you do not take one of these opportunities, or if a fast-food franchise employer does not offer some level of funding or reimbursement, you can still make some money during college to assist in paying down college debt. Consider paid summer internships as a double benefit, since they can give you résumé-building work experience and could lead to post-graduation employment. Your college placement office likely has a list of interested companies in your field.

By this point, contrary to the assumption inside the Matrix, you can see that you have a reasonable shot at qualifying for grants, scholarships, work-study, and part-time work. But once you've decided to go out and claim those dollars for your education, you need to drill down into the FAFSA process to understand what it takes to obtain scholarships and grants and then retain them.

For a good example of the steps to obtain and retain grants, let's focus on the Pell Grant, valued at up to $6,895 per year for 2022–23. According to Goldrick-Rab and Kendall, "[o]btaining the Pell for the first year of college requires completion of the FAFSA, eligibility, and enrollment (students must enroll at least half-time to get a partial Pell, and full time to receive a full Pell). Retaining the Pell Grant from year to year, and especially maintaining the size of the grant, requires all of those steps as well as making 'satisfactory academic progress,' which includes both a grade point average requirement and a specified pace of progress."[24] Specifically, you must maintain a minimum GPA of 2.0 on a 4.0 scale and make progress toward graduation within 150 percent of the normal time frame. For a four-year bachelor's degree, the graduation rule of 150 percent equals six years.

We understand the reluctance to fill out the FAFSA. It is a multipage form that requires a lot of information to complete. Even though the gurus at www.studentaid.gov assert "it takes most people less than an hour to complete and submit a new Free Application for Federal Student Aid (FAFSA)," including "gathering any documents or data needed, completing, and reviewing the application,"[25] in the 12 years that I submitted the FAFSA, I could never complete it in that time frame. Perhaps you can do it quicker than me. But, regardless of how long it takes you to fill out the form, completing the FAFSA is essential to your college financial program, so just buckle down and get it done.

Remember this important fact. To maintain eligibility for your federal financial aid, you must *renew the FAFSA application each year*, regardless of your circumstances. Even if nothing significant changes, you must still refile the FAFSA. Unfortunately, many first-year students who have been awarded Pell Grants fail to reapply. "Nationally, 15 percent to 20 percent of first-year Pell Grant recipients in good academic standing do not refile their FAFSA," say Goldrick-Rab and Kendall.[26] This sad fact contributes to the high attrition rate after the first year at many colleges. Apologies for beating the FAFSA submission drum. Hopefully by now you grasp its importance.

Many students are also unaware of the need to maintain satisfactory academic standing to retain their federal aid. A Wisconsin study found that "the percentages of students who were unaware of satisfactory academic progress requirements was similar across several key demographics, including first-generation college students whose parents do not have bachelor's degrees, continuing-generation students with at least one parent with a bachelor's degree, and students from both urban and rural communities across Wisconsin."[27]

These factors could also contribute to the large number of students who lose Pell Grants each year. Sadly, after obtaining the Pell Grant, "some 40 percent at community colleges" lose their Pell Grants each year for failing to meet "satisfactory academic progress standards."[28] If you receive a Pell Grant or another form of federal aid for community college, make sure this statement doesn't apply to you.[29] Reapply for your financial aid each year and maintain your academic standing.

Escaping the Matrix: Go Out and Find the Money for College

The notion that scholarships exist only for those gifted few who excel in academics is simply mistaken. While an average student can find money for college through many available grants and scholarships, you cannot simply expect the money to come to you. As in other areas of life, you have to work to find it. That generally means submitting applications to prove you qualify.

To all the Taylors who assume they could never qualify for scholarships or grants because they are just an average high school senior, there is money available to pursue college dreams. There is something unique about your circumstances that could yield a grant or scholarship. These could include the income of your family, your religious beliefs, your ethnic background or cultural heritage, the things you like to do inside and outside of the classroom, the games you like to play, the foods you like to cook, your creativity and resourcefulness. Whatever is unique about you can help generate grant or scholarship money to fund your college education.

Get paid for your initiative and industriousness. Seek out and find those scholarship opportunities. Don't neglect your initial FAFSA submission and annual resubmission, keep up your academic standing, and don't forget about work-study that can get you money and job experience. If you decide to go to college, target landing your share of scholarships and grants. Grab your piece of the pie. It's there for the taking.

CHAPTER 7

I Can Get an Athletic Scholarship

YOU'VE BEEN A COMPETITIVE ATHLETE since second grade. You love all team sports and excel at anything involving a stick, a ball, or a racket. You are particularly gifted in (fill in the blank). Your friends, family, and coaches have all encouraged your athletic aspirations and nurtured your hopes of winning an athletic scholarship to pay for college. Unlike Taylor, the high school senior in our last chapter who didn't think she could win an academic scholarship, you are certain you have what it takes to win an athletic scholarship.

Now hold on there, hotshot! Your friends, your parents, and your coaches all mean well, but athletic scholarships are extremely rare. Unfounded reliance upon getting one could be another mental trap inside the Student Loan Matrix that could end up sending you to a field of broken dreams. Let's break it down. Take a knee.

Of the erroneous assumptions within the Student Loan Matrix, the assumption *I can get an athletic scholarship to pay for college* can be the hardest to address because it is so closely tethered to an athlete's self-worth. Many student athletes believe, "If I don't play sports, if I can't ace a serve, throw a fastball, or score a goal, what good am I?"

I dealt with that same question in my youth. Well, sort of. In fifth grade, I was carried off the field on the shoulders of my Little League teammates after making the winning play in our town's championship game. The future was wide open! I could almost taste a college scholarship. But later on, in high school, after I lost my second base position to James "Beefy" Wilson two years running, I began to wonder about my future in college baseball.

A similar aspiration to compete in college-level sports arises in countless high school athletes who play football, basketball, field hockey, baseball, softball, lacrosse, tennis, or track. Because they are possessed of noteworthy talent, these athletes naturally think they will win an athletic scholarship. Without an unvarnished appraisal of a student's athletic ability, many high school students count on converting their athletic talent into a college scholarship to pay for college.

Unfortunately, that reliance can be a road to debilitating debt if the scholarship does not materialize. To obtain an objective appraisal of a high school athlete's true prospects, let's look at some actual college athletic statistics and build a realistic view of college athletic competitiveness based on hard data. The National College Athletic Association (NCAA) website at https://www.ncaa.org/ is a great place to start because it gives a comprehensive look at college athletics and includes charts that identify the number of high school students who play every college-level sport.[1] The NCAA website is a treasure trove of empirical data that reveals several eye-opening facts.

The sport that blew my mind was high school football. Naturally, one would think the prospects of getting an athletic scholarship in football would be excellent. It is popular, there are many players on a team, and football players are highly scouted as prospects for college teams. According to a recent NCAA report, over one million high school students play high school football. But of those, less than one-tenth go on to play college football at any level. And of those college level athletes, even fewer get scholarships.[2]

The lack of athletic scholarship opportunities is not limited to football. The recent Varsity Blues scandal[3] involving wealthy parents who bought access for their children to prestigious universities through less popular athletic programs revealed some interesting features about the college scholarship selection process.

Several of the programs, such as sailing and water polo, that the parents used to get their kids admitted into college didn't even offer scholarships. Their membership on a particular athletic team was simply a route for the student to get into highly competitive schools such as the University of Southern California in Los Angeles.[4] Reading between the lines of the news coverage, one can surmise that because those sports offer so few scholarships, the path is even more restricted for people of moderate means looking to reduce the cost of college through an athletic scholarship in lesser-known sports.

Many high school students cherish the hope that their athletic prowess can lead to a free ride in college. To be clear, some gifted students can and do qualify for full-ride athletic scholarships, and their successes are celebrated nationally. But the statistical reality of the situation demands that we examine the likelihood of a college athletic scholarship in detail.

The nearby chart shows the NCAA data for 2019 as of April 8, 2020, at each division level for each sport on offer in college. We analyze this particular year for two reasons: it is the most current published data and it gives a representative basis to estimate the probability of a current high school student competing in college athletics. Looked at another way, the chart shows the high risk that a high school senior *won't* qualify at a college level and therefore *won't* be awarded a scholarship.

On the NCAA chart, students can compare popular programs for both men and women athletes in sports such as basketball, lacrosse, and swimming. In the center highlighted column, the chart gives the "Overall % HS to NCAA" acceptance rate then gives the constituent rates in each of three divisions. Note that the rates on this chart do not show the number of *scholarships* awarded in each sport, only *the acceptance rate* into the sports programs. We'll address the actual scholarship rates later to draw an objective picture of an athlete's prospects.

Looking at basketball, the chart reveals that of the roughly half million young men who play high school basketball in the United States, only around 3.5 percent go on to play college ball. By comparison, over 150,000 fewer women play basketball in high school, so you might think that their prospects would be better. Not so. Scarcely 4 percent of them continue playing basketball in college.[6]

What about less popular sports? The odds for a lacrosse player who wants to continue their sport in college are slightly better. A little over 1 in 10 will continue playing—12.8 percent of the men and 12.5 percent of the women.

ESTIMATED PROBABILITY OF COMPETING IN COLLEGE ATHLETICS

	High School Participants	NCAA Participants	Overall % HS to NCAA	% HS to Division I	% HS to Division II	% HS to Division III
MEN						
Baseball	482,720	36,011	7.5%	2.2%	2.3%	2.9%
Basketball	540,769	18,816	3.5%	1.0%	1.0%	1.4%
Cross Country	269,295	14,303	5.3%	1.8%	1.4%	2.1%
Football	1,006,013	73,712	7.3%	2.9%	1.9%	2.5%
Golf	143,200	8,485	5.9%	2.0%	1.6%	2.2%
Ice Hockey	35,283	4,323	12.3%	4.8%	0.6%	6.8%
Lacrosse	113,702	14,603	12.8%	3.1%	2.5%	7.3%
Soccer	459,077	25,499	5.6%	1.3%	1.5%	2.7%
Swimming	136,638	9,799	7.2%	2.8%	1.2%	3.2%
Tennis	159,314	7,785	4.9%	1.6%	1.0%	2.3%
Track and Field	605,354	28,914	4.8%	1.9%	1.2%	1.7%
Volleyball	63,563	2,355	3.7%	0.7%	0.7%	2.3%
Water Polo	22,475	1,072	4.8%	2.7%	0.8%	1.3%
Wrestling	247,441	7,300	3.0%	1.0%	0.8%	1.2%
WOMEN						
Basketball	399,067	16,509	4.1%	1.3%	1.2%	1.7%
Cross Country	219,345	15,624	7.1%	2.7%	1.7%	2.7%
Field Hockey	60,824	6,119	10.1%	2.9%	1.4%	5.8%
Golf	79,821	5,436	6.8%	2.8%	1.9%	2.1%
Ice Hockey	9,650	2,531	26.2%	8.9%	1.1%	16.2%
Lacrosse	99,750	12,452	12.5%	3.7%	2.6%	6.2%
Soccer	394,105	28,310	7.2%	2.4%	1.9%	2.9%
Softball	362,038	20,419	5.6%	1.8%	1.7%	2.2%
Swimming	173,088	12,980	7.5%	3.3%	1.2%	3.0%
Tennis	189,436	8,596	4.5%	1.5%	1.0%	2.0%
Track & Field	488,267	30,326	6.2%	2.8%	1.5%	1.9%
Volleyball	452,808	17,780	3.9%	1.2%	1.1%	1.6%
Water Polo	21,735	1,217	5.6%	3.3%	1.1%	1.2%

Figure 14.[5]

The odds for track and field stars are worse, with around 5 percent of men continuing in college careers and about 6.2 percent of women.[7]

Competitive student athletes might look at this fact-filled chart as a roadmap to determine which individual sport offers them the best shot at making a college roster. For example, if you are a woman, check out ice hockey! Any way you look at it, the odds of actually making it onto a college athletic team are slim. And the odds of winning an athletic scholarship award are even slimmer.

A key point to keep in mind is that college athletic associations, rather than the colleges themselves, set the maximum number of athletic scholarships that member schools can award to student athletes for each sport. So the college coaches don't set the limits on scholarship awards. The coaches do have discretion to award fewer than the college association limits, but that is an internal choice, perhaps based on funding availability or other factors. They have no power to increase the number of scholarships.

Stick with me as we dive deeper now because it gets a bit convoluted. For scholarship purposes, the college associations have split collegiate sports into two major categories: Head Count sports and Equivalency sports.[8] A sport in the Head Count category has a stated scholarship cap, and the number of athletes receiving scholarship awards cannot exceed this number. To make it even more complicated, in a Head Count sport, an athletic scholarship can be awarded as either *full* or *partial*, meaning that students receiving athletic scholarships cannot be certain of receiving a full ride. Even partial awards count against the Head Count limit.[9]

All NCAA sports that are not designated Head Count sports are designated as Equivalency sports. The term *equivalency* refers to the fact that awards can be split into partial scholarships in any proportion up to the maximum number of scholarship awards allowed. For example, in the Equivalency sport of softball in an NCAA Division I school with a limit of 12 per team, the school could award a one-half scholarship to each of 24 softball players and not exceed the limit.[10] For this reason, full scholarships are relatively rare in Equivalency sports as compared to Head Count sports.

An additional caveat is that there is a top limit on the number of athletes who can be awarded even a partial scholarship in an Equivalency sport[11]—this limit is referred to as the maximum number of counters. As an example, for all NCAA Division I baseball teams, the maximum number of counters allowed is 27.

Some club sports, such as rowing and rugby, do not have an official governing association and consequently are not subject to the NCAA scholarship limits. However, for many of these sports, the respective teams have agreed to follow the rules of other sport associations regarding scholarships and other assistance. This rule is in place so a given college varsity-level program does not receive a significant advantage over a competing club program from another school.

The number of scholarships available at each division can vary significantly as shown in the following chart. By way of comparison, in track and field, both men's NCAA Division I and Division II are allotted 12.5 scholarships, while Division III gets none. A similar phenomenon can be seen in the women's divisions.

Now for specifics on the number of scholarships available. The two charts that follow are from ScholarshipStats.com and can be found at https://scholarshipstats.com/ncaalimits.[12] They show the limits on scholarships per team for both men's and women's sports during the academic year 2020–2021. We use this academic year because it reflects the scholarship limits after taking into consideration the pandemic disruptions. In addition to the NCAA scholarships, the chart also includes the number of scholarships available for the two other collegiate athletic associations—the National Association of Intercollegiate Athletics (NAIA) and National Junior College Athletic Association (NJCAA). The men's and women's charts show a slightly different distribution, but both reveal the low number of scholarships available.

ATHLETIC SCHOLARSHIP LIMITS: MEN'S TEAMS 2020–21

Men's Varsity Sports Scholarship Limit per Team:	NCAA I	NCAA II	NCAA III	NAIA	NJCAA
Baseball	11.7	9	-	12	24
Basketball *	13	10	-	-	15
Basketball—NAIA Div I	-	-	-	11	-
Basketball—NAIA Div II	-	-	-	7	-
Bowling	-	-	-	5	12
Cross Country—NCAA limits include T&F	12.6	12.6	-	5	10
Fencing	4.5	4.5	-	-	-
Football—NCAA I FBS	85	-	-	-	-
Football—NCAA I FCS	63	-	-	-	-
Football—Other Divisions	-	36	-	24	85
Golf	4.5	3.6	-	5	8
Gymnastics	6.3	5.4	-	-	-
Ice Hockey	18	13.5	-	-	16
Lacrosse	12.6	10.8	-	12	20
Rifle—Includes co-ed teams	3.6	3.6	-	-	-
Skiing	6.3	6.3	-	-	-
Soccer	9.9	9	-	12	24
Swimming & Diving	9.9	8.1	-	8	15
Tennis	4.5	4.5	-	5	9
Track & Field—NCAA limits include X-C	12.6	12.6	-	12	20
Volleyball	4.5	4.5	-	-	-
Water Polo	4.5	4.5	-	-	-
Wrestling	9.9	9	-	10	20
Average Athletic Scholarship	$18,013	$6,588	-	$8,093	$2,376

Figure 15.[13]

Take football as an example. The preceding chart shows that in football, NCAA Division I teams are limited to 85 scholarships per year, and these are split in some fashion among the four classes. The NCAA mandates that all football teams have a minimum of 63 players, and all teams can have up to 125 active players, including between 35 and 60 walk-on players. The average NCAA football roster is 105 players.[14]

A note is in order about the rules affecting the two Division I subdivisions. For the sport of college *football* only, NCAA Division I schools are divided into FBS and FCS subdivisions with differing limits, as shown on the chart. The NCAA's Football Bowl Subdivision (FBS), formerly known as Division I-A, is the top level of college football in the United States. The name Football Bowl Subdivision refers to a series of postseason "bowl" games, with a national champion determined by various polls ranking teams after the completion of the bowls.[15]

Unlike the "bowl" competition in the FBS, the Football Championship Subdivision (FCS), formerly known as Division I-AA, holds a multi-team bracket playoff tournament to determine its national champion. FBS teams are capped at 85 players on scholarship, while FCS teams are capped at 63 scholarships against a total roster of 125 players. NCAA Division II teams are capped at 36 scholarships, while Division III gets none.[16]

Now let's turn to the women's athletic program to identify the athletic scholarship available for each collegiate sport.

Note that for both men's and women's sports, the limits on athletic scholarships available make those scholarships extremely competitive and extremely rare. Note too that even if an athlete wins one of these highly competitive scholarships, the actual amount awarded can be relatively modest such as $6,588 for Men's Division II athletes.[18]

ATHLETIC SCHOLARSHIP LIMITS: WOMEN'S TEAMS 2020–21

Women's Varsity Sports Scholarship Limit per Team:	NCAA I	NCAA II	NCAA III	NAIA	NJCAA
Basketball	15	10	-	-	15
Basketball—NAIA Div I	-	-	-	11	-
Basketball—NAIA Div II	-	-	-	7	-
Beach Volleyball	6	5	-	-	10
Bowling	5	5	-	5	12
Cross Country—NCAA limits include T&F	18	12.6	-	5	10
Equestrian	15	15	-	-	-
Fencing	5	4.5	-	-	-
Field Hockey	12	6.3	-	-	-
Golf	6	5.4	-	5	8
Gymnastics	12	6	-	-	-
Ice Hockey	18	18	-	-	-
Lacrosse	12	9.9	-	12	20
Rifle—includes co-ed teams	3.6	3.6	-	-	-
Rowing	20	20	-	-	-
Rugby	12	12	-	-	-
Skiing	7	6.3	-	-	-
Soccer	14	9.9	-	12	24
Softball	12	7.2	-	10	24
Swimming & Diving	14	8.1	-	8	15
Tennis	8	6	-	5	9
Track & Field—NCAA limits include X-C	18	12.6	-	12	20
Triathlon	6.5	5	-	-	-
Volleyball	12	8	-	8	14
Water Polo	8	8	-	-	-
Average Athletic Scholarship	$18,722	$8,054		$7,870	$3,259

Figure 16.[17]

Combining Acceptance Data with Scholarship Data

Summarizing the 2019 data for high school football, some 1,006,013 students played football, and of that number, only 7.3 percent or 73,712 made it to an NCAA team in any of the three divisions. Of those 73,712 students, only 29,174 played NCAA Division I football.[19]

The NCAA Division I football teams were then and are now split into the FBS and FCS subdivisions discussed previously with 130 FBS teams and 127 FCS teams. To make things slightly more complicated, the FBS division goes by the Head Count rules, while the FCS division goes by the Equivalency rule. What you need to know is that FBS teams are allowed 85 scholarships each year, meaning only 85 individuals get a scholarship per year. Consequently, an aspiring college athlete would want to ask the recruiting coach at the college of their choice how many positions are available to be split among what number of athletes to determine the athlete's likelihood of landing a scholarship.

Interestingly, although FCS division teams are allowed 63 scholarships each year, they go by the Equivalency rule, which means more than 63 individuals can receive a scholarship at those schools. It also means very few full-ride scholarships awarded. What does this mean to you as an aspiring college athlete? The short answer is that landing a spot on a college roster is rare and landing an athletic scholarship on that roster is even rarer. Think of it this way: if you are the best player in your position, in your sport, in your state, you have a shot at an athletic scholarship. It's not impossible, but it's rare.

What Are the Odds I'll Land a Football Scholarship?

OK, what are the actual odds? Let's do the math. The numbers reveal a remarkable fact about your chances of landing a scholarship. We'll call it out when we get there.

There are 130 FBS teams with 85 football scholarships each for a total of 11,050 opportunities. There are 127 FCS teams with 63 scholarships each for a total of 8,001 opportunities. This means the total number of football scholarship opportunities available in all of NCAA Division I football is 19,051. Those 19,051 slots must cover all four year groups (first year through seniors), and since the other three classes already would have been allocated scholarships we can assume about one-fourth remain for the incoming class. If so, first-year students are competing for about 4,700 slots. This is not a precise calculation and depends greatly on the college you are targeting, but you get the basic idea.

Applying the same calculations for NCAA Division II, we find Division II teams total 100 with 36 scholarships available for a total of 3,600, split among four classes, for a total of 900 scholarships available to first-year students.

If we continue to perform the math, that means of all the 1,006,013 high school football players, only about 4,700 Division I athletes and 900 Division II athletes can be awarded a football scholarship.[20] Since Division III teams do not award scholarships, the total number of first-year scholarships available for all NCAA Division I, II, and III schools is 5,600. That's a little over one-half of 1 percent (0.56 percent). That's the remarkable fact we referenced previously. It puts your chances at *about 1 in 200.* Given the high expectations of many high school athletes, that number is remarkably low. Are you the best in your position in your sport in your state in your senior year?

The numbers are similar for men's basketball. There are 540,769 high school basketball players. Of those, 18,816 make it to an NCAA team, around half of those make it to a Division I team, and the other half make it to a Division II team. NCAA Division I basketball is a Head Count sport.

The charts reveal that Division I basketball teams are allowed to give 13 students scholarships; Division II teams are only allowed to give 10 students scholarships. There are 357 Division I teams and 308 Division II teams. Doing the math reveals there are about 7,721 scholarships available each year in NCAA men's basketball.

Again, incoming first-year students are competing for around one-fourth of these, which means in reality there would be a total of 1,930 scholarships available. This equates to about one-third of 1 percent (0.35 percent) of male high school basketball players or *about 1 in 300.* That number bears repeating—male high school basketball players have a 1 in 300 chance.

The odds are not the same in every sport, so student athletes can be cagey in their selection of high school sports programs. For example, if you're involved in less popular sports (e.g., lacrosse) there is a higher likelihood of scholarships, so you could consider actively pursuing a scholarship. But go into the endeavor with eyes wide open.

Even for those small percentages of high school athletes who successfully land athletic scholarships, the financial reward is rarely a full ride. Relying on that eventuality is setting yourself up for a fall. Note that according to the charts, the average men's scholarship award totals only $18,013 in NCAA Division I and $6,588 in Division II, while the average women's scholarship awards are slightly higher at $18,722 in Division I and $8,054 in Division II.[21] Although these are substantial sums toward college expenses, they may not go far to offset the cost of a private university with a $70–$80,000 annual price tag.

When compared to your chance of winning the lottery (1 in 25,000,000), your chance of winning an athletic scholarship at 1-in-200 or a 1-in-300 might not seem so bad. But those odds may not be good enough for you to bet your college future on.

It's also interesting to consider how few college athletes go on to make it to the pros. Here's a table from the NCAA showing the estimated probability of reaching that level.

ESTIMATED PROBABILITY OF COMPETING IN PROFESSIONAL ATHLETICS

	NCAA Participants	Approximate # Draft Eligible	# Draft Picks	#NCAA Drafted	%NCAA to Major Pro	% NCAA to Total Pro
Baseball	36,011	8,002	1,217	791	9.9%	-
M Basketball	18,816	4,181	60	52	1.2%	21%
W Basketball	16,509	3,669	36	31	0.8%	6.9%
Football	73,712	16,380	254	254	1.6%	-
M Ice Hockey	4,323	961	217	71	7.4%	-

Figure 17.[22]

Wait, what? Am I reading that right? Yep. As of April 8, 2020, of the 1,006,013 high school football athletes, some 73,712 participated in NCAA college football. But of those, only 16,380 were draft eligible, and only 254 college athletes actually made it to the National Football League.[23] That equates to 0.025 percent. It's hard to be the bearer of such deflating news. But to paraphrase Muhammad Ali, if you hope to make it into professional football, "You've got two chances. Slim and none. And Slim just left town."[24] That 0.025 percent gives you a lot more respect for those guys on the football field every Sunday, doesn't it?

Since we're on the topic of athletic scholarships, let's also discuss the recent ruling that college athletes can be "paid" for their work at institutions of higher learning. From an equity perspective, they should be paid, given the amount of time required of them to compete on nationally ranked teams and the value of the entertainment they provide. Informal research reveals that the time commitment for competitive Division I teams can range up to 30 hours a week for workouts, team meetings, film reviews, travel time, and game day preparation.[25] That 30-hour commitment is very similar to a work week.

Recently, the issue of paying student-athletes was addressed by the US Supreme Court. In a June 21, 2021, ruling, the Court ruled unanimously that "the NCAA's rules restricting certain education-related benefits for student-athletes violate federal antitrust laws."[26] Regarding how this will affect student athletic scholarships, the key takeaway is that the Court "refused to disturb the NCAA's rules limiting undergraduate athletic scholarships and other compensation related to athletic performance" and simply struck down "NCAA rules limiting the education-related benefits schools may make available to student-athletes"—such as rules that prohibit schools from offering graduate or vocational school scholarships.[27] The upshot is that NCAA rules prohibiting compensation of college athletes still stand, but the ability of student-athletes to profit from their athletic endeavors through Name, Image, and Likeness (NIL) endorsements is now wide open.

One year into the program, colleges with sophisticated NIL programs can be attractive to highly qualified student-athletes. For example, the University of Nebraska has pioneered an NIL program designed to teach the student-athlete how to build a business around themselves so that they can earn money from it over a period of years.[28] The program appears to be bearing fruit for some student-athletes. "Nebraska has been on the forefront of NIL since its introduction in July 2021" working with third-party entities known as collectives "to expand NIL and organize offerings for student-athletes since institutions were prohibited from involvement in NIL activities."[29]

But let's keep in mind that only the most highly qualified student-athletes can make the team in the first place, are competitive enough to get scholarships in the second place, and fortunate enough to win NIL endorsements in the third place. So, the slim (to none) prospects remain about the same for the vast majority of students to earn either scholarships or NIL endorsements to pay for college.

The Cost of Student Athletics

Sadly, despite the huge amounts of money, time, and effort put into college athletics, and despite the television coverage, the corporate sponsorships, and the ad revenue, most college athletic programs are not even breaking even. Ironically, athletes who enter college athletic programs may even end up paying some portion of the program to support their teams through student activity fees.

In a revealing article titled "March Madness Is a Moneymaker: Most Schools Still Operate in Red," Jo Craven McGinty reports that "[i]n 2019, athletic departments across all three NCAA Divisions generated $10.6 billion in revenue from all sports," but they "spent more than $18.9 billion."[30] That means overall athletic programs were operating in the red by some $8.3 billion. Given the television coverage and fan support, one would think college athletics would be generating funds for their schools. But rather than generating funds to offset other college costs and lower the cost of attending college, overall the athletic departments actually lost money. "The two biggest costs were financial aid for athletes ($3.6 billion) and coaches' compensation ($3.7 billion)."[31] Remarkably, college coaches earn more than college presidents. But you already knew that so let's not get sidetracked.

Here's the kicker: to make up that $8.3 billion deficit in 2019, the colleges in the three NCAA Divisions supplemented their tuition revenue "by institutional and governmental support and student activity fees."[32] In other words, many high school students who had planned to attend college on an athletic scholarship were unlikely to make the team or get an athletic scholarship but were very likely to pay college activity fees to support the team.

Escaping the Matrix: Realize Not Many Students Can Compete as College Athletes

The main point to remember is that because grants, academic scholarships, and financial assistance are available to all students, including athletes, high school athletes should avoid hanging their college dreams entirely on an athletic scholarship. If a student-athlete does happen to be competitive enough to win a scholarship in their sport, odds are they will need to continue pursuing additional funding because it is unlikely they'll get a full ride.

On the plus side, even though athletic money isn't as available as student-athletes might like to think, there *are* athletic scholarships out there. The wise course is to cover both the academic and the athletic scholarship bases. In addition, because injuries can occur at any point in your college athletic career, be prepared with a backup plan.

The benefits of an educational degree last a lifetime and will continue well past the conclusion of a college student's athletic career and the average professional athlete's career. Many adults continue to enjoy sports for recreation even after pro dreams fade. There's nothing that can stop someone from living an athletic lifestyle. But recalibrating expectations based on the view from outside the assumptions of the Student Loan Matrix can result in a student finding their true calling that much sooner.

CHAPTER 8

I Need Networking in College for Career Success

ONE OF THE SUBTLER ASSUMPTIONS that form the Student Loan Matrix is that college is important not for education's sake but for the sake of the networking opportunities it offers. People attend college not only hoping to graduate with a prestigious or marketable degree but also because it offers an introduction to a powerful fraternity/sorority organization, an opportunity to connect with a future Bill Gates, or an entrance into an alumni network that will open the doors to a more prosperous future.

Are you a student focused on one of these connections? Are you seeking to build ties with other attendees at the university of your choice? Ones that could be the means to guiding you into a successful career in business, on Wall Street, or in politics? The graduates of elite colleges who are in hiring positions know the rigor of their own academic experiences at their alma mater. Consequently, they may gravitate toward job candidates who have shared that experience. If you happen to have school ties from a prestigious institution, you might well look forward to a great career based on those ties.

That school tie is indeed remarkable if you happen to make it into the elite group of one-half of 1 percent (0.5 percent) of students attending Ivy League schools out of 17 million total undergraduates in the country.[1] But if you are one of the students seeking a college experience largely for the networking opportunities on offer, it might be useful to reevaluate whether you need them to succeed, and, in the event that you actually do need networking to succeed, whether you need college to obtain it. This is particularly true after COVID-era college students experienced mandatory online learning that severely limited social interaction at even the most prestigious institutions.

To be evenhanded here, universities do offer formal networking services to their alumni through university platforms and through such organizations as the Handshake Network that presents insights on the path from college to career from a network of students, universities, and recruiters.[2] Then too, a fellow alum could be predisposed to look kindlier on an application from someone who attended their alma mater than they might on an application from someone with whom they have less in common. But keep in mind that only about 1 in 200 job applicants is likely to be from their alma mater, so even if this is a real effect, it is rare.

It is also possible for a student to completely miss these opportunities despite initially intending to make use of the networking available at their college of choice. If you go to college specifically for networking opportunities but don't make use of the networking services on offer, you've wasted the time and money you spent for that purpose. Additionally, as many students have discovered, networking that is focused on social climbing eventually runs out of steam when people see through it. The most valuable networking arises from the ability to work with people and put your best foot forward. It's about doing consistently high-quality work in your field. And you can do that without college networking and even without a college degree.

How does the expectation arise that you need a college education to generate connections for networking purposes? While it can be tempting for a first-year college student to look to the school to provide a ready-made network, they should be wary of getting in over their heads financially at a high-dollar elite institution strictly for networking. Since all the Ivy League colleges, MIT, and Stanford offer "no loan" financial aid policies for low-income students who are accepted, the elite college experience is likely to be as affordable as an in-state public four-year college. But if you are a full-pay student, these elite colleges are more expensive. If you are targeting an elite institution and get accepted, the networking opportunity is an added benefit of which to make full use.

If you are not accepted at an elite college, it may be a better idea—and less risky in the long run—to take the harder path of forming those connections for yourself. Those who believe they need a networking experience in college to achieve career success may expect that by going to college they can create a long-term network that will generate future financial success. There is undeniable merit in the idea of networking for career success. But let's take a careful look at the assumption as it pertains to college.

College Networking: What Universities Have on Offer

The argument for college networking does have some valid features. One very favorable facet of networking that many universities provide are alumni organizations and job boards that let alumni hire other alumni. This gives their students a leg up in the area or state where the college has an alumni presence.

This is a networking feature that is potentially valuable to college attendees. Many colleges host job fairs or summits on available careers in certain fields. These types of networking opportunities can be helpful for both the job seeker and employer. A business associate noted that, as a job seeker, she has looked at alumni job boards for leads in the past and has had success applying to businesses run by alumni of her alma mater. She also noted that later in her career as a recruiter, she found that presenting in seminars at universities and posting on college job boards was a great way to bring in new talent.

Attending a specialty school known for a particular field and graduating with the highly regarded degree can also be a networking shortcut. For example, a design degree from the Rhode Island School of Design or a business degree from Babson College would place you in a favorable position to be hired in one of those fields because of the extensive networks in place for graduates.

However, the networking opportunities available to college students may be easy to miss for the average individual. As a point of comparison, how often have you walked past your school guidance counselor's office and made a mental note to stop in next week to talk about college selections and then failed to visit the office entirely? In between student organizations, social events, homework, and a part-time job, many college students may forget about their institution's career center in just the same manner. And colleges don't mandate networking. The value of the networking on offer in college is dependent upon your willingness to make use of it.

If networking is a major reason you're going to college and you fail to take advantage of networking opportunities, you're effectively paying tens of thousands of dollars for a service you don't exercise. Does your personal financial situation permit this college expenditure, or would you be better served to find an alternative route that doesn't land you deeply in debt?

THE LIMITS OF COLLEGE NETWORKING

Beyond the formal networking services on offer at universities, the value of informal networking as a guarantor of career success must be scrutinized. Many students believe they will meet individuals like Bill Gates in college who will later be of service in their careers and possibly enhance their income. Although this might be true for some people, it is not a reliable basis to incur college debt because it is too speculative. With the exception of fundraising enterprises, where a network of donors can be extremely valuable to an individual fundraiser, college networking for personal career success is of negligible value. Supporting this premise, recent research indicates that networking does not lead to significantly more income on average.[3]

In my experience, business success rises or falls on the value of the work produced and on the hard work performed by individuals developing their talent over long days and nights. While networking contacts may be useful to introduce an opportunity, long-term success arises from how a person takes advantage of that opportunity. It may well be true that by attending classes and extracurricular activities in college, you will have the occasion to interact with other students and that the interaction can potentially create connections that will last a lifetime. We can also acknowledge that some of these connections will take you further than your grades or what you learn in class.

That's the general benefit of networking in college. The problem is that the anticipated outcome is completely speculative. How can you measure the worth of the college networking or put a value to it as you attempt to weigh it within the scale of college debt? And how can you know that the college networking was the source of your success rather than your own industriousness?

Specifically, how can you measure the impact of networking except anecdotally? Given the uncertain nature of the connections you will make in college and how those connections will affect you 10, 15, or 20 years later, it is worth challenging the notion of college as an incubator of networking connections. For example, at my 25th college reunion, I got reacquainted with a classmate who had been brilliant at math in college and had become a successful accountant after graduating. He would have been a great networking guy to know in the accounting field after college because of the expected arc of his career. But in the middle of his career, he lost a battle with the bottle, crossed some ethical lines, and ended up in federal prison.

During the years he spent in prison, he would not have been a particularly good networking reference for a career in accounting. Later, he regained his balance and became an advocate for Alcoholics Anonymous. At that point he became a great networker for the 12-step program in AA. Would I have known any of this at college when I hoped to network with him professionally? No, it was just too speculative.

Maybe someone you meet will be good for your career later on, maybe not. Without hard data, is college networking a sound rationale for paying the economic cost to engage in it? The on-campus experience of college presents similar worthwhile values, such as the chance to interact with experts in your chosen field. But the link to actual hiring is tenuous unless your professors guide you toward a particular outcome. Perhaps some actual data in this area will prove my hypothesis incorrect. But what I generally see relates to the value of networking as a skill, such as the ability to meet people, rather than the value of networks formed among fellow students or professors in college.

A thought-provoking article titled "The Importance of Networking" on The Haven at College website gives several reasons why networking in college is worthwhile. This is an excellent reference to analyze the various reasons point by point and determine whether they support networking in your personal experience. The article first explains that "networking is a great way to gain information about your industry. Networking with leaders and peers in your field helps you hear tips and gain advice from others who are successful."[4] While this is quite true, this type of networking is not confined to college campuses and can be pursued outside of institutional learning once you determine your career field. It may be available to college students who attend conferences or special lectures and the like, but it is more frequently available to graduates already deeply involved in the workplace.

The article next explains how networking enables you to practice your "social game," preparing you for "interviewing and communicating with coworkers and leaders of a company."[5] Improving your social skills, especially as needed for the workplace, is certainly a valuable skill as referenced in chapter two. As the article explains, "networking is a great way to practice your social skills, make changes as needed, and practice more."[6] However, note that this practice also can occur either in or out of college. If you were considering attending college purely to practice your networking skills, you might consider less expensive alternatives.

The third benefit of networking in college is that it helps you find better opportunities, getting you in front of "people who know when jobs are being created or becoming available." The Haven at College writer advises you to "[b]uild a good relationship with the right people" so that "they may give you tips on future employment opportunities before they are announced to the public."[7]

This is helpful advice. College students can forge these types of relationships within student organizations or by building rapport with professors also active in their fields. But these relationships can also be forged in the working world by professionals who become involved in social clubs or attend conferences within their industry. Which would you prefer? A few hundred dollars spent on a club membership and attendance at a professional convention, or tens of thousands of dollars to pay off student debt?

The Haven at College also advises networking in college for the purposes of acquiring multiple mentors so you can "match your need with the mentor you feel can help you the most."[8] This is flat out great advice. One particular advantage of networking in college is that it gets your foot in the door. A college professor is more likely to talk to a student in their class than to a stranger, particularly a student who requests career guidance or a student who wants to work for the professor. A college professor is also much more likely to have an extensive network of associates in your field who could be beneficial for you to know during your career.

Many students seem to think that the best networking is with their classmates, as opposed to with the faculty, and are reluctant to knock on the professor's door during office hours. This tendency overlooks the true value proposition of networking in college—getting to know the profs. Take this advice to heart and focus on the professor network, rather than the student network. Then take this advice beyond the college experience and apply it to your career. Figure out a way to engage with faculty in the college setting and with senior leaders in the business setting; in clubs; in churches, mosques, or temples; and in professional associations within your field. Take it from an old guy, we are looking for young talent to step forward.

The Haven article also encourages students to find mentors in more than one field, such as an academic mentor and a financial mentor, which is likewise excellent advice. It recognizes the need for personal development in many areas at an early stage in one's career. This advice to seek out multiple mentors also applies beyond the college experience and will be applicable to your career after you land a job in your field.

The Haven at College cites a fifth reason that college networking is beneficial: it helps you stand out in a favorable way, so that you can do "positive things that help others remember you."[9] To this excellent method of standing out in a favorable way, again, you might ask whether the strategy is limited to the college experience. It is certainly good counsel, but does it apply only to college?

In sum, regarding networking as a basis for attending college, consider if the juice is worth the squeeze. While The Haven at College article makes several excellent points about the importance of networking, particularly within a business setting, the reasons for networking fail to explain why such networking is best achieved during the college experience, except in the case of the faculty. To those who believe they require the formality and dedicated resources of college institutions to give them a boost in start-of-career networking, consider whether you might be better served financially by making a presentation at a convention within your field. On the other hand, if you decide to attend college, take full advantage of the opportunity to engage with faculty members in your field. They are solid gold and many students overlook the value of such connections.

If you are introverted by nature, consider asking college friends in the dorm or via Zoom how they are finding ways to interact socially and establish connections to other people. They might recommend attending organizations such as the National Society of Professional Engineers that offer free or reduced-price student memberships[10] to gain social experience and to network. They might talk about church interaction in rural settings and socially distanced club interactions in urban settings. Maybe you could do that too.

In this era of technology and remote working, for better or worse, many of your connections could be virtual for some time. Offices outside of the home will become less and less obligatory. According to Peggy Noonan in the *Wall Street Journal*, the Partnership for New York City reported that during the latter phase of the pandemic, "less than 15 percent of office workers [were] back in the workplace they left a year ago."[11] Ms. Noonan went on to note that "the collapse of the commuter model" in New York City left "the office towers of Midtown empty."[12] Things have improved since then, but the remote work model looks like it is here to stay in some form or another. A lawyer I know has worked for a firm in the San Francisco area for two years and has yet to have an in-person meeting. Let that sink in for a minute and consider how it will impact the notion of networking in college.

The networking and social interaction that seemed to be an essential part of the college experience was simply unachievable for many during COVID. Even in pre-COVID times, networking was hard work and the virtual environment made it harder. It does not happen accidentally, and you somehow have to balance your desire to impress people with the humility to realize you are only at an entry level. Learning how to navigate this new social re-ordering will be a key element of your education. Somehow, either inside or outside of college, you will have to navigate the societal change occasioned by COVID. The social skills that will help you survive in the new era must be nurtured internally and without a playbook. And they must be developed whether or not you attend classes on campus.

This scenario is playing out in real time before our eyes as colleges and universities migrate from in-person to online classes and back as each COVID variant appears and recedes. In the process, students may feel they have been deprived overnight of the very networking interactions that formed the rationale for rubbing elbows with other students at elite colleges.

The whole COVID response on college campuses raises the question: How important to a college education experience were those networking interactions in the first place? If they could be removed from the college experience without consequence and without a reduction in tuition, how important were they?

In a lawsuit demanding refunds for the lost college experience, students at the University of Miami and at Drexel University cataloged the unfulfilled networking promise. Roy Willey, a lawyer at the Anastopoulo Law Firm in South Carolina, the firm that filed the cases against the University of Miami and Drexel University, maintains that the colleges weren't providing students with the social experience they were promised. An article titled "College Students Demand Coronavirus Refunds" points out that "[i]n addition to academics, tuition and fees cover face-to-face interaction with professors, mentors, and peers; access to facilities such as computer labs and libraries; and extracurricular activities and networking opportunities, the suits allege."[13]

To prove this point, the lawsuits cite direct quotes from each college's website that promote their residential experiences. For example, the University of Miami website touts, "Living on campus opens a world of interaction with other students, faculty, and staff members in many social, development, and academic activities."[14] The suits underscored the difference between the on-campus learning experience and the online learning experience. As of this writing there are some 70 lawsuits for refunds from universities following COVID campus closures. The prospects of students winning these lawsuits are clouded by the difficulty of determining the universities' contractual obligation to provide in-person versus online instruction, the legal argument of impossibility of performance during COVID, and the difficulty of proving the extent of the students' intangible loss.[15]

For our discussion about the relative necessity of the networking experience in college, these legal cases neatly frame the issue. The complainant students argue that social interaction with students, faculty, and staff is beneficial for their development and they missed out on a benefit when they did not receive it. The universities, on the other hand, argue that they did not promise in-person interaction and are not therefore under any obligation to provide networking. One would think that universities would defend the value of networking as a unique element of their stock in trade. Their unwillingness to do so undermines the premise that social interaction through networking is essential to obtaining a college education.

Clearly, some level of social interaction and networking is useful and necessary in college, but ask yourself if it is critical to becoming well educated, as we defined earlier, and if it is essential for you to obtain your college degree. It must not actually be essential since colleges continued to produce graduates during COVID when there was no networking available for social interaction.

It is certainly unusual for colleges to first claim the value of social interactions with faculty and students in their literature, then remove those interactions during lockdown, and subsequently claim that tuition and fees should not be refunded for the lost opportunity to experience social interactions. In a recent article titled “To Fight Coronavirus, Colleges Sent Students Home. Now Will They Refund Tuition?” Melissa Korn and Douglas Belkin point out the inconsistency of this position. “As colleges and universities nationwide shut down dorms and dining halls, cancel athletic events and commencements, and shift to remote instruction amid the growing threat of the novel coronavirus, many families had a pressing question: Will there be a refund?”[16]

There is no definitive answer. It depends on the school and their financial position. For example, during COVID, Stanford University moved all classes online and “eliminate[d] housing and dining charges for the spring quarter, which start[ed] March 30, for students who ha[d] left campus,” Belkin and Korn report.[17] But Stanford did not decrease college tuition. To which, senior Jessica de la Paz, age 22, observed, “It doesn’t seem fair to me to pay for an education that I’m not receiving.”[18] Like many students, Jessica felt she learned more from study groups and faculty office hours than from lectures. Without study groups and office hours, which are hard to recreate remotely, the full tuition charge was problematic for her.[19]

Likewise, at Georgetown College, a private Christian school in Kentucky, classes were moved online, and students were not given a rebate for room and board because the college was not in a financial position to do so.[20] For Jacob Locke, a junior from Alabama who anticipates college debt around $50,000, “the idea that some of that will be for services he couldn’t use was hard to accept.”[21]

These articles about the COVID experience on campus shed light on the fallacy of the assumption that networking in college is essential for your career success. Even though COVID concerns are fading in 2023, new strains continue to arise, and a more virulent strain could arise that requires campus lockdowns again, so it remains an issue. The campus responses to COVID concerns call into question the very premise that a student needs college for networking and that college networking is essential to obtain an education or to be successful in a career. They also highlight the desire of students to enjoy the normal social interactions that college can offer. While there is clearly value to social interactions that develop a cadre of professional and personal associates with whom one shares business and social interactions, college is not the only place to develop such relationships.

Escaping the Matrix: Your Network Starts with You, Not Your College Campus

Contrary to the notion that networking requires you to *schmooze your way to the top*, true networking involves building good relationships with experts and mentors in your field. It involves showing key people in positions of authority that you're a top performer and a hard worker. It involves becoming a hard worker through dedication and commitment to your craft and then being unabashed about your interest and capability to move ahead when the opportunity arises.

Zig Ziglar, the noted salesman and motivational speaker, was known for his saying: "success is when opportunity meets preparation."[22] If you have prepared yourself through hard work, senior leaders in your career field will be inclined to give you job tips, not because you *schmoozed* them, but because you have demonstrated your work ethic and they know your value. That type of networking generates deeper ties and more long-lasting value for both the senior and junior person. Be on the lookout for senior leaders who are willing to take an interest in your professional development.

In my professional experience, employers care more about concrete experience and demonstrated performance than a person's track record of networking in college or even the school name on a person's degree. For that reason, networking is more powerful in the working world after college. As an employer, I don't give much thought to where an employee obtained their degree or what college ties they may have. But if I hear from a professor that a standout student is coming my way, I pay close attention. My take is that other employers also care about an employee's experience, business acumen, interpersonal skills, and what they can do to benefit the company more than they care about the employee's college ties.

The COVID experience of locked-down campuses and online classes has taught us that while social interaction is desirable to equip you for the challenges of life, it is not an essential ingredient of the college curriculum. If networking were essential to the college experience, students would be well advised to take coursework in the topic.

It is quite true that interactions with students, faculty, and staff at universities can help a person prepare for a career. That said, if you decide you want those college networking opportunities, then be a discerning consumer of the educational product and make sure to take advantage of the opportunities on offer, such as engaging with professors, initiating social interactions with students, tracking postings on job boards, and pursuing alumni hiring opportunities offered at your university.

The key point is that there is no free ride for networking opportunities at college. Networking opportunities can arise from serendipity, or they can arise from hard work made known to key players—but in neither case are networking opportunities a guarantee of employment or a successful career. As you prepare for the college experience, ask yourself how much social interaction you require from college and whether you could find those interactions in some other social setting. Then, when you arrive on campus, your target will be in front of you.

CHAPTER 9

Going to College Is a Risk-Free Endeavor

THERE IS NO WAY to avoid the fallacy of the assumption that attending college is risk-free. The hard fact is that attending college after high school carries as much risk as any human endeavor and, in many cases, even more because of the student debt that can arise. Because it's more fun to contemplate an experience wrapped in visions of beautiful campuses and developing shared relationships, the idea that one is embarking on a very risky course simply gets crowded out of mind.

Many aspects of success in life depend on how you analyze risk. For example, how much do you need to study to avoid an F in algebra class? What is the risk that you'll be rejected by that person you find particularly attractive in biology? These thought processes require varying levels of risk assessment. The examples here are easier than analyzing the risk associated with college, which is complex. At 17, you very likely haven't yet developed the skills to navigate such complex terrain. This chapter presents some basic tools for you to use when you analyze the risks of attending college.

Let's start with a working definition of risk. I define it as "uncertainty about the positive and negative outcomes of a plan." To my thinking, risk is a way of describing the possibility of an adverse outcome. Assessing risk is a way to judge how big an impact that potential adverse outcome can have on your life. There are some risks you can be aware of and work to mitigate. However, there are other risks that you may not know about and therefore cannot mitigate.

For example, you can look both ways before crossing a street and avoid distractions in the road to reduce the risk of getting hit by a car. You can make sure you are in a safe area with lifeguards to avoid the risk of an undertow. You can also take precautions to avoid getting hit by lightning on a golf course. But there is still some risk associated with any activity. There is no way to eliminate risk altogether, but you can minimize it to a point where you will, in all likelihood, avoid it.

In the construction business, when bidding on a competitive project, I recognize several risks and do my best to mitigate them to stay in business. There is a risk that a subcontractor may go out of business. I mitigate that by requiring the subcontractor to obtain a performance bond for their work on the contract. I mitigate risks of weather delays with contract language that permits our company to extend the contract deadline for weather disruptions. There are risks of transportation delays, price inflation, and lead time delays that can be minimized or alleviated by taking specific actions to ensure a profitable job.

But as I noted, there are some risks that are more difficult to mitigate. For instance, there is a risk that unforeseen circumstances may arise (such as hitting an underground boulder when digging a foundation) that make the project more costly than anticipated. In construction work, you can mitigate unknown risk by building a contingency fund into your proposal on the project. But there is no guarantee that even a contingency fund will cover an actual circumstance. That's just the risk of doing business.

A high school student planning for college engages in a different type of risk analysis than I do for a construction business. It's complicated by the fact that college decisions have an emotional element. Even though a brief examination would reveal that going to college poses risks, it can be very tempting to write them off without due analysis—to just give in to Student Loan Matrix thinking. But you only have one college career, and you may not have a backup plan if things go south. You might think, "My parents will help me out with the bill," or maybe you simply assume, "Lots of people have done this; how hard could it be?" However, by attending college, you are making a significant financial commitment, and without considering the risks of that commitment, you could be left in the dark about the potential consequences. So avoid the temptation to simply write off the risk analysis.

Let's discuss the known risks at the time you are choosing your college. There are two major risks: that your degree won't generate enough salary to cover your debt payment and that you won't get a job in your field. We tackle both in this chapter.

The Risk That Your Degree Won't Cover the Debt

The biggest risk is that you will not land a job after graduating that generates enough salary to pay off your debt in a reasonable time. That risk has to do with your personal capability for college-level work, your determination to complete the work, the career field you are pursuing, and the market for your skills when you graduate. This risk can be exacerbated by your college major selection. To understand the nature of this risk, we will analyze which college majors have the best prospects for post-graduation employment. A related risk is not graduating at all so you can't find work in your intended field. Knowing your prospects of landing a job in your field can help you mitigate the risk of graduating without finding work.

To mitigate the risk of not landing a job with enough salary to pay your debt, students can access tools available to predict salaries in their field. As a general caveat, it is problematic to predict where the job market will be in four years, especially for more specialized careers. But a good starting point to research the job market is the Occupational Outlook Handbook from the Bureau of Labor Statistics at https://www.bls.gov/ooh/.[1] Other useful resources include tools on the payscale.com website to compare salaries, obtain salary surveys, and search wages at https://payscale.com. You can also find related tools on the salary.com website to determine your worth as an employee with a salary calculator, salary comparisons, and compensation data at https://salary.com. Finally, you can consult the annual salary survey from the National Association of Colleges and Employers (NACE) for detailed job projections by specific academic major at https://careers.unc.edu/wp-content/uploads/2022/02/NACE

-Salary-Survey_Winter-2022.pdf. With these tools you will be well armed to anticipate where the job market will be headed when you intend to enter it after graduation.

In an article titled "Some 43% of College Grads Are Underemployed in First Job," Melissa Korn details the job prospects for various college majors. She cites research by Matt Sigelman, chief executive of labor analytics firm Burning Glass and coauthor of a recent report that "looked at real-time job postings and more than four million résumés from people who graduated college between 2000 and 2017."[2]

Korn explains that "[c]ollege graduates who studied homeland security and law enforcement had a 65 percent probability of being underemployed in their first job out of school . . . Those with degrees in psychology and biology stood chances of 54 percent and 51 percent, respectively, of working jobs that don't require college degrees," while "[e]ngineers had only a 29 percent probability of being underemployed, the best outcome of any major."[3] The article goes on to state that "43 percent of college graduates are underemployed in their first job. Of those, roughly two-thirds remain in jobs that don't require college degrees five years later."[4] These are not encouraging statistics, but they are useful to understand if you are banking on a lucrative job after graduation.

The study gives a broad overview of the job landscape after college, reporting that "[g]raduates of liberal arts areas such as philosophy, foreign languages, ethnic and gender studies, history, and English have a better-than-even chance of landing a job that fits their education level."[5] The report notes that liberal arts careers "may not pay well, with teaching and social services popular destinations, but graduates can expect to fare better in terms of landing credential-appropriate roles than transportation, culinary services, agriculture, and public administration majors."[6]

Unfortunately, COVID disruptions on the job market left many graduates over the past two years dealing with the prospect of long-term unemployment. In an article titled "The Crisis of Unemployed College Graduates," authors Jeffrey Selingo and Matt Sigelman argue that colleges should help prepare prospective graduates to navigate a poor job market because since the start of the pandemic, hiring for entry-level college graduate positions had fallen 45 percent.[7] Written during the height of the pandemic, this circumstance may no longer apply to current graduates since unemployment rates normalized in 2022 and decreased in 2023. However, the job market in any given field can still be disrupted by COVID, which can have ripple effects on later hiring levels as the job market evolves.

New forms of COVID may cause turmoil in entry-level positions in some fields and, as COVID becomes less of a threat, may enhance opportunities in other fields. Students who are tracking such trends by using salary.com, payscale.com, and related tools can be alert to the new job prospects. As an example, Selingo and Sigelman note entry-level openings in the $50,000 range "for college graduates as logistics analysts, distribution managers, and loan officers [had] risen up nearly 30 percent since 2019."[8] Likewise, entry-level opportunities were expanding for "business and financial analysts, and software and web developers, both of which [paid] over $50,000."[9] Accordingly, a far-sighted student might preview the salary levels of starting positions in various fields to winnow career choices.

As you consider your potential majors and the risks of unemployment they might entail, research the job prospects available before you decide. If you make the choice to study a major with limited salary potential, be aware that you may need to minor in another field or seek gainful employment outside of your major field when you graduate. This is a good example of a risk-mitigation strategy.

The Risk of Not Graduating in the First Place

Another major risk in college is not graduating in the first place and therefore being unable to get a job that pays for the debt you incurred. You might have been surprised to learn in the opening chapters of this book that your prospects of actually graduating from college were a bit sketchy. The US Department of Education publishes the graduation rates annually in a National Center for Education Statistics study known as NCES 2020-144. Analyzing overall graduation rates for both public and private institutions of higher learning, the graduation rate was 63 percent. Specifically, the recent statistics show that "[i]n 2019, the overall six-year graduation rate for first-time, full-time undergraduate students who began seeking a bachelor's degree at four-year degree-granting institutions in fall 2013 was 63 percent. That is, by 2019 some 63 percent of students had completed a bachelor's degree at the same institution where they started in 2013."[10] That leaves about 37 percent who did not graduate in the six-year window.

You might be thinking, "I'm not going to pay tuition for six years of college! I'm planning to graduate in four years, max." OK, let's do the math and see what class hours you need to graduate then. If you take and pass 15 credits per semester, you'll graduate in four years. But if you take and pass only 12 credits per semester, the minimum to be considered a full-time student for financial aid purposes, you will graduate in five years. Taking fewer credits per semester means later graduation, and after a while, perhaps no graduation. There are also other indicators of your graduation prospects and the debt involved.

One objective indicator of individual prospects for graduating from a particular college is the percentage of Pell Grants awarded. In "Failing Our Kids," a *Dallas Morning News* article, authors Tamara Hiler, Lanae Erickson Hatalsky, and Megan John identify the frequency of Pell Grants as an indicator for student graduation outcomes from particular colleges. The authors noted that in 2013–2014, approximately 1.7 million full-time students took out student loans to finance their college education. In that year, the US awarded more than 1.1 million Pell Grants to students attending 1,100 institutions.[11] The correlation between Pell Grants and graduating with student loan debt is strong enough that the number of Pell Grants can serve as a leading indicator of graduation outcomes.[12] The *Dallas Morning News* article is somewhat dated, but its premise has held up over time and its analytical approach is still worthy of discussion.

The article reported that in 2014, data from the US Department of Education's College Scorecard indicated "nearly half of the students aren't graduating, many students aren't earning sufficient incomes even years after enrollment, and far too many are unable to repay their loans."[13] The authors identified the core institutional failure as "the very essence of what colleges spend billions of dollars purporting to do: provid[e] an education worthy of the time and cost associated with it."[14]

They then analyzed the reasons for this failure:

1. **Completion rates are chronically low.** "A typical four-year private, nonprofit college graduates only 55 percent of full-time freshmen within six years of enrollment, and in Texas, the average completion rate is 47 percent."[15] Perhaps more problematic, "at 761 of these schools, less than two-thirds of all full-time students earn a degree within six years of enrolling as a freshman."[16] No academic or public mechanism exists to identify these colleges as "dropout factories" or flag them for notice or intervention. In fact, "for private, nonprofit colleges, no bar exists whatsoever to trigger any form of intervention or scrutiny from the federal government."[17] Consequently, unsuspecting students may find themselves playing a bit part in a drama with a cast of thousands in which the outcome is already known.

2. **The wage outcomes are low for many students.** When the article was written, "[a]n adult with a high school diploma [could] expect to earn around $25,000 a year. At the average four-year private, nonprofit school, only 63 percent of students who started school with loans earned more than $25,000 six years later . . . omit[ting] graduates who were in graduate school as full-time students."[18] The dynamic between high school graduate salaries and college graduate salaries still holds true, though the amount has grown with inflation.

3. **Tuition and wage outcomes are unrelated.** The authors found "absolutely no correlation between the price of the school and the quality of the outcome for the student." In fact, "students attending schools with lower mobility outcomes (like completion rates, earnings, and repayment rates) are actually paying more for their educations than their peers attending higher-quality schools."[19]

4. **Pell Grants are a proxy for poor-performing schools.** Many high-performing schools enroll small numbers of low-income students. Because 94 percent of Pell recipients currently come from families with an adjusted gross income below $60,000, the number of awarded Pell Grants can act as "a good proxy for students who need

> college to be a mobility machine," explain Hiler, Hatalsky, and John.[20] These are students who need college to improve their lot in life. The irony is that the students who most need that boost are often the ones most damaged by the process. For the four-year private, nonprofit schools, the average rate of Pell students in the student body is 35 percent, while at the most selective colleges, the percentage of Pell Grants is often half of that.[21] But at "dropout factories, half [50 percent] of the students get Pell Grants, while non-dropout factories have 22 percent Pell students."[22] Based on this information, the prudent college applicant will want to inquire about the percentage of the student body receiving Pell Grants, thereby determining if their prospective college might be risky for them. It certainly makes sense to pose the question before matriculating.

This article underscores the risk of not graduating at all. The bottom line is that such poor graduation outcomes "do very little to increase economic mobility."[23] Because of this, students unwittingly experience the exact opposite of upward economic mobility. Using the Pell Grant metric could help you avoid dropout factories and the unpleasant outcome of debt incurred without a degree in hand to cover it.

When you're considering potential colleges, look at the percentage of students with Pell Grants at the school as a gauge for the risk of not graduating. If you are considering a for-profit college, be alert to that school's statistics for bachelor's degree attainment to mitigate your risks. If you want to dig deeper to investigate the empirical prospects for graduating from college for your individual age, gender, race, and chosen major, that information is available through the resources discussed in the book. The investigation is a worthy endeavor to avoid debt without a degree to pay for it.

Predictors of Success in College

SAT and ACT scores are common metrics used by colleges to determine whether the students that apply can handle the rigors of the curriculum. However, when it comes to the likelihood of a college student completing their degree, let alone doing so in a reasonable amount of time, these metrics are not the best predictors of success.

A student's grade point average (GPA) reflecting their academic record is a better predictor of college success than scores on SAT, ACT, and AP exams. The GPA telegraphs how hard you are willing to work rather than how smart you are. But your likelihood of successfully graduating from college is better reflected by another factor unrelated to either your academic record or test scores.

Surprisingly, it has less to do with you as an individual than with your family. The best predictors of success in college is simply your *parents' socioeconomic status*, according to a landmark study titled "Education and Socioeconomic Status" from the American Psychological Association.[24] Other key factors that point to success include your GPA, the level of math you took in high school, whether you won $25,000 or more in private scholarships, and your educational expectations for attaining a degree beyond a bachelor's degree.[25]

Unsurprisingly, if your parents have sufficient resources to offer you a head start in your studies and on the expenses of college, you are more likely to finish. This is not to discourage those who come from economically disadvantaged backgrounds. If that describes you, take this information as an incentive for you to beat the odds, prove the statistics wrong, and obtain your degree. It is meant to offer data so you can embark on your educational journey with eyes wide open to the obstacles you will need to overcome.

The Cost-Benefit Analysis

You may be assuming that you have to go to college to get a better job and to make a higher income. But that assumption may no longer hold true. Is the degree worth the debt? After working at a job since 2015, some graduates doubt if the juice is indeed worth the squeeze.

In his article titled "Recent Grads Doubt College's Worth," Douglas Belkin observed, "Recent college graduates are significantly less likely to believe their education was worth the cost compared with older alumni."[26] He cited the second annual Gallup-Purdue Index, which polled more than 30,000 college graduates during the first six months of 2015. From the data, he concludes,

"One of the main reasons is student debt, which is delaying millennials from buying homes and starting families and businesses."[27]

The statistics were daunting then and continue to be a cause for concern. In 2015, some 68.9 percent of college students graduated with debt, and the average debt load for a bachelor's degree at graduation was $29,669.[28] "According to the Index," says Belkin, "only 33 percent of alumni who graduated between 2006 and 2015 with that amount of debt strongly agreed that their university education was worth the cost."[29] Nope, the juice wasn't worth the squeeze for them.

The Gallup executive director for education and workforce development, Brand Busteed, is cited in the article as being startled by the "steep decline in the perception of whether a degree was worth the cost" and predicted the phenomenon we are witnessing today—the slackening demand for higher education. "When you look at recent graduates with student loans, it gets really ugly, really fast," he said. "If alumni don't feel they're getting their money's worth, we risk this tidal wave of demand for higher education crashing down."[30]

Substantial student debt also portends other difficulties for life after college. "Heavily indebted graduates were 17 percentage points more likely to delay buying a car and 16 percentage points more likely to put off buying a house," reports Belkin. "They also were more likely to delay marriage, start a business, have children, or move out of their parents' homes."[31] In other words, every major milestone toward adulthood is impacted in the lives of students who are heavily indebted.[32]

As more and more students become aware of the risks and conclude that the ends don't justify the means, higher education will need to change its policies or face collapse. Specifically, the entire enterprise will need to democratize and consolidate to survive the inroads presented by online and technical schools.

Escaping the Matrix: Is College Worth the Risk for You?

In an opinion piece, Preston Cooper offered an incisive look at the question, is college worth the risk? He performed a data-based analysis on a large number of college majors to arrive at some sobering facts. The analysis involved calculating the return on investment for nearly 30,000 different bachelor's degree programs. He then "estimated the median lifetime earnings for graduates of each program and subtracted tuition costs in the wages missed while enrolled."[33]

To establish a solid model, he "compared that number with a scenario in which those students didn't attend college, using the earnings of high school graduates as a baseline and then adjusting for demographics, cognitive ability, and family background."[34] Through this analysis, he was able to "compare the net boost in lifetime earnings that students would get from each college degree."[35] The results show that "28 percent of bachelor's degrees, weighted by enrollment, do not have a net positive return."[36]

Mr. Cooper points out the fallacy in many students' thinking regarding the college they attend rather than the major they pursue: "The students often obsess over where they get in, [but] their majors have the most sway over their future earnings."[37] Some majors in particular have definite financial advantages. "Programs in engineering, computer science, economics, or nursing all yield a high return, often increasing their students' net lifetime earnings by $500,000 or more," says Cooper.[38] Contrariwise, "a majority of programs in art, music, philosophy, and psychology leave their average students financially worse off."[39]

This begs the question, what is the risk that your intended college major will not pay off? More precisely, how can you know beforehand if a particular major will pay the freight on its college debt? An insightful article by Jon Marcus in the *Washington Post* titled "Will That College Degree Pay Off?"[40] chronicles the wealth of data that recently became available to answer that question. A sea change occurred when the US Department of Education began releasing data linking student debt to actual majors at actual colleges. For the first time, in 2019, data became available "about debt incurred for specific programs, rather than averaged among every student at an institution," reports the *Washington Post* article.[41]

By accessing the US Department of Education data, students can now find an accurate answer to the million-dollar question of a particular degree's actual economic value to the holder of that degree. Specifically, a student can research the public data at the US Department of Education College Scorecard at https://collegescorecard.ed.gov.[42] By entering your preferences, you can identify several colleges tailored to your exact requirements, then tweak the preferences to explore other options. The data in the scorecard has been aggregated from data submitted by the 77 percent of college students who received federal grants or loans, so it is reasonably comprehensive.[43]

The College Scorecard presents a treasure trove of specific information that a prospective student can apply to perform a cost/benefit analysis of their desired major at their selected colleges. Here's an example using the tool. A student seeking a bachelor's degree in English Literature at Oberlin College in 2022 had an 87 percent chance of graduating and could expect to earn a median annual salary of $44,000 after having paid a four-year net cost (after federal grants) of $140,000. In this example, the information was based on data collected from individuals who began at Oberlin College 10 years ago, regardless of their completion status. This remarkably granular information can definitively answer the fundamental question of whether the salary generated by a degree in your field of study will cover the debt to obtain that degree at a given college.

Because this exceptionally useful data is publicly available, high school students can conduct an inquiry to analyze their risk and to address their core concerns before even taking a step on the campus. This inquiry may point them in the direction of a particular major at a particular college, or in the direction of other alternatives such as education à la carte. The College Scorecard website even presents alternative pathways to a career such as apprenticeships and employer training programs. This brief discussion about the US Department of Education College Scorecard is what is known at some schools as a "foot stomper." It's on the test. Reread it. Cogitate on it. Then use the College Scorecard tool to minimize your risk of obtaining a degree that won't pay the freight.

In sum, college is not risk-free. But by analyzing the risk using tools such as the College Scorecard, you can make an informed decision to mitigate the risk. Consider how the various risks in college affect you personally, then act to minimize them.

CHAPTER 10

I'll Get a Job in My Field That Will Cover My Debt

WE'VE JUST BEEN TALKING about jobs that don't cover the cost of student debt, so why do we need a whole chapter on that very assumption? This chapter is needed to explain a simple rule of thumb that will help you clarify your approach to student loans. The rule is that your total student loan debt at graduation should not exceed your starting annual salary.[1] Since the average, or mean, starting salary of a college graduate has been identified as $58,862, to follow the rule of thumb you should have no more than $58,862 in student debt at graduation.

This powerful rule of thumb allows you to work backward from the expected starting salary in your field to determine an acceptable debt load to shoulder in college. That is an immensely useful piece of information. Think about your choice of major in college, not just from a subjective perspective of your personal interests, but also from an objective perspective of future potential earnings in a field that will cover your debt. Critical to this approach is knowing what job you want, in what field, and at what first-year salary.

The reason many people choose to attend college isn't for love of learning, better networking opportunities, or even a desire to be well educated. Their reason is more practical. They believe that higher education will lead to higher lifetime earnings from getting a good job, perhaps as predicted by the Hamilton Project and related studies discussed earlier. Students naturally assume that the right degree will lead to career opportunities sufficient to cover the cost of the student loans they took out to earn it. But this particular assumption can be a trap for the unwary. The better course of action is to determine your projected salary from the available data and then ensure your debt does not exceed that amount.

Many reliable sources, including NACE, cite $58,862 as the average starting salary of college graduates, so that figure would be a good cap for your college debt. In times of inflation, like 2022–23, that salary figure will rise as inflation rises. Therefore, as you pick your major, tailor your analysis of your own potential earnings with inflation in mind to ensure your expected salary is able to carry your expected debt load. Applying the rule should be done prospectively for undergraduate work. It is difficult to apply to graduate school debt because that debt can escalate far beyond undergraduate levels.

Lisa Bannon and Andrea Fuller analyzed the costs of graduate school at the University of Southern California, a private university in Los Angeles, in a *Wall Street Journal* article titled "USC Pushed a $115,000 Online Degree. Graduates Got Low Salaries, Huge Debts."[2] It revealed that graduates of USC's master's degree program in sociology were frequently saddled with massive debt and low pay. Their analysis revealed that "[r]ecent USC social work graduates who took out federal loans borrowed a median $112,000. Half of them were earning $52,000 or less annually two years later."[3]

Were they following the rule of thumb? Sort of. Social work is an exception to the rule of thumb because of Public Service Loan Forgiveness (PSLF). This program forgives the remaining debt after 10 years (120 payments) in an Income-Driven Repayment plan. Likewise, a borrower will have some forgiveness in PSLF under the Income-Based Repayment (IBR) if total debt exceeds annual income. The availability of the Grad PLUS loan coupled with PSLF can lead to exploitation by some colleges. Because the colleges know that the debt will be forgiven, they encourage their students to borrow through the Grad PLUS loan program for the inflated cost of the master of social work at their school.[4] Buyer beware.

The Bannon and Fuller article identified several representative students who had graduated from USC's sociology master's degree program with low pay and huge debts. Susan Fowler, a 37-year-old mother of two, owes about $200,000 from the master's degree program and earns $48,000 a year as a community mental health therapist in Mount Pleasant, Iowa. Similarly, Mauri Jackson, age 29, owes $167,000 for her time at USC and earns about $59,000 a year as a social worker. Likewise, Patrice Dorsey-Ross owes about $138,000 for her sociology master's program at USC and earns $16.95 an hour at a nonprofit, which translates to approximately $34,000 a year.[5] Beyond their undergraduate debt, these students added post-graduate debt without the additional salary they thought their new qualification would yield.

Clearly, starting salaries have not kept pace with escalating undergraduate or postgraduate costs.[6] But comparing first-year salary with rising costs of college is more of a college affordability issue than one about student debt. Remember, the rule of thumb compares student debt with first-year income, not college costs with income. When we compare debt to income, we see that debt at graduation has been growing faster than the net price of college. Earlier we noted that debt as a percentage of income grew from 33 percent to over 50 percent in the past 30 years.

How can you be prepared to pay your expected debt out of your expected starting salary? The key is the college major you choose. The college major will determine your first-year salary and your capacity to pay student debt. So, let's unpack that idea a bit. The Indeed Career Guide presents data showing the average salary for graduates by their college major in an illuminating article titled appropriately "Average Salary for College Graduates" produced by the Indeed Editorial Team.[7]

The 2021 article opens with a general observation: "While there are a few outliers, the general average salary for college graduates comes to about $58,000 according to a recent National Association of Colleges and Employers (NACE) salary survey. Those who majored in computer science, engineering, mathematics, health sciences, and business were the highest earners, with salaries ranging from $52,000 to $71,000."[8] Since compensation levels in general are affected by inflation and by supply and demand, consult the current Indeed Career Guide to obtain current information.

This data reflects the Hamilton Project notion of the median salary situated at the midpoint of a range of salaries. The 2021 report presents extremely useful statistics showing the average salaries generated by college majors at that time, in descending order:[9]

Engineering:	\$69,188
Computer science:	\$67,539
Math and sciences:	\$62,177
Business:	\$57,657
Social sciences:	\$57,310
Humanities:	\$56,651
Agriculture:	\$55,750
Communications:	\$52,056

The report then continues with college majors that generate lower salaries:

Fine arts:	\$48,871
Neuroscience:	\$48,190
Music:	\$48,686
Art and music education:	\$45,613
Drama and theater arts:	\$44,538
Visual and performing arts:	\$42,465
Studio arts:	\$41,762
Early childhood education:	\$39,097.[10]

This granular data shows the range of salaries available on either side of the median. For those who want to dig deeper and research current salary data, this resource also gives a detailed breakdown of recent graduate salaries by major industry, including business, marketing, health, finance, and technology.

Two articles by Andrew Van Dam, who publishes under the *Washington Post* byline "Department of Data," shed light on the consequences of college major selection. The first, titled "The Most-Regretted (and Lowest-Paying) College Majors," in the September 2, 2022, edition cites the Federal Reserve survey and notes that "nearly half of humanities and arts majors have studier's remorse in 2021 . . . Engineering majors have the fewest regrets; just 24 percent wish they'd chosen something different."[11] The article tracks the selection of majors over the past 35 years to reveal college major trends.

The second article by Andrew Van Dam addresses "college majors with the highest unemployment rates" in the September 16, 2022, *Washington Post* edition. Here, Van Dam analyzes Census Bureau data to present the rates of unemployment by college major for people 25 and older. Fine arts majors rank highest at 3.6 percent unemployment, environment and natural resources majors are in the middle at 2.6 percent, and education majors are the least unemployed at 1.6 percent, which Van Dam notes may be attributed to "seasonal factors."[12] These two Van Dam articles provide useful data points for high school students to consider as they map their course toward selecting a major.

As the Indeed Career Guide illustrates, different majors yield different salaries upon graduation. Even the highest-paid professionals still need to watch their pennies if they are obliged to pay off huge student debt. Their high salaries don't necessarily have extra room for onerous monthly loan payments. The Indeed Career Guide gives helpful tools to project salaries for various college majors upon graduation. Applying the rule of thumb to the projected salaries helps prospective college students determine their debt cap target.

Applying this analysis to graduate school economics reveals an even more sobering reality for students pursuing professional degrees. In a *Wall Street Journal* article titled "Some Professional Degrees Leave Students with High Debt but without High Salaries," authors Rebecca Smith and Andrea Fuller analyze recently released data from the US Department of Education.[13] From the data they conclude that "professional degrees like dentistry and veterinary medicine are leaving many students with immense college debt, threatening the outlook for fields that provide essential public services."[14] The same holds true for degrees in chiropractic medicine, physical therapy, and optometry, which generate a combination of high debts and modest salaries.[15]

The article noted that one student, Sara Jastrebski, completed veterinary studies at the University of Pennsylvania in 2021 with about $370,000 in student debt, which is about four times her starting salary of about $100,000 as an associate veterinarian. Likewise, the federal data shows that New York University (NYU) dentistry students who graduated in 2015 and 2016 accumulated median debt of $349,000 with median earnings around $82,000. Similarly, University of Southern California (USC) students had median debt of roughly $398,000 with median earnings around $91,000 to cover the debt cost.[16]

In each instance, the graduate debt exceeded the one-year salary debt maximum rule of thumb and measured roughly four times a single year of earnings. Because this high debt continues to incur interest, some graduates are concerned about ever retiring the debt. Dr. Jastrebski, the Penn veterinary graduate, determined she "would make more than $200,000 in payments over 20 years on [her] plan and still have a balance of about $700,000 because of accumulating interest."[17]

Before you decide to go for that postgraduate degree, think about the costs both in the short run and long run. As seen in the preceding, undergraduate students don't necessarily bear the worst debt loads. That distinction belongs to the postgraduate degree crowd.

For both undergraduate students and postgraduate students, similar questions arise. How can one strike a balance between the choice of a major and the resultant salary? What elements of the balancing should weigh most on the decision scale? When the cost of college is rising, and the relative marketability of a degree is falling, where should one land in the mix? A good way to address these questions is by calculating the rate of return.

The Rate of Return

The rate of return on college is often overlooked by students and parents. Yet the reason for going to college is frequently to generate higher earning potential, in which case the rate of return on investment should be top of mind. Informed students should be asking what major to pursue, at what college, and at what cost to ensure they attain a favorable rate of return on the college investment.

An informative article by authors Richard Vedder and Justin Strehle makes the case for thinking of the college experience as an investment that should yield a favorable rate of return. "Rising costs and declining benefits mean the rate of return on a college investment is starting to fall for many Americans," claim Vedder and Strehle.[18] They then query "whether it might not be better for more students to forego college in favor of less expensive postsecondary training in vocations like welding and plumbing."[19]

We dealt with this phenomenon earlier and noted that the financial rewards of a career in the trades could outstrip those of some college-educated professionals and could also forego the debt burden. But is there any data on this? Yes, indeed. Vedder and Strehle cite the New York Federal Reserve Bank statistics to point out "with some inexpensive vocational training, [prospective college graduates] could easily get jobs that pay much better."[20]

But how can a prospective student calculate the rate of return on their college education? How can they know whether their career choice can cover the cost of their schooling, particularly when "the payoff from a college education varies sharply depending on school and major."[21] Good news, there is just such a Return on Investment report for colleges available at https://www.payscale.com/college-roi. There is even a breakout for college majors at https://www.payscale.com/college-roi/major. Seek, and ye shall find!

The source of this extremely useful information is the big data maintained by the US Department of Education, and it is remarkably granular as noted previously. For example, you can determine the rate of return for an electrical engineer at a private school versus a state school. You can also determine that electrical engineers can earn twice as much as psychology majors. Knowing that this type of information is publicly available will allow you to determine the rate of return on your chosen major at your chosen institution.[22]

What about using your race, ethnicity, and gender to fine-tune your determination of the rate of return on your college investment and to see how these elements could help you in the process? That information can help you tailor your ROI determination. Vedder and Strehle observe, "the size of the college-earnings advantage also varies with race and gender. In recent years, male college graduates' earning power has decreased significantly, as it has for Whites and Asians. Not so for women, Hispanics, and Blacks, for whom the financial payoff to a college education has continued to rise."[23] So you can tailor the inquiry to your personal demographic profile.

One possible explanation for the phenomenon that college graduates often earn more than high school graduates could be that their degrees "act as signaling devices in the job market."[24] In the eyes of a prospective employer, a job candidate "with a bachelor's degree has always seemed brighter and more disciplined, ambitious, and reliable than someone with only a high school diploma."[25] But that old perspective is eroding, warn Vedder and Strehle: "As the proportion of adult Americans with college degrees grows beyond one-third, being a college graduate no longer necessarily denotes exceptional vocational promise."[26] In short, "the bachelor's degree is not the reliable signaling device it once was."[27]

This article by Vedder and Strehle generated a letter to the editor that supports the idea of considering college an investment and judging it by its rate of return. Chuck McGee, the letter's author, views colleges like any other business with a product to sell: "That product is a 'successful future.' "[28] Mr. McGee theorizes that the successful future produced by a college degree should be subject to the same value analysis as any other product. "When kids graduate with a four-year college degree and are working at McDonald's, maybe it's time to do a value analysis of what that degree is really worth."[29] In such circumstances, the return on investment does not justify the investment cost.

The marketplace is now producing unbiased real-time data on the economic value of college degrees in every major and from most institutions of higher learning. As noted previously, that data is being produced by the US Department of Education and is now readily available for individual use. Access this wealth of information at the DOE website at https://collegescorecard.ed.gov/ or through the College Affordability and Transparency Center at https://collegecost.ed.gov/. Use these remarkably precise tools to find the rate of return expected for your intended major at your specific college. Then apply the rule of thumb to limit your debt at graduation to no more than your first-year salary.

The phenomenon known as *underemployment* arises when the assumption that a college graduate will get a job in their career field collides with the reality of a shortage of jobs in that field. A student may have a degree from a good school but may not be able to find employment in their field. Or may not find employment at all. This was particularly acute for graduates during COVID restrictions.

In an article cited previously in chapter nine titled "Some 43% of College Grads Are Underemployed in First Job," author Melissa Korn relates underemployment for college graduates to return on investment for various majors.[30] "Students weighing their college options increasingly are focused on the return from that hefty investment, pursuing disciplines they think could lead to a steady and lucrative career," says Korn.[31] It is wise to consider the return on investment before attending college. Five years after graduation, while continuing to pay down their college debt, roughly 28 percent of college graduates are underemployed in jobs that don't even require a college degree.[32]

Don't fall into the trap of selecting a major without understanding the ramifications. Do some research before you select your major in college. Find one that you enjoy, that generates a good rate of return, and that won't leave you underemployed or unable to pay the debt you accumulated. Take some major time to get this major decision right.

Escaping the Matrix: Find a Major that Suits You and Covers Your Debt

Don't get caught in the Student Loan Matrix assumption that your college degree will automatically be your passport to a well-paying job in your field. Don't bet on it paying down your debt. Instead, think proactively. Plan for reality. Find a job in your field that will cover your debt.

You don't necessarily need to be mercenary and choose a major simply based on the expected salary after graduation. Rather, go into the process of deciding on a college major with eyes wide open about the potential salary consequences. Then, temper your choice of majors with an eye toward maximizing the educational experience of college while minimizing student debt. Look at the world around you in college. Research the career field you want to pursue, your job prospects in that field after graduation, and what those jobs will pay toward the debt you accumulated to get the degree.

The key is to identify the desired field of employment, determine the projected starting salary, and pursue the major that points you in that direction—all before you take on burdensome debt. Then work to cap your debt at the amount of your projected first-year salary. Following the rule of thumb will help you find a job in your field that will cover your debt.

CHAPTER 11

I Can Get a Loan without Collateral

AT THIS POINT, we have examined a range of assumptions that have led many students into the valley of student debt. We began this journey to forewarn high school students and their parents to recognize debt valley traps inside the Student Loan Matrix to avoid getting ensnared. Now, we tackle a particularly perilous assumption: *I can get a loan without collateral.*

Collateral is what other people hold over your head to make sure you pay back the money they loaned you. As a simple illustration, if you loaned a friend $100 to get their bike fixed, how could you be sure they would repay you? You can't hold on to the bike because it's in for repairs. But you could hold on to their Martin D-28 acoustic guitar as collateral. That way, if they somehow forgot to pay back your $100, you'd have a way to square things up by selling the guitar. Or, come to think of it, maybe you'd just want to keep the Martin.

If you yourself would want collateral for something as small as a $100 loan to your friend, why wouldn't a lender want collateral for a $100,000 college loan? Is it reasonable that a lender would loan you that money without collateral? If the lender doesn't require collateral to secure your student loan, how could it possibly continue to operate as a banking institution? The whole idea makes no sense. Yet, in today's student loan market, many high school students and their families fall into the assumption that they can get a federal loan without collateral. But how can that be?

That's because when they go to apply for a federal student loan, they actually get it without collateral. Generally speaking, when they go to the lender, they simply sign some papers and walk out with the student loan they wanted. In that transaction, apparently no collateral was required. No guitar, no car title, no nothing. Wait a minute, something's wrong with this picture. Could it be that the collateral they agreed to for that federal loan was something other than a car title or a bank account?

Let's think critically about the assumption that no collateral is required for student loans. Banks, as such, no longer make *federal* student loans, and more than 92 percent of student loans now are from the federal government, which does not require collateral. The remaining 8 percent of student loans are *private* loans from credit unions and other financial institutions. These are not only credit underwritten, but also often require a creditworthy cosigner. In effect, when a student gets a private student loan, their parents are their collateral.

Indeed, even federal student loans require a form of collateral; it's just hard to see. To find it, you need to look carefully at those papers you signed back at the lender's office. Reading very closely will reveal that the collateral you are pledging when you sign up for student loans is akin to a virtual form of indentured servitude. If you can't pay back the loan, you are in essence agreeing to have your pay garnished to "work off the debt." The papers you signed to get the student loan most likely included language informing you that your student debt could not be discharged in bankruptcy (discussed in chapter 12) and that if you fail to do so, the federal government can garnish your wages to pay the student debt.

There's the collateral. It's hard to see, and it's a little complicated, but there it is. That's what the lender holds over your head to ensure they get their money back. Because this feature of the student loan experience is particularly hazardous, in this chapter we'll take some time to examine its genesis.

How Did This Happen?

The current situation did not arise overnight. Interlocking interests of colleges, lenders, and Congress percolating over time made this unusual financial brew possible. For shorthand, we'll refer to these interlocking interests as the "education–industrial complex,"[1] which is analogous to the "military–industrial complex" first propounded by President Eisenhower.

In his farewell address on January 17, 1961, President Eisenhower coined the term "military–industrial complex" to describe an informal alliance between the military, the defense industry, and politicians in which all three entities benefited, ultimately at the expense of the taxpayer. The military obtained necessary weapons, the defense industry benefited from being paid to supply those weapons, and Congress benefited from defense industry lobbying contributions to reelection funds. Eisenhower's speech warned against this "iron triangle" that could lead to detrimental effects of "undue influence."

We now see emerging in America an "education–industrial complex" with comparable features to the phenomenon described by President Eisenhower. In this new iron triangle, the military has been replaced by academia, and the defense industry has been replaced by the lending industry, and Congress has been replaced by, well, Congress. Just as the military–industrial complex brought undue influence into the hands of the defense industry, so too has the education–industrial complex given academia undue influence over students who are hoping to improve their lives through a college education.

We use the same term "education–industrial complex" to highlight the influence that educational institutions have brought to bear on government policies and to spotlight the relationship between lenders and colleges that operate hand in glove to promote student loans at the expense of students and their families. Because Congress has ensured the student loans cannot be discharged in bankruptcy, lenders readily offer money to students to pay for college even when the banks know or should know the students lack the means to repay that debt.

The Education–Industrial Complex at Work

Let's uncover the workings of this education–industrial complex. An excellent starting point is a 2021 documentary titled *Borrowed Future: How Student Loans Are Killing the American Dream,* written and directed by David DiCicco, produced by Dave Ramsey,[2] and hosted by Anthony Oneal, author of the book

Debt-Free Degree.[3] This documentary is so impactful that it should be required viewing for all aspiring college students.

The film includes commentary by Dave Ramsey, the financial expert, and uses interviews with several college graduates with substantial student debt to trace their career arcs. The film then retraces the same career arc back to its beginning and poses questions to a group of current high school students who are planning on acquiring debt to pay for their college educations. We will discuss the documentary in some detail here.

Early in the film, Seth Frotman, the executive director of the Student Borrower Protection Center, identifies an insidious root cause of student borrowing as the "unfortunate thought that we don't need to worry about student debt because it's 'good debt.'"[4] He notes that simply placing the word *student* in front of the word *debt* makes us think it is different from *bad debt*. That subtle distinction has crept into our thinking and is causing grievous harm in the form of massive borrowing as detailed in the 2019 College Board report, *Trends in Student Aid*.[5]

Digging into the mental outlook that underlies this borrowing trend, Dave Ramsey identifies one key issue as the disassociation between what we think and what we feel about student debt. "The problem is that you don't register emotionally that it's money" when you take out a student loan, Ramsey explains.[6] He contrasts this lack of emotional connection when taking out a student loan with the emotional experience you have when you take out a loan to buy a $20,000 car. In the case of the car purchase, you respond emotionally to the debt because you know the car itself is collateral. If you fail to make the payments, the car will be repossessed. But in the case of student debt, no such emotional response arises, perhaps because the collateral is invisible, even though the collateral is far more substantial and the consequences of failing to pay student debt are far more severe.

How did we become blind to the fact that we cannot acquire student debt without some form of collateral? The *Borrowed Future* documentary answers this question by tracing a series of well-intentioned congressional responses to the rising demand for higher education in the 1960s and 1970s. (Spoiler alert: yes, it's the baby boomers.)

The National Defense Education Act of 1958[7] that originated the student loan program was created shortly after the Sputnik launch as a way to counteract the seemingly superior Soviet educational system. Originally, under the 1958 act, the lending program was limited to student loans of $1,000 per year, and the money itself came directly from the US Treasury. Students could borrow a relatively modest amount of taxpayers' money for school under the expectation that when they completed their higher education, they would return the investment by contributing their knowledge and skills back to society. So far, so good.

Then things began to evolve. The demand for education mushroomed from the 1940s to the 1970s when children born between 1946 and 1964 came of age. Then, as each major demographic group matured after these baby boomers, the demand for education rose again. Data compiled by the Department of Commerce and Bureau of the Census show that between 1940 and 1990, the demand for higher education mushroomed. For example, among Black Americans it increased nearly ninefold from 1.3 to 11.3 percent, while among White Americans it increased nearly fivefold from 4.9 to 23.1 percent. Likewise, the percentage of Hispanic Americans completing higher degrees rose to 9.2 percent by 1990.[8]

The *Borrowed Future* documentary observes that as the demand for higher education grew, and the supply failed to keep pace, tuition costs rose. Thus, the need to fund those costs grew proportionately. It became necessary for the federal government to bring in banks to meet the rising demand to fund college education costs. Even though the government was now no longer obliged to foot the education bill out of the US Treasury, the government still guaranteed the loans made by the banks. This meant the banks would be paid whether the student made the payments or not. As part of this new arrangement, banks were entitled to collect interest on the loans.

When the demand for college attendance rose even higher in 1972, banks could no longer keep up with the demand. At this point, Congress came up with another solution known as the Student Loan Marketing Association, or "Sallie Mae." The name sounds sort of like a character out of a Li'l Abner comic strip. Nothing to see here, folks, it's just a marketing association.

Initially, Sallie Mae was "a government-sponsored enterprise designed to funnel money into the student loan program."[9] It did this by buying student loans from the banks. This in turn allowed the banks to create more cash flow. Here we see well-intentioned people doing reasonable things to address the complex problem of meeting a high demand for college funding with a low supply of funds. But over the next few decades, Sallie Mae grew beyond its humble beginning to become a dominant player in the student loan industry.

Then, in 2004, Sallie Mae became a fully independent entity, entirely separate from the federal government. When Sallie Mae became independent, it naturally acquired a profit motive, just like any other business. Interestingly, even though the organization changed from a governmental entity to an independent for-profit organization, the sunny name did not change. Its mission, however, evolved into a secondary market for such lenders as Fargo, Citizens Bank, Discover, and Wells Fargo. The banks that sold loans to Sallie Mae, such as Fifth Third Bank, were entirely independent, although they often had forward purchase agreements that were effectively lending a Sallie Mae product.[10]

In 2005, about a year after Sallie Mae became an independent entity, Congress amended the Bankruptcy Code, which had the effect of making private student loans more difficult to discharge through bankruptcy as discussed in more detail in chapter 12. Generally speaking, the Bankruptcy Abuse Prevention and Consumer Protection Act of 2005 (BAPCPA) provided more protection to creditors by expanding the number of exceptions to what could be discharged in bankruptcy.[11] Specifically, BAPCPA amended section 523(a)(8) of the Bankruptcy Code to increase the types of educational loans that could not be discharged in bankruptcy. Under the act, absent proof of "undue hardship," loans from "for-profit" or "non-governmental" entities could no longer be discharged.[12]

The technical changes to the nature of the loans that were subject to discharge did not alone effectuate a large increase in the amount of student loan debt. But the fact that the undue hardship rule now applied to almost all forms of student debt and the fact that lenders could now rely on the federal bankruptcy code to ensure loan repayment began to open the floodgates on student debt. In a sense, the inability to discharge student loans in bankruptcy became the collateral for the student loans.

As the *Borrowed Future* documentary reveals, the current student debt crisis arose from a cascade of well-intentioned responses to the issue of high demand for college funding. Apparently reasonable steps were taken over several decades by well-meaning bankers, lawyers, and educators in response to a persistent demand for college funding caused by the rising tide of baby boomers. Although well-intentioned in their origin, the financial interests of colleges and lenders that grew out of that response can now work against student interests. Armed with this knowledge, students and their parents can be alert to dangers in the loan marketplace.

Since most student loans today (roughly 92 percent) are federal, how can you tell if you have a private or federal loan? To determine whether your student loan is federal or private, simply log into www.studentaid.gov, which houses all federal loan information. If your loan is listed there, it's federal; if not, it's a private student loan.

Let's review. Academia relies on student tuition to fund its programs, so students apply for loans when they can't afford to pay for college costs up front. Because the government either originates or backs the student loans, such loans can be issued without tangible collateral. Lenders can accept the government backing in the place of the usual collateral (like a car title), and the lenders can therefore issue student loans. There are a number of lenders in the field with portfolios of loans that have migrated. To track them you almost need a scorecard. In brief, the federal loans that were formerly serviced by Sallie Mae were later transferred to Navient who then transferred them to Aidvantage, which was a division of Maximus.[13] Got that?

Since July 1, 2010, all new federal education loans have been made through the Direct Loan Program. Banks no longer make Federal Family Education Loan (FFEL) Program loans, although they may still have some FFEL loans in their portfolios. The FFEL Program is now in a wind-down situation, with the remaining volume decreasing every year. Banks no longer service loans in the US Department of Education Direct Loan Program.[14]

The overall result of this evolution is that colleges accept student loans without collateral because they are government backed. None of this is nefarious. But that doesn't mean student interests are well served in the process or protected by the schools. In fact, the loans may actually work against the interests of the students and their parents. The availability of student loans provided by some lenders through private student loans and by the US Department of Education through the Direct Loan Program may allow students and families to get in over their heads without realizing it and allow colleges to continue raising tuition.

To see the education–industrial complex in operation, note who ultimately pays when students default on their loan payments. Would that be Congress? Nope. The lenders that loaned the money? Nope. The universities that created the conditions for the loans and benefited from their issuance? Nope. After attempts to garnish the debtor's wages fail, or the debtor passes on, the default cost falls on the taxpayers. Additionally, under current student loan guidelines, some loan balances that are not paid in 20 to 25 years are transferred to taxpayers through federal loan forgiveness. That is the education–industrial complex in operation within the Student Loan Matrix. This current policy to transfer debt to taxpayers through forgiveness is distinct from the president's August 24, 2022, announcement of debt forgiveness that was discussed earlier, but the stuckee is the same.

This issue underscores the competing payment incentives that exist between colleges and their students. An insightful article by Alex Mitchell, titled "College Is Broken: Reflections and Predictions,"[15] explains the stark difference in the motivations of colleges and the motivations of the students. He points out that "[t]he college already got paid by either the government or the student loan company and there is simply no penalty for their lack of performance in student education and career placement (save for some very limited publicly funded university penalties)."[16]

Since the colleges have already been paid, they have little incentive to actually further the student's career objective. Nor does the government have any incentive "to provide education in areas where jobs are in the highest demand."[17] These competing incentives between the colleges and their students are not likely to be resolved any time soon because Congress has been reluctant to act. An article by Rebecca Ballhaus and Andrea Fuller shows why proposed legislation has stalled. The proposed legislation is designed to resolve the issue either by "capping what borrowers can take out" or by "tightening eligibility requirements to better ensure borrowers can repay."[18]

What Can Parents and Students Do?

Since no help is currently forthcoming from Congress, students and parents need to make their own plans to survive college debt, which includes figuring out their own cap on the PLUS loans that they can handle. Consider the plight of Rhiannon and Michael Funke, both age 43, who "owe a combined $778,000 in federal student loans for multiple graduate and undergraduate programs."[19] Here is an example of what can happen under a regimen of unlimited borrowing. Wisdom dictates caution, particularly for parents who want the best for their children. Knowing about the issue beforehand allows you to limit the debt.

Unlike undergraduate debt, for which the government imposes a borrowing limit, "[t]he Parent PLUS and Grad PLUS programs let people borrow the total cost of [college] attendance—room and board, books, and personal expenses on top of tuition—for as many years as it takes to get the degree," explain Ballhaus and Fuller.[20] Many sign up and regret it, perhaps because they incorrectly believed the government would not let them borrow more than they could reasonably repay.

"Lawmakers and administration officials in both parties acknowledge that the [PLUS] programs have left many borrowers with balances they will struggle to repay. Yet Congress has repeatedly punted on changing the programs," the article reports.[21] The reasons include "resistance to restricting disadvantaged students' access to funds, fear of angering schools, and the fact that the programs—on paper—have historically made money for the government."[22]

The last two reasons are particularly troubling. The authors cite Jason Delisle, a senior policy fellow at the Urban Institute think tank, who estimates that eliminating the Parent PLUS program "would cost the government $1 billion to $3.6 billion a year."[23] So that's a nonstarter. In addition to government economic interests, those organizations most resistant to capping or restricting the PLUS programs "are the universities, especially expensive private ones, which urge students and parents to take out PLUS loans to cover shortfalls in tuition and fees."[24] I'm searching for a word to describe this institutional behavior. Perhaps you have one in mind.

On separate occasions when both President Obama and President Trump attempted to rein in the program, they were vigorously opposed by colleges and universities. Consequently, the programs remain intact with the result that student loan debt in the United States exceeds $1.7 trillion and is second only to home mortgage debt.[25]

Economic incentives of these institutions are the underlying issue driving this phenomenon. In the education–industrial complex, each of the three key players has an economic reason to burden students with college debt. They each benefit from it. The economics of the arrangement reveal that the lenders have no incentive, the colleges have no incentive, and the government has no incentive (three out of three) to alter the flow of funds from students through lenders to schools.

Likewise, none of the three have any particular incentive to further the student's career objectives, to provide education in disciplines with the highest demand, or to reduce the student debt load—all of which could help the student who is holding the debt. "The only true incentive these colleges have is one that is too distant for many," explain Ballhaus and Fuller, which is "the ability to continue to recruit new students who will pay their ever-increasing tuition rates."[26] This failure of goal congruence between the interests of the college and the interests of the student contributes to the rising student debt default rate.

The US Department of Education reports that as of September 30, 2022, loans in default, defined as 270 days without a payment, totaled some $105.2 billion in the Direct Loan Program plus $63.7 billion in the FFEL program. That's a total of $168.9 billion of the $1.6345 trillion in federal student loans outstanding, or about 10 percent of the debt portfolio.[27] However you look at it, student debt presents a conundrum that high school students and parents must address with a well-considered plan before college.

How Did This Happen?

Trends identified previously in this book show some alarming facts. First, tuition has increased exponentially, along with other college costs such as housing. Second, graduates are struggling to find jobs after graduation, and the underemployment jobs they do find often don't pay enough to cover student loans. Third, because of increased college costs and poor job outlook, student loan defaults are at an all-time high, so many of these loans are not getting paid off.

Despite these trends, each succeeding year high school graduates continue to enroll in colleges and universities with tuitions well beyond their ability to pay and proceed to take out government-backed loans with no apparent collateral. A 2020 study from NerdWallet noted that 62 percent of the class of 2019 graduated with student debt that averaged $28,950.[28] The message of incapacitating debt is becoming increasingly clear.

Student Loans and Families

In a Hechinger Report article titled "Stuck in It until I Die," author Meredith Kolodner notes that Parent PLUS loans have spiked, causing financial disaster for low- and middle-income families. Ms. Kolodner cites a family that borrowed $40,000 to support their college student and ended up owing $100,000 in Parent PLUS loans over time because of compounding interest.[29] The family was trying to make payments of $1,300 a month out of a $13-per-hour maintenance worker wage and simply couldn't do it. When the education–industrial complex squeezes, it doesn't just squeeze the students, it squeezes parents as well.

In fact, people over 50 are one of the fastest-growing categories of student loan borrowers. In "The Faces of Student Debt," published in the *Washington Post*, the hard reality emerges. Authors Danielle Douglas-Gabriel and John D. Harden cite Federal Reserve data to uncover the startling fact: "Between 2010 and 2015, the number of outstanding loans by borrowers 50 and older grew by 80 percent—more than 32 percentage points higher than the growth of borrowers below 50 years old, according to Federal Reserve data."[30]

What would explain an 80 percent jump in outstanding loans among borrowers over 50? In a *Wall Street Journal* article, Tawnell D. Hobbs and Andrea Fuller identify a key factor in this growth of older borrowers: "There is no cap on what parents can borrow" through the Parent PLUS loan program, "no matter their income."[31] Many parents will do anything to provide a better future for their children, including taking on a debt burden that far exceeds their capacity to repay. And since Parent PLUS loans come with a high interest rate, paying them off can be especially difficult.[32] When it comes to Parent PLUS loans, despite their upbeat sounding name, parents need to be particularly cautious.

Many families are finding repayment impossible. A detailed picture of repayment rates on Parent PLUS loans first came to light recently when the government released data on the subject. At Baylor University, only 28 percent of "parents had begun paying back Parent PLUS loans after two years of being required."[33] They had borrowed a median of $59,000 to pay the tuition and fees for their children, which run to about $50,000 annually, "not including room and board."[34]

As a consequence of the growing population of senior citizens holding student debt for 20 years or more, defaults among our elder generation are on the rise according to a recent GAO report.[35] Few seniors imagined their golden years darkened by such financial turmoil. They thought they were doing the right thing by supporting their child's hope of attending the college of their choice. They did not realize that doing so could be their financial ruin.

An article in the *New Yorker* by Hua Hsu, titled "Student Debt Is Transforming the American Family,"[36] poignantly depicts the plight of families in similar situations. The article traces the circumstances by which Kimberly, "an intrepid, committed student" at New York University, found herself in financial distress. "[H]er family had sacrificed to help finance her education, and she had taken out considerable loans," explains Hsu. Kimberly "had looked forward to putting her degree to good use while chipping away at the debt behind it."[37] But the salary from the job she was offered did not cover the debt.

Hua Hsu's article references Caitlin Zaloom, an anthropologist at NYU, who has studied the role of college debt in contemporary American family life. "Since 2012, Zaloom has spent a lot of time with families like Kimberly's," reports Hsu. "They all fall into America's middle class—an amorphous category, defined more by sensibility or aspirational identity than by a strict income threshold. (Households with an annual income of anywhere from $40,000 to a quarter of a million dollars view themselves as middle class.)"[38]

The *New Yorker* article by Hsu cites Zaloom's book, *Indebted: How Families Make College Work at Any Cost* (included in the resources section at the end of this book), as concluding that "the challenge of paying for college has become one of the organizing forces of middle-class family life."[39] To research the book, Zaloom and her team "conducted interviews with 160 families across the country, all of whom make too much to qualify for Pell Grants (reserved for households that earn below $50,000) but too little to pay for tuition outright."[40]

Zaloom observed that the parents interviewed had "done all the things you're supposed to, like investing and saving and not racking up too much debt."[41] But that has not solved the problem. "What actually unites them, from a military family in Florida to a dual-PhD household in Michigan, is that the children are part of a generation where debt—the financial and psychological state of being indebted—will shadow them for much of their adult lives."[42]

In sum, the burden of student debt caused by the mistaken assumption that a student loan can be obtained without collateral falls on the entire family. For young adults, student debt can put life on hold, delaying home ownership, marriage, children, and the attainment of a stable financial footing. For their parents, it can mean a decline into poverty in their later years as they spend what was intended to be their retirement fund paying off their adult children's student loans.

How have we reached the point where college debt has evolved from a means to uplift aspiring students into a means to lock them and their parents in hock?

Escaping the Matrix: Know Who Will Pay the Loans if You Fail to Repay

As Benjamin Franklin famously warned, "the taxman cometh." At some time or another, the bill will come due for the student loans taken out to fund an education. Through wage garnishment or the federal tax burden, the lenders are guaranteed a return on the money they invested in you, plus interest.

The point of this discussion is not to rail against the education–industrial complex. Rather, the point here is to uncloak its workings so prospective college students have enough warning to steer clear and avoid the dangers of this assumption in the Student Loan Matrix. To aid in that effort, here are some useful references to map the terrain that lies ahead for students and their parents.

The www.studentloanhero.com website is focused on helping student borrowers get answers to critical loan questions and provides a wide range of relevant research in an accessible format. Be aware that if you become a customer of any of the lenders featured on their site, the Student Loan Hero site gets a referral fee.

Use www.creditkarma.com/calculators/debtrepayment to figure out efficient strategies to pay back loans after you have obtained them. The debt repayment calculator will show you how long it will take to pay off your debt and allows you to choose from making the minimum payment or a fixed amount of your choosing, or lets you select a time when you would prefer to be debt free.

For a broad look at life strategies, the Realworld Playbook, located at www.realworld.co, is a customized platform that offers members access to over 90 playbooks across health, finance, work, government, and life. Regarding college debt, it addresses questions like "How do I start to repay my student loans?" and "How can I open a checking account?" with play-by-play guidance. These are all tools to help navigate the rocky terrain created by the assumption that you can get a loan without collateral.

The problem of student debt is systemic. Vested banking and institutional interests operate contrary to the long-term economic interests of students and their families. Student loans are issued by lenders without collateral because they are backed by the government. Owing to this arrangement, the amount of the loan became untethered from the student's ability to repay. Consequently, colleges can charge ever-increasing tuition and fees to the students and their parents. Ultimately, if the student defaults, the taxpayers get stuck with the tab. What can we do about this? We've got to solve it individually.

The ideal is to graduate debt free through identifying affordable college programs, landing some combination of grants and scholarships, and undertaking outside work or work-study to complete college with a minimum of student loans. However, if a student performs a thorough risk assessment and still determines they want to take out loans, they need to be aware of the resources to get information on the loans and of the appropriate repayment strategies.

Without a clear understanding of the loans and their repayment strategies, the net effect of the education–industrial complex rules (granting student loans without collateral and without a true determination of capacity to pay) will result in unwary students and their well-meaning, supportive parents continuing to bear the brunt of the resulting debt debacle. The least prepared to shoulder this burden will be the most affected by it.

As students consider the fact that they don't want to repay student loans through their taxes, or see the debt garnished out of their wages, or push the burden onto their parents, or have their hard-earned social security checks reduced in retirement, they need to consider how to stay on top of the loans they do take out. Since the loans aren't generally dischargeable in bankruptcy, students are going to have to *pay me now or pay me later*.

CHAPTER 12

I Can Discharge My College Debt in Bankruptcy

SINCE YOU FIRST SAW the football field depiction of $1 trillion in the preface to this book, you may have been wondering in the back of your mind: Why *has* national student loan debt become so large? Why *does* it surpass a football field stacked up with $100 bills over the goal posts? Why *does* student loan debt exceed all other forms of debt except home mortgages? What is so unique about student debt? This chapter presents an explanation with evidence that has been hiding in plain sight.

Without giving it much thought, many students who are headed to college assume if the debt burden should become too difficult to bear, they could discharge it in bankruptcy. It would only make sense that college debt would be treated like any other debt and could be discharged in bankruptcy. This, however, is the final mistaken assumption in the Student Loan Matrix. In some ways it is the granddaddy of them all. Like the other assumptions, it can cause enormous pain.

As you sit in your beautiful dorm at the college of your choice thinking big thoughts, does it even enter your mind what could happen if you can't pay off your student loan debt? Of course not. The sun is shining. You've just chosen your major. Your entire life is in front of you. The lender's money is in hand to cover the costs of college, and you are imagining the exciting career before you. At this moment, the debt burden you are incurring as a college student will not have to be paid off for years to come. In this magic moment, you are pretty certain you'll get a well-paying job in your field that will cover the monthly debt payment. And if an emergency occurs, or you can no longer afford to make payments on the student debt, you naturally assume you can deal with the debt using the same laws that allow Americans to deal with other form of debt—the US Bankruptcy Code. Right? Well, not so fast. Let's take a minute to examine this.

The federal and private debts you incurred by signing those promissory notes are stickier than other kinds of debt and will remain with you until fully repaid, which, as we have seen, could require decades. Consequently, if you need to take on debt to attend college, it's important to have a full understanding of what you're getting in to and the possible ways of getting out. For this, you need to understand the unavailability of bankruptcy as a legal protection from student debt and that the risk of default shifts from the lender to you as the borrower.

The Federal Bankruptcy Code

How does the shift in default risk occur? In a nutshell, the language of the Bankruptcy Code at 11 United States Code § 523(a)(8), often referred to as BAPCPA 2005, specifically excludes student loans from being discharged in bankruptcy. The actual statutory language is a bit hard to decipher, but it is worth a read because this language is the organizing principle of the entire education–industrial complex. Understanding it offers the key to escaping the Student Loan Matrix. Here is the statutory language with key words bolded. Warning: it's very confusing.

> *(a)* ***A discharge*** *under section 727, 1141, 1192 [1] 1228 (a), 1228 (b), or 1328 (b) of this title* ***does not discharge an individual debtor from any debt*** *. . .*

(8) ***unless excepting such debt from discharge under this paragraph would impose an undue hardship*** *on the debtor and the debtor's dependents, for—*

(A) (i) ***an educational*** *benefit overpayment or* ***loan made, insured, or guaranteed by a governmental unit, or made under any program funded in whole or in part by a governmental unit*** *or* ***nonprofit institution****; or (ii)* ***an obligation to repay funds received as an educational benefit, scholarship, or stipend; or***

(B) ***any other educational loan that is a qualified education loan,*** *as defined in section 221 (d) (1) of the Internal Revenue Code of 1986, incurred by a debtor who is an individual* [emphasis added].[1]

Now there's some complicated legalese. To truly decipher this statutory language, you would need to consult a lawyer, and frankly, who wants to do that? But you can get a working idea of the meaning from this brief summary: a bankruptcy court cannot discharge an educational loan unless paying the debt would impose undue hardship on the borrower and the borrower's dependents.

Legislative History of the Bankruptcy Code

Because this statutory language is so dense and its impact so profound, let's review its legislative history starting in 1976. As described previously in chapter 11, student loan programs began in the mid-1950s and were about two decades old when the new bankruptcy law was enacted in 1976.

As detailed by Richard Pallardy in an informative article titled "History of Student Loans: Bankruptcy Discharge,"[2] the perceived need for a bankruptcy law amendment began in the early 1970s, when journalists and legislators began raising concerns about student debtors abusing the bankruptcy system by trying to evade their debt after graduation. Prior to this time, like most other forms of financial obligation, student loans *could* be discharged in bankruptcy proceedings. The only debts exempted from discharge were some types of tax debt, debt from criminal activity, and spousal and child support debt.[3] There was very little actual evidence for the underlying statutory rationale that student debt dodgers were a problem. In fact, a GAO report to Congress in 1976 found that less than 1 percent of student loans were being discharged in bankruptcy.[4]

Despite this negligible evidence of a problem, the 1976 Education Amendments altered two decades of precedent and declared that henceforth student loans could not be discharged in bankruptcy, barring any undue hardship, until after the student had paid on the debt for a period of five years following the start of the repayment period.[5] Consequently, the "largely baseless claims that student debtors were abusing the bankruptcy system" led to the first of a series of escalating restrictions on discharging student loan debt in bankruptcy.[6] One could argue that by solving a nonexistent student loan abuse problem, Congress unintentionally created a very real student loan debt crisis.

Further legislative changes relating to bankruptcy law and student loans consisted of a series of minor adjustments, each gradually tightening the rules around students who sought to discharge their debt in bankruptcy. In 1978, the Bankruptcy Reform Act moved the student loan provision for bankruptcy discharge from the Higher Education Act to the Bankruptcy Code at 11 USC 523(a)(8).[7] Then in 1984, the exception to discharge was expanded to cover private student loans, but only if the loans were made through a program funded in part by a nonprofit organization. (This was eliminated in 2005.)

In 1998, the option to discharge student loans after a specified number of years in repayment was eliminated. Since 1998, demonstrating undue hardship in an adversarial proceeding has been the only option remaining to plead for discharge in bankruptcy.[8] With the amendments to the Bankruptcy Code passed in 2005, Congress prevented bankruptcy discharge of "qualified education loans," which includes all federal and most private student loans.[9] In addition to this brief recap, since 1976, there have been a number of other legislative amendments to the US Bankruptcy Code that are useful to understand, but grueling to read, so they are detailed in the endnotes.[10]

The consequence of this drumbeat of legislative actions to tighten the rules around discharging student loans in bankruptcy can be seen in the following graphic. Rather than showing the federal student debt burden that now totals

$1.6345 trillion, this chart depicts the issue from inside the federal perspective over time by tracing the federal *asset* of student loans on the US Government Financial Statement.

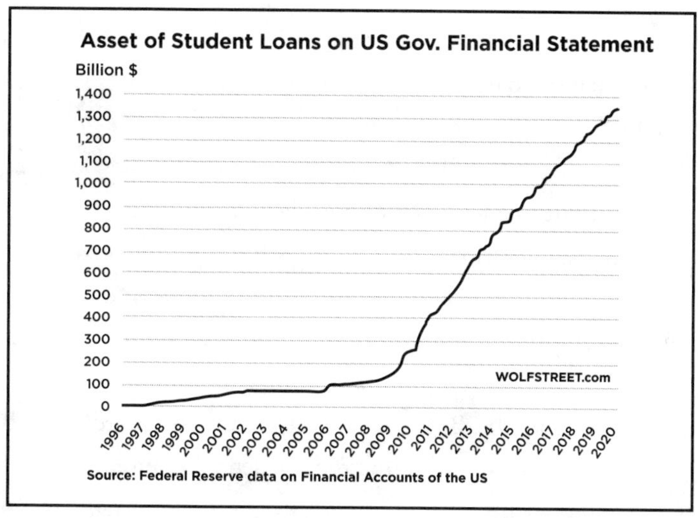

Figure 18.[11]

The asset chart depicts an inflection point as occurring around 2010. Why do you think it occurred then? What would have changed so dramatically?

Proving Undue Hardship under the Bankruptcy Code

The statutory condition for forgiveness of student loan debt in bankruptcy turns on the phrase, "undue hardship on the debtor and the debtor's dependents." At first glance, this phrase seems to hold out some relief for debtors. But that relief is illusory because "undue hardship" is near impossible to prove in court. One expert has estimated that "only about one in 2,500 student loan borrowers who file for bankruptcy succeed in obtaining a full or partial discharge of their student loans."[12]

To determine if particular circumstances constitute an "undue hardship," for which one could qualify for relief, many courts use the Brunner test while others use the totality of the circumstances test.[13] Under the more widely applied Brunner test, the court considers three factors to decide if repayment of your student loans would cause undue hardship and the debt should be discharged in bankruptcy:

1. Based upon your current income and expenses, you cannot maintain a minimal standard of living for yourself and your dependents if you are forced to repay your loans.

2. Your current financial situation is likely to continue for a big part of the repayment period.

3. You have made a good faith effort to repay your student loans.[14]

As the language in the Brunner test telegraphs, the hurdle has been set very high to qualify for discharge of student debt. Because that hurdle is so high, very few student debt bankruptcy cases are even brought to litigation, much less won outright. This explains why student loan debt is generally not discharged in bankruptcy, even though the statute seems to offer relief through the notion of "undue hardship." Since the statute requires undue hardship to discharge student debt in bankruptcy, it has effectively tightened the flow of discharges to the point of closure.

The Consequences of the Tightened Bankruptcy Code

The rippling consequences of this tightened bankruptcy code are seen in the rise of student debt and the increasing number of loan defaults. The tightening has had the effect of incentivizing lenders to offer money to uncreditworthy applicants since the risk of default has shifted from the lender to the borrower. Because loaned funds are readily available to students, universities have had no incentive to reduce college costs. Rising college costs have coincided with readily available funds and tightened bankruptcy rules.

Whether college costs are rising from internal economic forces or as a consequence of readily available funds or from both is outside this discussion. The legislative and policy solutions to these issues are likewise outside this discussion. The important points for students and parents to remember are that: (A) student loans cannot be discharged in bankruptcy, so (B) students and parents must limit their appetite for loans to their individual circumstances, not the availability of funds.

To understand the interconnection between the bankruptcy code, the lenders, and the colleges, it is useful to consider the policies at play. By 2015, the consequences of the tightened restrictions on student debt bankruptcies were beginning to be seen. A prescient law review article by Preston Mueller, JD, titled "The Non-Dischargeability of Private Student Loans: A Looming Financial Crisis?" published by the *Emory Bankruptcy Developments Journal,*[15] describes the circumstances under which Congress excluded private student loans from discharge in bankruptcy and then discusses the predictable consequences. This article draws a correlation between decreased banking risk, higher student debt loads, and higher student debt defaults.[16]

Mr. Mueller observed that granting "student loans the privileged status of being non-dischargeable in bankruptcy skews lenders' incentives."[17] The lenders' incentives play out differently for private and federal loans, but both lenders are incentivized to make student loans by the tightened bankruptcy code. Private lenders pursue credit underwriting for private student loans, which means they rely on FICO scores, debt-to-income ratios, and duration of employment, and generally require a creditworthy cosigner such as a parent, since most students do not satisfy these criteria on their own. So private lenders grant loans tied to creditworthiness.

On the other hand, the federal lenders do not consider the borrower's ability to repay federal education loans.[18] Although private student loans do have loan limits, the federal Parent PLUS and Grad PLUS loans have no aggregate limit, and the annual limit is capped only at the cost of attendance minus other aid. As a result, the federal PLUS loans have essentially granted students an unlimited line of credit without consideration for the consequences if the individual student is unable to make the payment. The combination of unlimited PLUS loans and unavailability of bankruptcy discharge has had the effect of steadily increasing debt. This long-term trend has been thoroughly documented by the College Board in a report appropriately titled "Trends in Student Aid 2022."[19]

Focusing on *private* student loan debt, we can see it has risen remarkably and surmise that the Bankruptcy Code protection for lenders contributes to that continued rise. In 2005, some $6.6 billion in private student loans were granted by lenders. This number had climbed to over $10 billion by 2008.[20] Bringing that 2008 figure forward to 2021 reveals total *private* student loan debt (not *federal* student loan debt) had reached $123.14 billion according to the MeasureOne Private Student Loan Report, Q3 2021.[21]

That means that in the 16 years from 2005 to 2021, the private student loan debt increased 18-fold, from $6.6 billion to $123.14 billion. The fact that the private student loan industry experienced such prodigious growth is extraordinary. Recall that this private loan figure accounts for only around 8 percent of the total student loan portfolio, while the other 92 percent is owned by the federal government. Both portfolios have seen eye-popping growth over the last two decades. Whether or not the bankruptcy code change was the underlying cause of this growth, students and families need to guard themselves against the inability to discharge student debt in bankruptcy.

In sum, the exemption of private student loans from discharge in bankruptcy began as a legislative response to a perceived need to prevent student loan fraud in the early 1970s. Over time, that purpose appears to have faded from view, but the effects of the US Bankruptcy Code on student loan debt continue to this day. Clearly, it is a contributing factor in the ballooning level of student debt in the United States, and students must be alert to the consequences of taking on debt.

Garnishment of Student Debt

Because student debt cannot be discharged in bankruptcy, and because the lion's share of student debt is federal, and because the government can recover its debts using garnishment and offset, and because garnishment and offset are true pain point for students, let's get a better understanding of garnishment and offset.

Garnishment refers to the ability of the federal government to withhold a percentage of your wages administratively to pay off a debt. Such debts might include child support or, in this case, student debt. The regulations allow the government to withhold 15 percent of your wages for student debt, but also require that you be left with at least 30 times the federal minimum wage per week after garnishment.

Offset refers to the ability of the federal government to seize your federal income tax refund and a portion of Social Security disability and retirement benefit payments to repay your federal student loan debt. The offset for both is 15 percent. The offset cannot exceed an amount that leaves you with at least $750 per month after the offset.

Now, let's reflect back on that moment when you applied for the federal college loan and you signed the student loan papers at the lender's office. Remember how you thought to yourself, "Man, this is easy"? Yes, it was indeed easy to sign your name. It was indeed easy to obtain the loan from the federal lender. But now you see why it was so easy. If you default and can't pay off your student loan, the US Treasury can garnish your wages and offset your income tax refund and your Social Security disability and retirement checks.[22] Unlike the ease of signing the loan application, the prospect of living on $750 a month in your retirement after the Social Security offset is not so easy. But how likely is it?

Sadly, according to Government Accounting Office (GAO) data published in GAO 17-45, the government garnished some 114,000 borrowers in 2015, an increase of some 407 percent from those garnished in 2002. Garnished collections yielded $171 million.[23] The percentage of people in this dire situation is relatively small, but the situation is troubling. Some 114,000 people with outstanding student debt, who had contributed 6.2 percent of their salary through monthly payroll deductions into their Social Security accounts for an average of 35 years, saw their monthly Social Security checks garnished. That's a hard situation late in life. Isn't there some relief? Well, no.

The Honorable Robert E. Nugent, a retired bankruptcy judge from Wichita, Kansas, wrote about the heartbreaking scenes he witnessed over the course of 20 years sitting on the bankruptcy bench. He recounted how he had "presided over many student loan cases of people who had borrowed tens or hundreds of thousands of dollars that they couldn't pay."[24] Judge Nugent notes with unrelieved gloom, "There's a reason no rational commercial lender would have made these loans: there's no way these borrowers will earn enough to repay them.

Sadly, there was little I could do for these unfortunate people."[25] From his two decades of service on the bankruptcy bench, Judge Nugent concluded that for the vast majority of people whose student loans were unable to be discharged in bankruptcy, those debts "become virtual debtors' prisons."[26]

This section is not meant to pile on the bad news. Rather, it's intended to give students and their families a time telescope with which to look out into the future to identify specific problems well in advance so they can avoid the problems altogether when they get to college. The Parent PLUS loan program qualifies as just such a problem. An article by Josh Mitchell titled "The US Makes It Easy for Parents to Get College Loans—Repaying Them Is Another Story" notes that some three million parents have taken on student loan debt through the Parent PLUS program offered by the US Department of Education.[27] These loans were granted with little inquiry into the parent's ability to repay the loan. In the usual application process, the lender would not inquire about a borrower's financial status such as their income, debt level, savings, or credit scores, yet they would extend loans that could well be beyond the borrower's ability to repay.[28] A PLUS lender's lack of curiosity about your ability to repay is a signal to protect yourself from possible garnishment by being absolutely certain of your creditworthiness for the loan and your ability to repay.

Creditworthiness of Student Loan Borrowers

Here it is useful to note there is a split in how private lenders and federal lenders handle creditworthiness. Because federal lenders of student loans don't consider creditworthiness, student loans can be granted to borrowers with otherwise disqualifying credit scores. Although the subprime threshold credit score is 620, almost 40 percent of the federal loans described in Mr. Mitchell's article went to borrowers below that threshold, indicating a high risk of default.[29]

Federal student loan applications don't inquire about creditworthiness, but private lenders of student loans do. If the student borrower is not creditworthy, they are required to have a creditworthy cosigner, who is usually the parent. Consequently, in most cases, private student loans have "two fish on the hook"—the student and their parent. If the student defaults, they can require the cosigner parent to repay the debt. In addition, if the student graduates, they will become a "proven asset" for the lender and thus be more capable of repaying the loan. This is why private student loans have very low default rates. The main risk for the lender is the possibility that the student doesn't graduate. They reduce that risk by lending only to students at selective schools, where the risk of not graduating is lowest.[30] Federal student loans do not have the same guardrails as private loans, so they have a higher risk of default.

For a historical perspective on what can happen when a large number of subprime loans are granted to large numbers of people with the highest risk of default, recall the circumstances of the housing boom in 2006 when housing prices peaked and the housing bust in 2011 when they cratered. "Subprime mortgages peaked at nearly 20 percent of all mortgage originations in 2006," when the housing market began to implode, notes Mr. Mitchell.[31] Compare the 40 percent approval rate noted for student loans with this 20 percent approval rate for subprime mortgages before the housing boom. That 40 percent approval rate for student loan borrowers with the highest risk of default goes a long way to explaining the current wave of student loan defaults.

One would think that if a lender knows that your creditworthiness as a borrower predicts you can't pay back the loan, the lender would not fork over the money. But no, the lenders decide based on risk to them of nonpayment. They know that your loan can't be discharged in bankruptcy. No surprise then that according to the GAO, between 2010 and 2015, the number of borrowers who had "wages, tax refunds, or Social Security checks reduced because of unpaid student debt increased 71 percent."[32] No surprise either that some 41,000 Parent PLUS borrowers had their paychecks garnished in FY 2015.[33]

To paint the picture of how easily PLUS lenders can loan money to uncreditworthy borrowers, Mr. Mitchell described an actual Parent PLUS scenario. At the time in 2006 when Sherry McPherson filled out an application for a $16,000 Parent PLUS loan to cover her son's tuition, she was an unemployed single mom who had just retired from the Army following an injury in Iraq. She had a large credit-card debt, a car loan, and a subprime credit score.[34]

She recalled telling the school's financial aid administrator that she didn't think she would get the loan because of her difficult financial circumstances. The financial aid administrator simply said, "Look, all we need is your Social Security number." Said Ms. McPherson, "They approved me in three minutes."

Predictably, she has not been able to repay the loan. Unpredictably, her Parent PLUS loan balance has more than doubled.[35] Ms. McPherson represents a sad study in the dangers of granting student loans to subprime borrowers without considering creditworthiness. It's a reason for students and parents to be extremely wary of the PLUS process. Just because you can get a Parent PLUS loan doesn't mean you should take it.

As we've seen, there is no real prospect of escaping student debt through discharge in bankruptcy. And forget sliding by unseen—remember that much of the government recoupment consists of collecting tardy payments through wage garnishment and the offset of income tax refunds and Social Security benefit payments.

If that wasn't bad enough, much of the payment that borrowers can scrape together ends up going to pay the interest portion of the bill rather than to paying down the principal. On this point, Rebecca Safier, writing on the Student Loan Hero website, stated, "Of the $1.1 billion garnished from benefits as of 2016, more than 70 percent had gone to paying off fees and interest, rather than the borrower's actual debt."[36] For many people, student debt is an oppressive ball and chain that they must drag to their grave. Think about this now, before you apply to college, so you don't join that sad army of debtors after your college career. Use the time telescope to look into the future before you sign up for a boatload of debt.

Forgiveness of Student Debt

As we noted in the beginning of the book, there's a growing governmental movement to forgive student debt and the president has proposed a debt cancellation plan. If it is implemented, how much will that plan affect the national level of student debt? The Congressional Budget Office (CBO) "estimates that the cost of student loans will increase by about an additional $400 billion in present value as a result of the action canceling up to $10,000 of debt issued on or before June 30, 2022, for borrowers with income below specified limits and an additional $10,000 for such borrowers who also received at least one Pell Grant."[37] Under the proposed plan, some $400 billion in debt would be canceled, or about a quarter of the current outstanding student debt balance of $1.74 trillion.

Readers may wonder how the federal cancellation of a debt this large could actually take place. A moment's reflection will reveal that the debt doesn't simply vanish when the government no longer requires college students to repay it. Instead, a football field stacked with $100 bills about 2.5 feet high (a quarter of the total student debt load) will be effectively transferred to the American people to be paid at some point in the form of taxes.

When scrutinized carefully, the term *student loan forgiveness* is better described as a shift in the burden of repayment. The term simply refers to the process by which the responsibility for student debt is transferred from the student who incurred the debt to the taxpayer who didn't. People on all sides of the political spectrum may debate the wisdom of this transfer, but because a high school student graduating after June 30, 2022, is not eligible for debt forgiveness under the plan, it is not relevant to our discussion.

The debt forgiveness aspect of the president's plan doesn't impact the current 17-year-olds who will be taking out student loans in the future. Nor is it likely that the current 17-year-olds' college debt will be forgiven four years from now when it comes time for the newly minted graduates to repay it. They will be obliged to follow the loan policies in effect as of that date.

However, there is a distinct possibility that the US Department of Education loan policies will have changed when current high schoolers graduate from college. Most significantly, they could see a major change under the department's proposed guidance for a new Income-Driven Repayment (IDR) plan. If the proposed IDR plan is adopted and survives court challenges,[38] the effect on student loan repayment practices and amounts would be substantial. Under the IDR plan, your monthly loan repayment would be calculated, not on your loan balance, but on your discretionary income, which is what remains after you pay for essentials like housing and food. In effect, the remainder of the loan balance would be converted into a grant.

Let's take an example under the current Income-Based Repayment plan (IBR) and contrast it with an example under the proposed Income-Driven Repayment (IDR) plan to get an idea of the impact on your monthly payment. The Department of Education currently determines discretionary income (what's left over after paying for essentials like housing and food) by taking your household income and *subtracting 150 percent of the federal poverty guideline* for a family of your size and location. For a family of three in Texas with a household income of $58,000, subtract non-discretionary income of $34,545 (150 percent of the poverty guideline) to determine your discretionary income of $23,455. The current Income-Based Repayment (IBR) amount would be a percentage of that $23,455.

Under the new Income-Driven Repayment plan (IDR), the baseline amount of discretionary income is reduced dramatically when the threshold for discretionary income gets raised from 150 percent of the federal poverty guideline to 225 percent. So the new IDR plan would lower the discretionary income for the stated $58,000 household income from $23,455 to only $6,182.50 ($58,000–$51,817.50 = $6,182.50), which is about a fourth of the baseline used in the old IBR plan. Applying the US Department of Education debt repayment terms for that amount yields a monthly payment of just $26 under the new IDR plan.

In addition to reducing the size of the baseline identified as discretionary income, the new IDR plan also reduces the percentage of discretionary income that must be paid out of that baseline each month. Under the new IDR plan the repayment is pegged at 5 percent of discretionary income, down from the current requirement of repaying 10 percent of monthly discretionary income. Finally, in addition to the baseline and the percentage being lowered, the repayment period would also be adjusted downward. For borrowers whose initial debt was less than $12,000, it will be reduced to 10 years. For all other borrowers it will remain at 20 years.

Reducing the baseline, the percentage, and the repayment period under the new IDR program will significantly reduce the monthly payment from what borrowers currently pay. For example, a family of four with $75,000 in household income would see a drop in the repayment from $278 per month to $52 per month.[39]

In one sense, this new IDR reduction appears to be a great boon to students laboring under a debt burden.[40] But the question facing recent high school graduates remains how to avoid the burden of non-dischargeable debt in the first place. The student debt does not simply disappear; it doesn't vanish under either the debt forgiveness plan, the Income-Based Repayment plan (IBR), or Income-Driven Repayment plan (IDR).[41] It only makes sense that the debt will all have to be paid in some form eventually—by current taxpayers or by future taxpayers. As you consider your college experience, think about how you can avoid accumulating debt in the first place. If you can't avoid accumulating debt, think about how you're going to make the necessary payments to avoid defaulting.

Escaping the Matrix: If You Take Out Loans, Have a Plan to Pay Them Back

If you decide you want to go to college, it's better to graduate debt free than to carry a debt burden for years after college. But if you can't manage to graduate debt free, try to pay down college costs during the college years through savings, scholarships, earnings, and thrifty living. Then have a plan to pay back the rest of it when you graduate. Veterans and active members in the US Armed Forces can sometimes earn forgiveness through the Public Service Loan Forgiveness program—another reason to consider military service.

For civilians, remember the rule of thumb is to cap total student debt at your projected annual salary after you graduate. That means pursuing education à la carte or working for Target or Walmart to take advantage of scholarships on offer can be a great benefit. That also means keeping your eye on the prize of walking debt free at graduation and tracking your progress year by year.

If you incur debt pursuing higher education, the debt doesn't have to stall your life. It doesn't have to trap you and your family into a modern-day indentured servitude without escape. If you plan ahead to manage your worst-case debt scenario, you can avoid taking out more debt than you can afford to repay. This may involve choosing a less expensive college option, taking longer to graduate so you can fund your education with a more intensive work schedule, or applying for more grants and scholarships.

Step out of the Student Loan Matrix thinking, prepare for your financial obligations, and take charge of your borrowing. Then you will be the owner, rather than the borrower, of your own future.

Conclusion

SPIRALING STUDENT DEBT affects you regardless of who you are or how you identify yourself by demographic categories:

- rich, poor, or middle class
- rural, urban, suburban, or exurban
- academically gifted, average, or challenged
- male, female, nonbinary, LGBTQ, or transgender
- Christian, Jew, Muslim, Hindu, agnostic, atheist, or nonreligious
- Democrat, Republican, Independent, Libertarian, Green, or Constitution Party
- White, African American, Asian, Native American/Alaskan Native, Native Hawaiian/ Pacific Islander, multiracial, or Hispanic

Regardless of where you place yourself on this spectrum of identities, student debt is prowling for you. The debt simply doesn't care about your personal characteristics, your politics, or how you identify yourself to the world. It is indifferent to whom it ensnares. But it only ensnares the unwary. Build your defenses against this lurking danger.

When undergraduates walk across the stage to accept their diploma and wake up the next day to discover a debt burden that could hound them the rest of their lives, something is wrong. When they discover they may not be able to find work in the field they have studied for four years, something is wrong. When they discover that their level of pay won't allow them to pay off their student debt for decades and their financial burden will prevent them from stepping into adult life, something is wrong. Things simply can't go on as they are. The college financial system is broken. Things have got to change.

The Changing Map of Higher Education

The good news is that change is coming. All over the nation, perhaps instigated by the COVID pandemic, students are wising up to the fact that a college campus does not need to be a modern paradise with such attractions as a "lazy river pool complex" and "steaks cooked to order" in the campus dining hall.[1]

Students are beginning to realize that they must take responsibility for their own education, that learning is available online, and that social interaction is available off campus. As thought leaders push for low-cost education for both the student and the taxpayer, the next generation of higher education is being built on a new model.

Many states are already implementing plans to recognize, expand, and support community colleges as a vigorous form of continuing education that can be delivered at a low cost. Other states are offering free college or College Promise programs to low-income or academically gifted and committed students who qualify. High school graduates are turning to trade schools, apprenticeships, and vocational trainings that they used to spurn.

If higher education is going to survive when other educational options increase, it's going to have to change. We are now on the cusp of a tectonic transformation, and we will experience this transformation in several ways, predicts Alex Mitchell in a HackerNoon article featured on www.medium.com.[2]

1. Students will grow in their reliance on online education, sometimes called massive open online courses (MOOCs). With courses offered by EdX, Coursera, Khan Academy, and Udacity, students will be able to educate themselves "in almost anything for free."[3]

2. Code schools, often called coding boot camps, are going to continue to evolve and expand. As they do so, "new models for sustainable funding and profitability" will emerge.[4] Code schools will teach students to become software developers using Python, JavaScript, C#, and other programming tools to communicate with computers. Graduates of these code schools will thrive in information technology positions.

3. Trade schools that apprentice students in fields like carpentry or electronics are being reinvigorated. Companies like NextGenT can "offer many technical certificate programs in high-demand fields like cybersecurity."[5] This will enable students in the future to target career fields with a wider array of options to achieve needed training.

4. In order to compete with these proliferating low-cost educational options, colleges will begin offering other payment options. These might include income share agreements (ISAs), in which a student agrees to "pay a percentage of their future income" to their lender, rather than paying for their education up front.[6] Or "get-paid-to-learn options" where companies pay employees a salary to further educate themselves rather than the students themselves paying their education costs.[7] Some companies with the get-paid-to-learn option include Lambda School, Modern Labor, and Career Karma.

Imagine how education will be delivered 10 or 15 years down the line. Alex Mitchell foresees a world where "mid-tier private colleges" that do not make a shift in the way they operate may cease to exist, while community colleges will grow in size and influence.[8]

Can you picture code and trade schools gaining such prominence that they are regarded as a new Ivy League capable of offering "robust curriculum to developers, data scientists, designers, product managers, and more"?[9] Can you conceptualize the current Ivy League and top research universities as the only "old-guard" colleges that remain?[10]

The aggregate sum of student loan debt has climbed to such a level that it will collapse "in value as defaults skyrocket," making obsolete the debt option that has held so many individuals seeking higher education in bondage for so long.[11] The world of the future will see every city in the US offering free associate's degrees at public community colleges.[12] And beyond an associate's degree, US companies will begin to pay their employees to further their education because they know educated workers do a better job.

While there is no way to accurately predict the future, there currently exists empirical evidence of emerging trends in education that do not leave the student in smothering debt. Mr. Mitchell's article offers encouragement that the next generation of higher education is now being built and will open new opportunities.

In case you think these predictions are based on mere speculation, consider that data published in 2021 by the US Department of Education revealed that some 579 institutions of higher learning disappeared over the previous three-year period.[13] Citing US Department of Education statistics, a recent article notes, "Closures of for-profit colleges and universities (across the board, from those certificate-granting institutions to those that award bachelor's degrees) accounted for about three-quarters of the 579 institutions that disappeared over that three-year period."[14] Similarly, the number of public nonprofit four-year universities also declined.

These statistics indicate we may be approaching a tipping point. Instead of the robust growth trend in the number of college students and institutions seen in the 1960s, 1970s, and 1980s—the very trend that spurred the tightened bankruptcy code and the rise of Sallie Mae—the number of institutions of higher education is now shrinking. This shrinking trend will likely be exacerbated over time as the offspring of baby boomers move past childbearing age, and fewer children are born to the couples now delaying parenthood for economic and other reasons.

Additionally, the trend will likely speed up in the near term as economic forces and COVID variant concerns continue to constrain college institutions and their ability to charge tuition for distanced learning. The world of higher education our grandchildren face will not be the one our children face today.

In the Here and Now

Before we march off into future land, we've still got to face the music in the here and now. Until the educational landscape has been reshaped by the forces now being unleashed, each student must plan and execute their own escape from the Student Loan Matrix assumptions. With the information you now know, you won't have to wait for higher education to change to start your own future with little to no debt. You've neutralized the assumptions that make up the Student Loan Matrix, and now your future is in your hands.

Education goes beyond simply attaining a diploma by completing 120 hours of college classroom work. In fact, there are rumblings of a move to cut college completion from 120 to 90 hours. An article by Scott L. Wyatt and Allen C. Guelzo titled "College Doesn't Need to Take Four Years" argues, "[d]ropping back to a three-year degree would be a recruitment attraction for students concerned about the costs of tuition, especially if four-year degrees increasingly cease to guarantee middle-class employment."[15]

Education means equipping yourself with the tools to deal with life's challenges and the skills to thrive in any business, organization, or enterprise you choose to join or run. Students just like you are already employing creative ways to educate themselves, escape or manage student loan debt, and seize their own future, rather than passively receive it.

One very bright college-bound high school senior was offered four different options for college from three nationally recognized universities and one lesser-known college. The elite universities offered varying financial packages, but the lesser-known college offered a full ride. This bright student chose the lesser-known college, enjoyed her experience there immensely, and received her diploma debt free. She then went on to graduate from a competitive law school, land a prestigious federal judge clerkship, and join a large law firm with a specialized practice, all without the benefit of an elite undergraduate university degree. In a similar situation, you may decide that a degree from a prestigious university gives you a competitive advantage in the workplace and is indeed worth a heftier price tag. But count the cost of both options.

A recent college graduate from Hawaii paid off $53,000 in student loans in less than a year. He did it by working diligently at multiple part-time jobs. According to an article posted by Lauren Day on KHON2,[16] Kamaka Diaz was motivated to act when he realized the interest included in his repayment plan would drive the total cost of his education from $53,000 to some $70,000. At that point, he determined to work his way out of debt as soon as possible and avoid the compounding debt interest. To save on expenses, he lived in his parents' home, and to work off his debt, he "made videos, planted trees, shipped things, delivered things, did yardwork," and even "dressed up as Buzz Lightyear for a three-year-old's birthday party."[17] The result of his single-minded dedication was that "Kamaka Diaz paid off $53,757 in 11 months."[18]

In like manner, a young woman I met hiking the Appalachian Trail paid off $60,000 in debt from college in a year of concerted effort. Upon graduating with a large debt, she was shocked to think that her life choices would now be dictated by her student loans. Like the Hawaiian student, she decided to accelerate paying off her debt. She took a demanding job in the Northern Tier oil fields that paid well. She kept expenses down by eating ramen, living in a converted shipping container, and splitting costs with a roommate. In just over a year, she had repaid the debt. She then decided to hike the Appalachian Trail and transition back to a normal lifestyle.[19]

If the decision to attend college is still somewhere off in the future, there are several ways to start planning to avoid the financial pitfalls of student debt and to manage it creatively should you decide to take it on. Have a look at the resources available to financially prepare for your future education and pay particular attention to 529 plans. These state-based plans are rock solid financial planning tools for college, but only about 10 percent of eligible students take advantage of them.

Investigate your prospective college major with an eye toward whether its projected annual salary can indeed pay back the debt you will incur for that major. In other words, think backward from your projected annual salary for the major you wish to pursue to gauge how much debt you can take on. Try to avoid a career in a relatively low-paying field after pursuing the requisite major at a relatively high-cost university. You'd rather have those two financial elements reversed.

Admittedly, at age 17 it's hard to know what you want to do with your life when you become an adult. It's an authentic dilemma. If you are unclear what career you'd like to pursue, one option we've discussed is to embark on a gap year before college and give it some unhurried thought. Let your high school classmates move on at their pace while you move on at yours. As a bonus, you may figure out what major you want to pursue in light of the interests you discover during the gap year. But if you do decide to take a hiatus, be aware that only 90 percent of students who take a gap year end up going on to college, and those that do are only about half as likely to graduate. So think it through. A gap year may point you in the direction of a career you hadn't considered in high school. If so, calculate the level of debt to take on and what university credential you'll need to qualify for the new career you've selected.

Another way to avoid the financial pitfalls of the college choice is to postpone it for a bit and pursue a trade for a few years. After you have stabilized your financial footing, go to college and get your degree. At that point, you may have a clearer idea of the field in which you'd like to specialize. An example might be a plumber who later decides to become a mechanical engineer, or an electrician who later decides to become an electrical engineer. In my business experience, I've met two certified professional engineers (PEs) who followed that exact route. If you decide to take the trade route, be mindful that nontraditional college students are much less likely to graduate, in part because they have to work to pay the bills and may have families they need to support at the same time. So give it a good thought before you make your long-term plan.

Don't forget, many businesses offer educational financial assistance for their employees. These can be extremely useful to young adults just beginning their careers. Walmart and Target are two such companies that provide truly remarkable educational assistance to both part- and full-time employees. Likewise, Starbucks has a great program with Arizona State University. Using this business assist route, you can test the waters of the college experience while working at a big-box store, getting paid, building seniority, and gaining maturity, and all without landing in deep debt.

A Blueprint for Success

Despite the costs, college is still a worthy endeavor for many students. It can enable career specialization, instill confidence, and—if resources are adequately utilized—provide some interesting and lucrative career opportunities. We encourage you to be realistic and practical as you consider whether you wish to attend college and, if so, in what capacity.

If you choose to pursue a college degree, have a plan to graduate debt free on the big day. Instead of deciding to attend the best college you get into, recalibrate your thinking to attend the best college you can graduate from debt free. If you decide a degree with higher prestige is worth going into debt for, have a plan to pay it off quickly. Think of the two recent graduates who paid off their debt in a year.

Before going to a high-cost university, understand the cost of all the components of the program that you are paying for and act accordingly. Consider the advantages of reducing debt by attending community college on the 2+2 plan. Two more years at home after high school won't kill you. In fact, two years of community college while living at home with your parents can save both you and your family thousands of dollars in loans and interest later.

Be mindful in your selection of a college and your selection of a major. When choosing a major, look for one in a field you enjoy with open positions, and look for one that can pay for your desired lifestyle. All the better if it is also in a field where you can make a real contribution to society. Make use of the tools and strategies available to you to minimize your projected debt burden. Apply for scholarships and grants. Don't rely entirely on possible athletic scholarships since they are rare and can present unforeseen pitfalls. Remember that there are private scholarships and federal grants waiting for students motivated enough to fill out the FAFSA, submit an application, and pursue them.

Finally, don't forget that you can make a contribution to society and get paid for doing it through public service in such programs as the Peace Corps. Check out www.publicservicecareers.org for sound career advice on degrees in public service. As you create a strategy for funding your future, consider how work-study, military service, and education à la carte could give you valuable work experience while paying for college.

You've had a close look at the 12 assumptions that comprise the Student Loan Matrix and seen through them. It is my hope that, having done so, you will become free to navigate the world of higher education while avoiding a great expense of time and treasure. Now that you and your family are aware of the dangers lurking on the path, you can move forward safely, stepping into a considered future, whatever that future may be.

Chart your course to achieve the education that works best for you. Make sure you obtain the skills you need to survive and thrive in the post-COVID world. Don't be a passive participant in your own future. Use the information you've gained from this book to map out a route to graduate debt free. I wish you all the best in your journey and look forward to hearing whether the book was a helpful guide. Enjoy!

List of Figures

Resources for Further Reading

TO CONDUCT YOUR OWN RESEARCH for college decision-making, consider the following resources for further reading.

Accessible Online Courses

The EDX website, https://edx.com, offers over 250 online courses generally focused on engineering training. Each course costs an average of $400 to $500, including courses taught by Harvard and other Ivy League schools. Upon conclusion, you will receive a certificate to show your ability to complete the coursework. You might also enjoy the Great Courses program from the Teaching Company at https://www.thegreatcourses.com/, with videos of a wide range of courses.

The US Department of Education Data

The seminal DOE website, https://www.ed.gov, allows you to navigate the policies and programs the government has set forth. You will also find interesting studies showing a wide array of useful statistics about those who attend college and their majors. This is where you will find the statistics regarding graduation rates within six years. Make a priority of accessing the wealth of information on college majors at various institutions on the DOE website at https://collegescorecard.ed.gov/ or through the College Affordability and Transparency Center at https://collegecost.ed.gov/.

Education Statistics

The website of the National Center for Education Statistics (NCES), sponsored by the US Department of Education, is found at https://nces.ed.gov. It provides digests of educational statistics and is a good source for researching questions such as comparative rates of retention at public, nonprofit, and for-profit institutions.

College Ranking Sites

U.S. News & World Report Annual Ranking. The granddaddy of college ranking sites is the *U.S. News & World Report* annual ranking at www.usnews.com/best-colleges. Started in the mid-1980s, this annual ranking covers such categories as Top Public Schools, Engineering Programs, Historically Black Colleges and Universities (HBCUs), and the Ivy Leagues. These rankings are based on an algorithm of peer ranking submissions that are submitted annually by heads of admissions, provosts, and presidents at each of 222 liberal arts schools and 388 large universities.

Some caution is warranted if students intend to use this ranking site for college selection purposes. Malcolm Gladwell deconstructs the *U.S. News* peer ranking algorithm in a thought-provoking podcast titled "Lord of the Rankings" (July 1, 2021). Mr. Gladwell's probing analysis reveals that the designated college officials actually rate their peer colleges *subjectively* based on a score from 1 to 5, rather than *objectively* using a rating system of fixed metrics.

Consequently, the *U.S. News* college rankings are not based on "social science research" that might justify the weight they are sometimes given by students, and perhaps more so, their parents, in the college selection process. While they might be an initial starting point for comparison, as Mr. Gladwell observes, the *U.S. News* rankings could best be described as "an assessment of their feelings of other schools," rather than an assessment of any objective criteria.[1] Subjective feelings among college administrators about other schools that might be competitors may not be the best gauge for students to calibrate their own college decisions or to give their parents bragging rights.

Gladwell's observations are reinforced by Dr. Christopher L. Eisgruber, President of Princeton University, who casts doubt on the utility of students relying on the *U.S. News and World Report* ranking for their college selection process. In a *Washington Post* article titled "I Lead America's Top-ranked University. Here's Why These Rankings Are a Problem,"[2] he observes, "My university has now topped the *U.S. News & World Report* rankings for 11 years running. Given Princeton's success, you might think I would be a fan of the list. Not so. I am convinced that the rankings game is a . . . slightly daft obsession that does harm when colleges, parents, or students take it too seriously."[3] That's not the ringing endorsement that you'd expect from the president of the highest-ranked university in *U.S. News & World Report*'s annual rating.

Despite these criticisms of the *U.S. News* ranking system, it remains a useful tool to gauge the reputation of a college. In an article titled "College Ranking Rebellion Seems Likely to Fail,"[4] Josh Zumbrun notes that "most of the data used to determine the rankings can be derived from public information," and that for the ranking of undergraduate institutions, only "20 percent of the score is assigned from a survey asking institutions to assess each other."[5] The key is to consider what you really want out of a college. Then you can determine for yourself how much weight to give its *U.S. News* ranking.

US Department of Education College Scorecard. Since the *U.S. News & World Report* rankings operate through subjective criteria, it would be helpful to find something like a Consumer Reports rating for colleges that takes a more objective approach for comparison purposes. In this vein, Dr. Eisgruber recommends the "College Scorecard," produced by the US Department of Education, because it "allows anyone to compare colleges on several dimensions without the distraction of rankings."[6] This fact-based scorecard gives an objective basis for comparison.

That idea of an objective comparison is also advocated by Colin Diver, JD, former President of Reed College and former dean at University of Pennsylvania Carey Law School. In a book titled *Breaking Ranks: How the Rankings Industry Rules Higher Education and What to Do about It* (referenced later), Diver recommends rankings based on individual characteristics of higher education, such as "instructional quality and learning gains," "affordability," and "student selectivity." Diver's ideal ranking system would be published by an impartial nonprofit like Consumer Reports, rather than a for-profit organization like *U.S. News.* Such a ranking system would assign a numerical listing to perhaps the top 25 schools, and then list the remaining schools in unranked clusters to eliminate "faux precision."[7] Until such a system is developed, students are free to assign their own weight to the various ranking systems available.

The *Wall Street Journal* College Rankings. The *Wall Street Journal* compiles an annual ranking site at www.wsj.com/collegerankings that offers a wealth of specialized data. The format allows you to view college rankings within areas of specialty, as well as various helpful statistics, such as percent of students graduating and percent obtaining jobs in their desired career field—two key factors to consider in selecting a college.

Other College Rankings. Other college rankings that are worth perusal are available from Niche, Kiplinger, Money, Princeton Review, Times Higher Education's World University Rankings, and Washington Monthly. Each provides a valuable prism to identify the benefits of various schools under consideration.

Educational Practices

The American Association of Higher Education and Accreditation (AAHEA), an independent, membership-based, nonprofit organization dedicated to building human capital for higher education, offers a website at www.aahea.org. AAHEA provides information about higher education on issues that matter in a democratic, multiracial society. AAHEA also promotes and disseminates examples of effective educational practice to address those issues.

Books

We recommend several books that address various strategies to graduate debt free and think through the financial aspects of the college experience. Each has a useful focus and can be considered as part of a strategic approach to escaping the Matrix.

Debt-Free Degree by Anthony ONeal walks students from middle school through each of the four years of college with useful information on how to avoid unnecessary expenses and cut costs.

Graduate from College Debt Free by Bart Astor gives the perspective of a financial planner and analyzes the financial aid process to help students find ways to minimize out-of-pocket costs.

Confessions of a Scholarship Winner by Kristina Ellis is a fun read with useful guidance on how to maximize scholarship awards. Ms. Ellis is a maven in the field who personally won $500,000 in scholarships and shares her secrets of success.

How to Graduate Debt Free also by Kristina Ellis gives the perspective of a recent college graduate and focuses on low-income or first-generation students who may have limited access to the information otherwise.

Who Graduates from College? Who Doesn't? by Mark Kantrowitz presents some 700 tables and charts that give aspiring college students a data-based guide to increase their prospects for graduating from college. To move to the head of the class, check out his related books *How to Appeal for More Financial Aid*, *Filing the FAFSA*, and *Secrets to Winning a Scholarship*. Each delivers reliable information from a true subject matter expert.

Indebted: How Families Make College Work at Any Cost by Caitlin Zaloom uses a case study approach to describe how parents and students are forced to take on huge college debts with no certainty that the investment will pay off. The book paints a portrait of middle-class America trying to navigate the complexities of institutions tasked with determining who is eligible for student aid.

Breaking Ranks: How the Rankings Industry Rules Higher Education and What to Do about It by Colin Diver, JD, gives an insider's view of the rankings industry. As a former President of Reed College and former dean at University of Pennsylvania Carey Law School, Mr. Diver brings educational and legal acumen to the issue of college rankings.

Finally, to get a feel for how the college experience can differ from school to school, check out a landmark work titled *Colleges That Change Lives: 40 Schools That Will Change the Way You Think about Colleges*. This educational guide was first published in 1996 by Loren Pope, formerly the education editor of the *New York Times*. It identifies 40 liberal arts colleges and their core philosophies. Each has a different focus, but all are invested in developing critical thinkers, societal leaders, and moral citizens. The profiles in the book give students a feel for what features and benefits they might look for in various college environments.

Endnotes

Preface

1. The federal student loan debt can be accessed through the StudentAid.gov site at: https://studentaid.gov/sites/default/files/fsawg/datacenter/library/PortfolioSummary.xls. This site reports that *federal* student loan debt outstanding as of September 30, 2022 (the end of the federal fiscal year), was $1.6345 trillion, with some 43.5 million borrowers owing an average of $37,575.
2. The total student loans outstanding for both federal and private debt can be determined by consulting the G.19 report of the Federal Reserve Board at https://www.federalreserve.gov/releases/g19/HIST/cc_hist_memo_levels.html. As of September 30, 2022, the G.19 report shows an outstanding balance of $1.76786770 trillion (abbreviated as $1.768 trillion). The Federal Reserve Board combines the federal student loan data listed previously with private student loan data from MeasureOne to arrive at this figure. The most recent publicly available report from MeasureOne, dated Q3 of 2021, can be found at https://fs.hubspotusercontent00.net/hubfs/6171800/assets/downloads/MeasureOne%20Private%20Student%20Loan%20Report%20Q3%202021%20FINAL%20VERSION.pdf. The G.19 report does not show the number of borrowers. However, by estimating that about 14 percent of federal student loan holders borrow from private sources, and about 80 percent of private student loan holders borrow from federal sources, about 1.5 million people have private student loan debt outstanding and no federal student loans outstanding. Adding the 1.5 million private debt holders to the 43.5 million federal debt holders yields a total of about 45 million borrowers with either federal or private student loans outstanding. That would put the average total student loan debt outstanding at about $39,000. Using this methodology, this $39,000 figure is best seen as an estimation, rather than a definitive number. Information provided by Mark Kantrowitz, December 15, 2022. Used with permission.

3. *See* the Alliant Credit Union website depiction of dollar bill dimensions at: https://www.alliantcreditunion.org/money-mentor/the-dollar-bill-believe-it-or-not.
4. A single $100 bill measures 0.0043 by 6.14 by 2.61 inches, so $10,000 measures 0.43 inches tall. One million dollars in a single stack measures 43 inches tall, which equals 10 stacks about 4.3 inches high each. *See* https://www.alliantcreditunion.org/money-mentor/the-dollar-bill-believe-it-or-not. Graphics created by Reed Sullivan and Russell Brown. Used with permission.
5. The $1 billion depiction is reached by dividing the volume of $1 billion dollars (398.7802 cubic feet) by the area of the five pallets (80 square feet) to arrive at the height of 4.98 feet or roughly 5 feet.
6. The $1 trillion depiction is reached by dividing the volume of $1 trillion (398,780.2 cubic feet) by the area of a football field (63,000 square feet) to arrive at the height of 6.33 feet in $100 bills covering the field. The height of $1.768 trillion on the football field would be 6 inches above the 10-foot goalpost crossbar.
7. According to the Federal Reserve Board's G.19 report, auto loan debt tallies $1.397653 trillion. The Federal Reserve Bank of New York estimates it as slightly higher at $1.52 trillion but may not be as accurate as the G.19 report since it is an estimate rather than a tabulation. According to the Household Debt and Credit Report published by the Federal Reserve Bank of New York, credit card debt stands at $925 billion. *See* https://www.newyorkfed.org/microeconomics/hhdc. The Federal Reserve Bank of New York also publishes a figure for home mortgage debt that tops $11.669 trillion. So student loan debt is about one-sixth of home mortgage debt.
8. In this book we refer to the "student loan or student debt problem." But it can also be described as a "college completion problem." Undergraduate students who drop out of college are more likely to default on their student loans, and these students represent the majority of the defaults. When students drop out, they have the debt, but not the degree to help them repay the debt. Identifying this phenomenon as a student debt problem, however, allows us to analyze the issue from the perspective of a high school student who aspires to attend college and then work preemptively to help them solve the problem.
9. This information is from the National Postsecondary Student Aid Study (NPSAS), which has been published every 3 to 4 years since 1987 and presents a cross-sectional study of how postsecondary students finance their education. An analysis of the 2015–16 NPSAS and 2017–18 NPSAS-AC reports revealed that in 2016, the average Parent PLUS loan debt at graduation was $27,158

and was borrowed by 10.1 percent of parents of undergraduate students. Two years later, in 2018, the average Parent PLUS loan debt had risen to $30,812 and was borrowed by some 9.5 percent of parents of undergraduate students. Parent PLUS loans are included in the total estimated $37,000 average debt per borrower. Because a relatively low number of parents take on the loans, Parent PLUS loans represent about 8 percent of the total average debt amount. Analysis by Mark Kantrowitz, interviewed December 15, 2022. Used with permission.

10. *See* the Federal Reserve Board's Survey of Consumer Finances (SCF) report at https://www.federalreserve.gov/econres/scf/dataviz/scf/chart/#series:Education_Installment_Loans;demographic:all;population:1;units:mean;range:1989,2019. Household debt includes the debt of all borrowers in the household, which can include debt for married borrowers as well as children who borrowed and still live in the household.

11. According to the Beginning Postsecondary Students Longitudinal Study 12/17 (BPS: 12/17), some 66 percent of students graduate with a bachelor's degree from a public four-year college within six years. The BPS: 12/17 is the second and final follow-up study of some 22,500 students who began postsecondary education in the 2011–12 academic year. These students were first interviewed as part of the 2011–12 National Postsecondary Student Aid Study (NPSAS:12). The BPS study is unique in that it includes both traditional and nontraditional students, follows their paths through postsecondary education over the course of six years, and is not limited to enrollment at a single institution. *See* "Beginning Postsecondary Students Study 12/17," by Michael Bryan, Darryl Cooney, and Barbara Elliott. *See also Who Graduates from College? Who Doesn't?* by Mark Kantrowitz, 2021, Table 308.

12. Mark Kantrowitz, *Who Graduates from College? Who Doesn't?* Cerebly, Inc., 2021, Table 308. For college students at four-year public colleges, the figure is 35 percent (Table 308). For all college students, the figure is 41.0 percent. For full-time students, the figure is 44.8 percent, based on Tables 2 and 2B.

13. Kantrowitz, *Who Graduates from College? Who Doesn't?* Table 308. For-profit college graduation rates vary by the level of attainment. For bachelor's degrees, 25 percent graduate in six years, but only 14 percent graduate in four years. The graduation rate at for-profits is somewhat better for two-year associate's degrees at 35 percent and decidedly better for one-year certificate programs at 57 percent. *See Who Graduates,* Tables 628 and 631.

14. Of course, debtor prisons no longer exist in the US, and you can't be arrested for a failure to pay your student loans. However, if you are sued for failure to pay student loans you can be arrested for failing to show up in court. *See* an interesting article by Carrie Pallardy dated December 31, 2018, on the SavingForCollege website at https://www.savingforcollege.com/article/can-you-be-arrested-for-not-repaying-your-student-loans.

15. *See* the GAO report on Financial Aid Offers at https://www.gao.gov/products/gao-23-104708. The report presents sobering statistics that should make students and parents wary of the information presented in college financial aid letters. Because colleges in the study were competing with other colleges for top students, they tended to underreport the financial costs and blur the fact that loans do not act like grants in reducing costs. Given the esteem in which universities and colleges are generally held, and the expectation of fair dealing with which students and parents approach financial aid letters, a college's failure to accurately report college costs is doubly offensive.

16. Because students and parents can be vulnerable to this financial aid letter sleight of hand, protect yourself by inquiring if your college financial aid letters comply with the GAO guidance. Specifically, ask about these 10 best practices that the GAO recommends colleges implement in issuing financial aid letters.

1. Direct and indirect costs are itemized.
2. Provide a total cost of attendance that includes key expenses.
3. Estimate the real net price.
4. Separate the free money, loans, and work-study.
5. Don't include a PLUS loan.
6. Label the type of aid being offered.
7. Label the source of aid.
8. Include actionable next steps.
9. Emphasize the key details and distinctions in the different aid.
10. Don't refer to the financial aid offer as an "award."

Students and their parents who know to be alert for errors or omissions in the financial aid letters can avoid being sucker punched by misleading financial data. Caveat emptor. *See also*, "Financial Aid Letters Don't Reveal the Real Cost of College," by Michelle Singletary, *Washington Post*, December 7, 2022, at https://www.washingtonpost.com/business/2022/12/07/financial-aid-gao-report/.

17. The National Association of Colleges and Employers (NACE) is a leading source of information on the employment of the college educated. According to the NACE Starting Salary survey, the mean starting salary for the class of 2021 was $58,862. *See* https://www.naceweb.org/job-market/compensation/salary-projections-for-class-of-2022-bachelors-grads-a-mixed-bag/.

18. For bachelor's degree graduates, unemployment rates are now below pre-pandemic levels which is a favorable sign for college graduates. *See* https://www.bls.gov/charts/employment-situation/unemployment-rates-for-persons-25-years-and-older-by-educational-attainment.htm.

19. Lawrence Mishel, Elise Gould, and Josh Bivens, "Wage Stagnation in Nine Charts," Economic Policy Institute, January 6, 2015, https://www.epi.org/publication/charting-wage-stagnation/.

20. Andrea Koncz, "Salary Trends Through Salary Survey: Historical Perspective on Starting Salaries for New College Graduates," NACE, August 2, 2016. *See* Figure 1, "Adjusted Average Salaries for Bachelor's Degree Graduates, 1960–2015," https://www.naceweb.org/job-market/compensation/salary-trends-through-salary-survey-a-historical-perspective-on-starting-salaries-for-new-college-graduates/.

21. College Board, "Trends in College Pricing 2022," Figure CP-2, Average Published Tuition and Fees in 2022 Dollars by Sector, https://research.collegeboard.org/trends/college-pricing/highlights#:~:text=In%202022%2D23%2C%20the%20average,%25%20before%20adjusting%20for%20inflation).

22. This debt calculation of $1,200 is only a "best guesstimate" extrapolated from related data and is not based on empirical data. In an indication of the relative insignificance of student debt in popular thought at that time, college debt at graduation was not even being reported by governmental or educational associations in 1972. Anecdotally, this $1,200 figure squares with my personal college experience. After summer jobs, work-study, parental support, and an ROTC monthly stipend of $100, my debt at graduation in 1975 was about $1,000. Beyond anecdotal evidence, reliable data from 20 years later shows that by 1992, the unadjusted average debt at graduation of $9,300 had risen to 33 percent of the unadjusted average starting salary of $28,030. Mark Kantrowitz, "Average Student Loan Debt at Graduation," SavingforCollege.org, July 23, 2020, https://www.savingforcollege.com/article/average-student-loan-debt-at-graduation.

23. Kevin Gray, NACE, "Salary Projections for Class of 2022 Bachelor's Grads a Mixed Bag," January 10, 2022, https://www.naceweb.org/job-market/compensation/salary-projections-for-class-of-2022-bachelors-grads-a-mixed-bag/).

24. Kantrowitz, "Average Student Loan Debt at Graduation." "This table shows historical figures for average debt at graduation and the percentage graduating with student loans for recipients of bachelor's degrees, associate's degrees, and certificates. It also includes historical figures for the average parent loan debt at graduation for bachelor's degree recipients. These figures are not adjusted for inflation."

25. Koncz, NACE, "Salary Trends Through Salary Survey."

26. Kantrowitz, "Average Student Loan Debt at Graduation." The percentage increase of average debt over the past 20 years has been particularly noteworthy. "Over the last two decades, average debt at graduation has increased by 86 percent for bachelor's degree recipients, by 136 percent for associate's degree recipients, by 146 percent for certificate recipients, and by 194 percent for parents." However, the rate of debt increase over the past 10 years has begun to slow. "Over the last decade, average debt at graduation has increased by 21 percent for bachelor's degree recipients, by 39 percent for associate's degree recipients, by 50 percent for certificate recipients, and by 53 percent for parents."

27. For an informative summary of college cost trends, *see* the College Board's "Trends in College Pricing," https://research.collegeboard.org/media/pdf/trends-in-college-pricing-student-aid-2022.pdf. Figure CP-9 depicts the average net price for public four-year institutions since 2016–17 and notes "the average net tuition and fee price paid by first-time, full-time, in-state students enrolled in public four-year institutions has been declining after adjusting for inflation; it was an estimated $2,250 in 2022–23." Figure CP-10 depicts average net price for private nonprofit four-year institutions since 2017–18 and notes "the average net tuition and fee price paid by first-time full-time students enrolled in private nonprofit four-year institutions has been declining after adjusting for inflation; it was an estimated $14,630 in 2022–23."

28. College Board, "Trends in College Pricing 2022," Figure CP-2. Note that the data before 1986–87 is from the "Integrated Postsecondary Education Data System (IPEDS), US Department of Education, National Center for Education Statistics, weighted by full-time equivalent enrollment," while the data shown for 1987–88 forward is from the "Annual Survey of Colleges, the College Board, weighted by full time undergraduate enrollment." Consequently, it is reliably accurate.

29. Private college costs will be significantly higher than the average. According to the 2022–2023 NACE data, after receiving grant aid, full-time students at *private* nonprofit four-year colleges will need to cover "$28,660 in tuition and fees and room and board . . . in addition to $4,140 in allowances for books and supplies, transportation, and other personal expenses." *See* https://www.naceweb.org/store/2022/2022-nace-student-survey-report-and-dashboard-4-year/.

30. It's hard to imagine how my grandchildren will pay for college in 15 years. I hope they read this book. Maybe as a bedtime story after *Goodnight Moon*, a well-worn book in their home. (*Goodnight Moon* by Margaret Wise Brown, illustrated by Clement Hurd, Harper & Brothers, September 3, 1947.)

31. This 70 percent figure has not been updated since 2019 because (1) the analysis is based on a quadrennial study using projections in between survey years and the new survey has been significantly delayed, and (2) the pandemic has interrupted the analysis. Keep in mind that the aggregate limit on federal student loans for dependent undergraduate students is $31,000 ($57,500 for independent students). Current evidence indicates that students in bachelor's degree programs, but not associate's degree or certificate programs, are increasingly bumping up against these limits. Information provided by Mark Kantrowitz, December 15, 2022. Used with permission.

32. National Center for Education Statistics (NCES), "Graduation Rates," https://nces.ed.gov/fastfacts/display.asp?id=40.

33. White House website, Statements and Releases, "Fact Sheet: President Biden Announces Student Loan Relief for Borrowers Who Need It Most," August 24, 2022, https://www.whitehouse.gov/briefing-room/statements-releases/2022/08/24/fact-sheet-president-biden-announces-student-loan-relief-for-borrowers-who-need-it-most/.

34. Andrew Chung, "Six States Urge US Supreme Court to Keep Block on Biden Student Debt Relief," Reuters, November 23, 2022. On November 23, 2022, the state attorneys general from Arkansas, Iowa, Kansas, Missouri, Nebraska, and South Carolina "asked the US Supreme Court to reject President Joe Biden's bid to reinstate his plan to cancel billions of dollars in student debt." The lower court had dismissed because of a lack of legal standing, which was appealed to the Eighth Circuit Court of Appeals. The Eighth Circuit issued a preliminary injunction with a ruling that suggests that they will find the state AGs have legal standing. The US Department of Education appealed to the US Supreme Court. The Supreme Court agreed to consider the case, with arguments to be held in February 2023 and a decision issued thereafter. *See*

https://www.reuters.com/world/us/six-states-urge-us-supreme-court-keep-block-biden-student-debt-relief-2022-11-23/.

35. Jackie Lam, Bankrate website, September 13, 2022, "Will Biden Forgive Private Student Loans?," https://www.bankrate.com/loans/student-loans/private-student-loan-forgiveness/.

36. "Colleges Love Loan Forgiveness," *Wall Street Journal*, August 26, 2022, Op Ed, p. A14.

37. The Income-Driven Repayment (IDR) aspect of the president's announced plan has received less attention than the debt forgiveness but could potentially realign the contours of the student debt program. As discussed in more detail in chapter 12, under the new IDR plan, the threshold for discretionary income gets raised from 150 percent of the federal poverty guideline to 225 percent and the repayment term gets shortened. Together these two policy changes could effectively act as a grant to the borrower and greatly reduce the amount repaid.

38. Not all private colleges are in the $75,000–$80,000 range. According to the College Board's "Trends in College Pricing 2022," the average sticker price of attendance at a private nonprofit college is $57,570. The average at a public in-state four-year college is $27,940, which is roughly half the sticker price of a private four-year college. These averages are before the sticker price is discounted by grants and other aid to arrive at net price.

Introduction

1. M. H. Miller, "Been Down So Long It Looks Like Debt to Me," *The Baffler* no. 40, July 2018, http://www.thebaffler.com/salvos/looks-like-debt-to-me-miller. Putting this article in context, NYU has been the subject of more newspaper stories about students graduating with a bachelor's degree and a six-figure debt than any other college. In 2021–22, students at NYU borrowed $705,932,583 in federal student loans, nearly three-quarters of a billion dollars. But NYU is only the fourth-worst offender. The top honor goes to Grand Canyon University at $835,477,803, followed by Liberty University at $743,989,990 and Southern New Hampshire University at $709,900,337. Information provided by Mark Kantrowitz, December 15, 2022. Used with permission.

2. Miller, "Been Down So Long." In retrospect, Mr. Miller could have pursued two other options. Income-Based Repayment became available in 2009 and Public Service Loan Forgiveness in 2007. They would have recalculated his payments for federal loans on a percentage of his income, as opposed to the amount he owed, and he could have had the remaining debt forgiven in 10 years after 120 payments. This is not meant as a critique of Mr. Miller or

his choices. Rather, it is a wakeup call for students today to be aware of the programs that might be available.

3. Miller, "Been Down So Long."
4. Miller, "Been Down So Long."
5. Miller, "Been Down So Long." On the other hand, rather than thinking of this payback period as a net negative, it could be considered as a cost of doing the business that's necessary to get a degree. When you borrow money to pay for something in a business, you sometimes choose a loan with a maturity that matches the life of the acquisition. The average work-life of a college graduate is about 40–45 years. Spending 27 of those years repaying the student loans is about two-thirds of the typical work-life. From a business perspective, the student loan payments do not consume all of the earnings premium attributable to the college degree. From a life perspective, however, paying off student debt for 27 years is a hard pull.
6. Miller, "Been Down So Long."
7. *The Matrix*, written and directed by the Wachowskis (Warner Bros. Pictures, Burbank, CA, 1999).
8. Wachowskis, *The Matrix.*
9. Wachowskis, *The Matrix.*
10. Wachowskis, *The Matrix.*
11. Given that more than two-thirds of students hold student loan debt when they graduate with a bachelor's degree, to actually graduate debt free might be an unrealistic goal. Student loan debt is unavoidable for many college students. Of those who apply for financial aid, the vast majority graduate with debt. This book is intended to reveal a range of options that students can use to minimize the impact of student loan debt on their lives, even if it may not be possible for them to graduate debt free.
12. *See* Sallie Mae, "How America Pays for College" at https://www.salliemae.com/about/leading-research/how-america-pays-for-college/.
13. Salle Mae, "How America Pays for College."

Chapter 1: I Gotta Go to College

1. *Caddyshack*, directed by Harold Ramis, written by Harold Ramis, Brian Doyle-Murray, and Douglas Kenney, produced by Douglas Kenney (Orion Pictures, 1980).

2. Despite the drumbeat behind it, the "I gotta go to college" assumption does not influence a fair percentage of high school graduates. As of October 2020, less than two-thirds (62.7 percent) of high school graduates aged 16 to 24 were actually enrolled in college or university. About a third of high school students are deciding they don't gotta go to college. *See* the Digest of Education Statistics and Projections of Education Statistics published by the National Center for Education Statistics (NCES) at the US Department of Education at https://nces.ed.gov/programs/digest/.

3. To be clear, this book does not advocate against going to college. It advocates against getting buried in college debt. College is the most reliable path to a good job, a fulfilling life, and financial success. But those outcomes are not guaranteed, and one does not necessarily need a bachelor's degree to achieve them. A key argument for education in society is that as educational attainment increases, a person's income increases, and their prospect of unemployment decreases. *See* this chart from the Bureau of Labor Statistics: https://www.bls.gov/emp/chart-unemployment-earnings-education.html. For a deeper dive into the true purpose of a college education, check out *What's the Point of College?: Seeking Purpose in an Age of Reform*, by Johann N. Neem, PhD, Johns Hopkins University Press, August 13, 2019, at https://www.amazon.com/Whats-Point-College-Seeking-Purpose/dp/1421429888. Neem argues that the purpose of college is to prepare students for the rest of their lives, rather than just their first paying job, by enhancing their capacity for rational analysis and independent judgment.

4. According to Salary.com, the average fast-food manager earns about $40,000 to $50,000 a year. *See* https://www.salary.com/research/salary/posting/fast-food-restaurant-manager-salary. The average fast-food worker earns about half that. *See* https://www.salary.com/research/salary/benchmark/fast-food-worker-salary.

   Fast-food managers may not require postsecondary education, but less than half of them have only a high school diploma, so this field follows the general rule that more education leads to more advancement.

5. Kristen Broady and Brad Hershbein, "Major Decisions: What Graduates Earn over Their Lifetimes," *Up Front* (blog), The Brookings Institution, October 8, 2020, http://www.brookings.edu/blog/up-front/2020/10-08/major-decisions-what-graduates-earn-over-their-lifetimes.

6. That million-dollar figure was updated in 2007 to $1.2 million by Mark Kantrowitz, who cited the US Census Bureau report and added the net present value and an annualized rate of return on investment. *See* Mark Kantrowitz, "The Financial Value of a Higher Education," *Journal of Student Financial Aid* 37(1):18–27, NASFAA, July 2007.

7. The Georgetown University Center on Education and the Workforce conducts research in the areas of jobs, skills, and equity with the goal of better aligning education and training with workforce and labor market demand. In a research study titled "Buyer Beware: First-year Earnings and Debt for 37,000 College Majors at 4,400 Institutions" the center found that first-year earnings for the same degree in the same major can vary by as much as $80,000 for graduates of different schools. *See* the Georgetown study at https://cew.georgetown.edu/cew-reports/collegemajorroi/.
8. The US Department of Education also publishes an enlightening College Scorecard that provides data on debt at graduation and then links to the income level several years after graduation disaggregated by degree level and field of study. *See* https://collegescorecard.ed.gov/. For example, median debt at graduation from MIT is $13,418 and the median earnings 10 years after graduation are $111,222, while for Ohio State University, the median debt is $20,500 and median earnings are $55,332. The report is updated annually based on data submitted by colleges to the US Department of Education. This resource should be read in conjunction with the Georgetown University Center on Education and the Workforce report discussed previously.
9. Broady and Hershbein, "Major Decisions."
10. Broady and Hershbein, "Major Decisions."
11. Broady and Hershbein, "Major Decisions."
12. While this is true compared with a lawyer who doesn't have student loan debt, we should also consider what his net income would be if he hadn't incurred the debt because he never went to college or law school in the first place. In most cases, the net income would be much less without the additional education.
13. Josh Mitchell, "Rising Education Levels Provide Diminishing Economic Boost," *Wall Street Journal*, September 6, 2020, https://www.wsj.com/articles/rising-education-levels-provide-diminishing-economic-boost-11599400800.
14. Mitchell, "Rising Education Levels."
15. Broady and Hershbein, "Major Decisions."
16. Salary.com, "Pipefitter Salary in New York," December 15, 2022, *see* https://www.salary.com/research/salary/benchmark/pipefitter-salary.
17. Salary.com, "Police or Sheriff's Patrol Sergeant Salary in New York," December 15, 2022, *see* https://www.salary.com/research/salary/alternate/police-or-sheriffs-patrol-sergeant-salary/new-york-ny.
18. Information provided by Mark Kantrowitz, December 15, 2020. Used with permission.

19. *See* Duke tuition information at https://finance.duke.edu/bursar/TuitionFees/tuition. Additional information provided by Mark Kantrowitz, December 15, 2020. Used with permission.
20. Michelle Singletary, "On College Decision Day, Don't Sentence Your Child to Decades of Debt," *Washington Post*, April 27, 2022, https://www.washingtonpost.com/business/2022/04/27/may-1-college-decision-day/.
21. Michael Lewis, *Moneyball: The Art of Winning an Unfair Game* (New York: Norton, 2004).
22. Lewis, *Moneyball.*
23. The "Federal Direct Parent PLUS Loans" originated in the Higher Education Act of 1965, at 20 USC 1087e.
24. Today's Military, https://www.todaysmilitary.com.
25. "Post 9/11 GI Bill (Chapter 33)," US Department of Veterans Affairs, https://www.va.gov/education/about-gi-bill-benefits/post-9-11/.
26. The Yellow Ribbon program is administered by the US Department of Veterans Affairs. *See* https://www.va.gov/education/about-gi-bill-benefits/post-9-11/yellow-ribbon-program/.
27. McDonald's, Archways to Opportunity, "Tuition Assistance," https://www.archwaystoopportunity.com/tuition_assistance.html.
28. Taco Bell, "Start with Us, Stay with Us," https://www.tacobell.com/education.
29. Bill Murphy Jr., "Managers at In-N-Out Burger Make $160,000 a Year. Here's How It Works," *Inc. Magazine*, January 26, 2018, https://www.inc.com/bill-murphy-jr/managers-at-in-n-out-burger-make-160000-a-year-heres-how-it-works.html.
30. Murphy, "Managers at In-N-Out Burger Make $160,000."
31. Chipotle, "Chipotle Education Benefit," https://chipotle.guildeducation.com/partner.
32. Kentucky Fried Chicken, "REACH KFC Educational Grant Program," https://kfcfoundation.org/reach/.
33. Chick-fil-A, "Chick-fil-A Remarkable Futures Scholarships," https://www.chick-fil-a.com/remarkable-futures-scholarships.
34. Papa John's, "Dough and Degrees," https://www.papajohns.com/doughanddegrees/.
35. Starbucks, "College Achievement Plan," https://www.starbucks.com/careers/working-at-starbucks/education/.

36. Scholarship America, "Burger King Scholars Program," https://scholarshipamerica.org/scholarship/burger-king-scholars-program/.

37. For Family Dine-In Restaurant Scholarships, *see* Bob Evans and Wayne White Scholarship at https://appalachianohio.org/grow/scholarships/scholarship-opportunities/wayne-f-white-and-bob-evans-scholarship-fund/; Cracker Barrel Foundation at https://crackerbarrel.versaic.com/login; IHOP Bob Leonard Memorial Scholarship at https://www.scholarshipsonline.org/2015/06/bob-leonard-memorial-scholarship-ihop.html; Perkins Family Restaurant Scholarships at http://www.free-4u.com/perkins_family_restaurants_community_service_scholarships.htm; Shoney's Boy Scout Navigators Scholarship at https://www.shoneys.com/our-story/news/shoneys-boy-scout-navigators-scholarship-program-provides-536000-in-scholarships-for-students-in-at-risk-communities/; and lastly, to research other restaurants check out the National Restaurant Association Educational Foundation at https://chooserestaurants.org/programs/scholarships-grants/scholarships/.

38. Denny's, "Denny's Hungry for Education Scholarship," https://www.dennys.com/hfe.

39. Praveen Paramasivam, "Target Launches Debt-Free Education for Frontline Workers," *Reuters*, August 4, 2021, http://reuters.com/world/us/target-launches-debt-free-education-frontline-workers-2021-08-04.

40. Paramasivam, "Target Launches Debt-Free Education."

41. College Financial Aid Advice, "Sam Walton Scholarship," updated May 25, 2022, https://www.college-financial-aid-advice.com/sam-walton-scholarship.html.

42. Kara, Staff Writer, "Want Tuition Reimbursement? These Companies Will Pay for School," Hip2Save, May 9, 2022, https://hip2save.com/tips/companies-tuition-reimbursement/.

43. One company that enthusiastically endorses the IRC 127 (26 U.S. Code §127) program is AGM Container based in Tucson, AZ. It's owner, Howard Stewart, offers a $5,250 annual tax-free reimbursement to all employees and has experienced notable success in training and retaining employees. One employee worked her way up from an entry level position at minimum wage to sales associate making $140,000 a year by earning a degree through the program. Interview with Howard Stewart, March 14, 2023. Used with permission.

Chapter 2: I Need a College Degree to Be Successful

1. Allysia Finley, "Rebellion in the Faculty Lounge," *Wall Street Journal*, May 21, 2021, http://www.wsj.com/articles/rebellion-in-the-faculty-lounge-11621619432.
2. Dana Wilkie, "What Happened to the Promise of a 4-Year College Degree?" SHRM article, October 21, 2019, http://www.shrm.org/resourcesandtools/hr-topics/employee-relations/pages/what-happened-to-the-promise-of-a-4-year-college-degree.aspx.
3. Wilkie, "What Happened."
4. Wilkie, "What Happened."
5. Wilkie, "What Happened."
6. Sherry Turkle, "The Flight from Conversation," *New York Times*, April 21, 2012, https://www.nytimes.com/2012/04/22/opinion/sunday/the-flight-from-conversation.html.
7. Leil Lowndes, *How to Talk to Anyone: 92 Little Tricks for Big Success in Relationships* (McGraw Hill, 2nd Edition, September 22, 2003), page 42.
8. Sanford C. Wilder, *Four Dimensions of Listening*, Educare Unlearning Institute, presented in Grafton, Illinois, February 4, 2022. Course material available at http://educareunlearning.com/. Used with permission.
9. Wilkie, "What Happened."
10. Wilkie, "What Happened."
11. Wilkie, "What Happened."
12. Tim Berners-Lee, "Steve Jobs and the Actually Usable Computer," *W3C* (blog), October 6, 2011, https://www.w3.org/blog/2011/10/steve-jobs/.
13. *See* US House of Representatives, The Chance to Compete Act, HR6967, at https://oversight.house.gov/wp content/uploads/2022/03/Summary.ChancetoCompete.HR6967 Hice-Khanna.pdf.
14. Roy Maurer, "House Passes Federal Hiring Reform Bill," SHRM Article, January 25, 2023. Mr. Maurer reported that "The Chance to Compete Act—legislation that alters the recruiting and hiring process for federal government jobs to incorporate skills-based assessments—passed the US House of Representatives by a vote of 422–2 on January 24. The bill also facilitates the use of more robust assessments over the self-assessment questionnaires currently used for nearly all federal jobs." *See* https://www.shrm.org/resourcesandtools/hr-topics/talent-acquisition/pages/

house-passes-federal-hiring-reform-bill.aspx#:~:text=The%20Chance%20 to%20Compete%20Act,%2D2%20on%20Jan.%2024.

15. Olafimihan Oshin, "Maryland to Drop College Degree Requirement for More State Jobs," *The Hill*, March 16, 2022. Maryland was the first state to eliminate bachelor's degree requirements for most government jobs. Maryland Governor Larry Hogan announced an initiative in March 2022 to drop college degree requirements for thousands of state jobs under a program called Skilled Through Alternative Routes (STAR). Those eligible for the STAR initiative "are 25 years of age or older, are active in the labor force, have at least a high school diploma, and have developed their skills through alternative institutions such as community college, apprenticeships, military service, and employment." According to the announcement, "47 percent of the 2,869,000 workers in the state are considered STARs." *See* https://thehill.com/homenews/state-watch/598494-mayland-to-drop-college-degree-requirement-for-more-state-jobs/.

16. Emma Williams, "Gov. Cox Launches Skills-First Hiring Initiative for State Government," Media Release by the Office of the Governor, December 13, 2022. "Utah Gov. Spencer Cox announced the state's efforts to eliminate the requirement for bachelor's degrees in its employee recruitment and emphasized similar support by local governments and the private sector." The rationale is to open up more job opportunities. "Degrees have become a blanketed barrier-to-entry in too many jobs," Gov. Cox said. "Instead of focusing on demonstrated competence, the focus too often has been on a piece of paper. We are changing that." *See* https://governor.utah.gov/2022/12/13/news-release-gov-cox-launches-skills-first-hiring-initiative-for-state-government/#:~:text=SALT%20LAKE%20CITY%20(Dec.,too%20many%20 jobs%2C%E2%80%9D%20Gov.

17. PennLive.com, "Gov. Josh Shapiro Signs Order Eliminating Four-year Degree Requirement for Thousands of Pennsylvania Jobs," *Pittsburgh Post-Gazette*, January 19, 2023. On January 18, 2023, Pennsylvania's Gov. Josh Shapiro signed an executive order eliminating a college degree requirement for most state government positions. *See* https://www.post-gazette.com/news/politics-state/2023/01/18/josh-shapiro-college-degree-requirement-jobs-workforce/stories/202301180096.

18. Douglas Belkin, "Rush to College Might Be a Mistake," *Wall Street Journal*, June 1, 2017, at http://www.wsj.com/articles/rush-to-college-might-be-a-mistake-1496289603.

19. Belkin, "Rush to College Might Be a Mistake."

20. Mark Kantrowitz, *Who Graduates from College? Who Doesn't* (Cerebly, Inc., 2021) Table 228, et sec, pp. 169–170. The outcomes are better for students who pursue an associate's degree or certificate program after taking a gap year.
21. Kantrowitz, *Who Graduates.*

Chapter 3: Tuition Is the Total Cost of College

1. Sticker shock refers to the shock of learning the full cost of college attendance when applying for admission. This may arise in a scenario referred to as "undermatching" where a highly qualified student selects a lower tier university after they realize the cost of the higher tier school. *See* https://thecollegeinvestor.com/38195/what-is-undermatching/ by Mark Kantrowitz. "Public policy advocates have claimed that very selective colleges are more affordable for low-income students, despite the higher cost of attendance." However, qualified students from low-income backgrounds may still "shy away from selective or private colleges and universities." The combination of a high-cost college with a high financial aid financing model is often blamed for this undermatching. When the student sees the total costs involved they may experience sticker shock and walk away.
2. The free tuition programs are "last-dollar" financial aid programs. They assume that all other financial aid, such as the Federal Pell Grant and the New York TAP Grant, are applied first to tuition and that the free tuition programs like the Excelsior Scholarship cover the rest. Between the federal and state grants, many low-income students already have close to "free tuition" so they might only get a few hundred dollars from the program. That's in contrast with middle-income families, who may get thousands of dollars from the program. Nevertheless, the free college programs like the Excelsior Scholarship are beneficial in getting college-capable low-income students to pursue a college education because the word "free" is a more powerful marketing message than the term "no loans." Information provided by Mark Kantrowitz, December 15, 2022. Used with permission.
3. *See* New York Excelsior Program at https://www.hesc.ny.gov/pay-for-college/financial-aid/types-of-financial-aid/nys-grants-scholarships-awards/the-excelsior-scholarship.html.
4. New York Excelsior Program.
5. Stacy Teicher Khadaroo, "Is 'Free College' Really Free?" *Christian Science Monitor*, May 16, 2019, https://www.csmonitor.com/USA/Education/2019/0516/Is-free-college-really-free.

6. Khadaroo, "Is 'Free College.'"
7. Khadaroo, "Is 'Free College.'"
8. *See* the GAO report on Financial Aid Offers at https://www.gao.gov/products/gao-23-104708.
9. Information provided by Mark Kantrowitz, December 15, 2022. Used with permission.
10. Mark Kantrowitz, "Information."
11. NACUBO, "Before COVID-19, Private College Discount Rates Reached Record Highs," May 5, 2020, https://www.nacubo.org/Press-Releases/2020/Before-COVID-19-Private-College-Tuition-Discount-Rates-Reached-Record-Highs.
12. For comprehensive figures, *see How to Appeal for More College Financial Aid: The Secrets to Negotiating a Better Financial Aid Offer . . . and Getting More Financial Aid in the First Place* by Mark Kantrowitz, Cerebly, Inc., 2019. For a guide to appeal the offer *see* https://www.trinityschoolnc.org/uploaded/College_Counseling/How_To_Appeal-Financial_Aid.pdf.
13. NACUBO, "Before COVID-19." Another study concluded that 80 percent receive gift aid, which is slightly lower than the NACUBO study, but still a decided majority of students. For a more detailed analysis *see* http://www.studentaidpolicy.com/who-pays-full-sticker-price-for-a-college-education.html. Be wary of the statistics indicating the number or percentage of students who receive financial aid because the actual amount of financial aid per individual student may turn out to be very low. This is particularly true if the college awards token institutional grants that boost their statistics. Also, be alert to the practice employed by a number of colleges called "front-loading grants," in which students get a better mix of grants vs. loans during the first year, and the mix changes when grants diminish in later years.
14. Philip Levine, "Dump the Discount Rate," Inside Higher Ed, August 14, 2019, http://www.insidehighered.com/views/2019/08/14/why-discount-rate-flawed-statistic-tracking-college-finances-opinion.
15. Amanda Ripley, "Why Is College in America So Expensive? The Outrageous Price of a US Degree is Unique in the World," *The Atlantic*, September 11, 2018, http://www.theatlantic.com/education/archive/2018/09/why-is-college-so-expensive-in-america/569884/.
16. Ripley, "Why Is College in America So Expensive?"

17. Holman W. Jenkins Jr., "Liz Truss Is a Human Sacrifice to the Inflation Fires," *Wall Street Journal*, October 1–2, 2022, p. A15. The article also references college inflation.

18. Mitch Daniels, "Student Loans and the National Debt," *Wall Street Journal*, September 2, 2022, p. A15.

19. Daniels, "Student Loans." For information about how many students graduate debt free in other states, *see also* the "Project on Student Debt," at http://ticas.org/interactive-map/. Select "Indiana" to see a 59 percent figure corroborating the 60 percent asserted by Daniels.

20. The 8 percent inflation rate figure reported at https://finaid.org/savings/tuition-inflation may need adjustment for current inflation. Over the last 10 years, based on College Board data, the inflation rate averaged 3.1 percent for tuition, fees, room and board for private nonprofit four-year colleges and averaged 2.7 percent for public in-state four-year colleges. The College Board data is not a true index, so it may understate the actual inflation rate. Also note that the past 10 years included several years of historically low inflation. The takeaway for each student is to include an inflation rate factor when you calculate your college costs. Information provided by Mark Kantrowitz, December 15, 2022. Used with permission.

21. Because Harvard is one of about 70 colleges with a "no loans" financial aid policy, its financial aid packages only include grants and student employment, not loans. A student can still borrow to cover the family contribution, but not as part of the financial aid package. Only 20 percent of Harvard students graduate with student loan debt, which is much lower than the national average. That result is partly because Harvard has a wealthier mix of students and partly because of their no-loans financial aid policy. Information provided by Mark Kantrowitz, December 15, 2022. Used with permission.

22. Trends in College Pricing: Highlights, College Board, https://research.collegeboard.org/trends/college-pricing/highlights.

23. Rachel Cruze, "How Long Does It Take to Pay Off Student Loans?," Ramsey Solutions, Oct 4, 2022, https://www.ramseysolutions.com/debt/how-long-does-it-take-to-pay-off-student-loans. "A typical student loan is structured to take 10 years to pay off. But research has shown it actually takes 21 years on average." *See* One Wisconsin Institute, "Impact of Student Loan Debt on Homeownership Trends and Vehicle Purchasing," at https://drive.google.com/file/d/0B8LurBVUNQZfQVhYZWZvamlfd00/view?resourcekey=0-nFC8857PHI2stfLraRIVbg.

24. Information provided by Mark Kantrowitz, December 15, 2022. Used with permission.

25. Sara Goldrick-Rab and Nancy Kendall, "The Real Price of College," The Century Foundation, March 3, 2016, https://tcf.org/content/report/the-real-price-of-college/?agreed=1. This 2016 study is an excellent research resource for analyzing the total cost of college. To obtain updated information, we recommend accessing the 2020 NPSAS data at https://nces.ed.gov/surveys/npsas/.
26. Goldrick-Rab and Kendall, "The Real Price."
27. Goldrick-Rab and Kendall, "The Real Price."
28. Goldrick-Rab and Kendall, "The Real Price."
29. The new formula itself will still be complicated, but it will be simpler from the student's perspective.
30. Goldrick-Rab and Kendall, "The Real Price.
31. Goldrick-Rab and Kendall, "The Real Price."
32. Abigail Johnson Hess, "It Costs over $70,000 a Year to Go to Harvard—But Here's How Much Students Actually Pay," Make It, CNBC, April 6, 2019, https://www.cnbc.com/2019/04/05/it-costs-78200-to-go-to-harvardheres-what-students-actually-pay.html.
33. Molly Webster, "I've Spent $60,000 to Pay Back Student Loans and Owe More Than Before I Began," *New York Times*, March 18, 2021, https://www.nytimes.com/2021/03/18/opinion/student-loans-cares-act.html.
34. Webster, "I've Spent $60,000."
35. Webster, "I've Spent $60,000."
36. Webster, "I've Spent $60,000."
37. Webster, "I've Spent $60,000."
38. Webster, "I've Spent $60,000."
39. Webster, "I've Spent $60,000."
40. Ms. Webster's loans appear to have been in the FFEL Program, which is not eligible for the payment pause and interest waiver. Other students in this predicament might have become eligible by consolidating their FFEL loans into a Federal Direct Consolidation Loan. Information provided by Mark Kantrowitz, December 15, 2022. Used with permission.
41. Loans made in 2008–09 and 2009–10 under the Ensuring Continued Access to Student Loans Act (ECASLA) were transferred to the US Department of Education at the end of the one-year financing if the FFEL lender was unable to repay the financing. Information provided by Mark Kantrowitz, December 15, 2022. Used with permission.

42. To make the situation more complicated, the borrowers could have chosen to move the loans into the Direct Loan Program to qualify for the payment pause and interest waiver by getting a Federal Direct Consolidation Loan. This was entirely up to the borrower. Aside from temporarily setting the interest rate to zero under the CARES Act, consolidation did not otherwise change the interest rate. Information provided by Mark Kantrowitz, December 15, 2022. Used with permission.
43. For an enlightening discussion of opportunity costs in college, *see* Kim Butler and E. P. Hagenlocher, *Busting the College Planning Lies: How Unknown Opportunity Costs Kill the Goose and the Golden Egg* (Kindle, Busting the Money Myths Book Series, October 27, 2022).
44. *Animal House*, directed by John Landis, written by Douglas Kenney, John Landis, Chris Miller, and Harold Ramis, produced by Ivan Reitman, Matty Simmons (Universal Pictures, 1978).
45. "Minimum Wage," United States Department of Labor, Wage and Hour Division, https://www.dol.gov/agencies/whd/minimum-wage.
46. "Trade Apprentice Salary," ZipRecruiter, accessed Jun 12, 2022, https://www.ziprecruiter.com/Salaries/Trade-Apprentice-Salary.
47. A significant number of students work a full-time job while in college, sometimes to their detriment. A student who works 40 or more hours a week is about half as likely to graduate with a bachelor's degree within six years. Information provided by Mark Kantrowitz, December 15, 2022. Used with permission.
48. The average award for bachelor's degree students is $4,202 with 8.1 percent receiving private scholarships for undergraduate studies. *See* https://www.savingforcollege.com/article/college-scholarships-statistics.
49. Graphics designed by Reed Sullivan and Russell Brown using data from the US Department of Education, National Center for Education Statistics, National Association of Colleges and Employers, and the College Board. *See* https://research.collegeboard.org/trends/student-aid/highlights; https://nces.ed.gov/programs/digest/d21/tables/dt21_330.10.asp?current=yesand; https://educationdata.org/financial-aid-statistics; and https://www.naceweb.org/job-market/compensation/salary-trends-through-salary-survey-a-historical-perspective-on-starting-salaries-for-new-college-graduates/.
50. Sullivan and Brown, Department of Education, etc. data.
51. Sullivan and Brown, Department of Education, etc. data.
52. Sullivan and Brown, Department of Education, etc. data.

53. Graphics designed by Reed Sullivan and Russell Brown using analysis provided by Richard Craft, AIF, ChFC, CPFA, CLU, Wealth Advisory Group, Berwyn, PA, 2022.

54. Sullivan and Brown, using analysis provided by Richard Craft.

55. *See* the NPSAS report at https://nces.ed.gov/pubs2018/2018466.pdf.

56. *See* https://www.whitehouse.gov/wp-content/uploads/2022/03/edu_fy2023.pdf.

Chapter 4: Community College Is a Step Sideways

1. *See* Dallas at https://www1.dcccd.edu/catalog/GeneralInfo/TuitionCost/tuition.cfm; *see* Seattle at https://www.google.com/search?q=Seattle+Central+College+costs&ie=UTF-8&oe=UTF-8&hl=en-us&client=safari; *see* Chicago at https://www.ccc.edu/departments/pages/tuition-and-fees.aspx; *see* New York at https://www.google.com/search?q=City+College+of+New+York+cost&ie=UTF-8&oe=UTF-8&hl=en-us&client=safari; *see* Philadelphia at https://www.google.com/search?q=Community+college+of+Philadelphia+cost&ie=UTF-8&oe=UTF-8&hl=en-us&client=safari.

2. Abigail Endsley, "How to Transfer Community College Credits to University," Pearson Accelerated, August 24, 2020, https://pearsonaccelerated.com/blog/community-college-transfer-credit.

3. The contributor wishes to remain anonymous. This information is used with permission.

4. Melissa Korn, "Default Rates for Certificate Graduates on Par with College Dropouts, New Data Show," *Wall Street Journal*, October 5, 2017, https://www.wsj.com/articles/default-rates-for-certificate-program-graduates-on-par-with-college-dropouts-new-data-show-1507225501.

5. Korn, "Default Rates."

6. Korn, "Default Rates."

7. Korn, "Default Rates."

8. Korn, "Default Rates."

9. Korn, "Default Rates."

10. Jon Marcus, "High-Paying Jobs That Don't Need a College Degree? Thousands of Them Sit Empty," NPR, February 14, 2023, at https://www.npr.org/2023/02/14/1155405249/high-paying-jobs-that-dont-need-a-college-degree-thousands-of-them-are-sitting-e. The article updates a similar NPR article from

2018 and attributes the reference to 30 million jobs that don't require a degree to the Good Jobs Project of The Georgetown Center on Education and the Workforce at https://goodjobsdata.org/.

11. Stacy Berg Dale and Alan B. Krueger, "Estimating the Payoff to Attending a More Selective College," National Bureau of Economic Research (NBER) Working Paper Series, 1999, https://www.nber.org/system/files/working_papers/w7322/w7322.pdf, p. 30.
12. Dale and Krueger, "Estimating the Payoff."
13. Casey Gendason, owner of Casey Gendason Guidance, Dallas, TX, information provided on November 4, 2022. Used with permission.
14. Gendason, "Information."
15. *See* National Center for Education Statistics (NCES) report BPS 12/17 at https://downloads.regulations.gov/ED-2016-ICCD-0093-0008/attachment_2.pdf.
16. NCES, BPS 12/17 report.

Chapter 5: I Can Live Inexpensively on Campus

1. Thomas Jefferson, The University of Virginia. The Academical Village was built to foster cross-disciplinary exchange. "Jefferson's design housed faculty from a range of specialties around a central lawn. Students lived in single rooms between professors' homes. At the head of their shared lawn stood the library (also known as the Rotunda)." *See* https://www.virginia.edu/visit/grounds.
2. *See* the Integrated Postsecondary Education Data System (IPEDS) report to the National Center for Education Statistics at https://nces.ed.gov/ipeds/use-the-data.
3. Lynn O'Shaughnessy, "Federal Government Publishes More Complete Graduation Rate Data," Cappex, https://www.cappex.com/articles/blog/government-publishes-graduation-rate-data.
4. Sara Goldrick-Rab and Nancy Kendall, "The Real Price of College," The Century Foundation, March 3, 2016, https://tcf.org/content/report/the-real-price-of-college/?agreed=1. For updated information, access the 2020 NPSAS data at https://nces.ed.gov/surveys/npsas/.
5. Goldrick-Rab and Kendall, "The Real Price."
6. Goldrick-Rab and Kendall, "The Real Price."
7. Goldrick-Rab and Kendall, "The Real Price."

8. *See* the 2021 Consolidated Appropriations Act at https://www.cms.gov/cciio/programs-and-initiatives/other-insurance-protections/caa and the specific FAFSA simplification provision at https://www.nasfaa.org/fafsa_simplification.
9. Goldrick-Rab and Kendall, "The Real Price."
10. Ali Breland, "If the Tuition Doesn't Get You, the Cost of Student Housing Will," *Bloomberg Businessweek*, August 13, 2019, https://www.bloomberg.com/news/features/2019-08-13/if-the-tuition-doesn-t-get-you-the-cost-of-student-housing-will.
11. Breland, "Student Housing."
12. Breland, "Student Housing."
13. Breland, "Student Housing."
14. Casey Gendason, owner of Casey Gendason Guidance, Dallas, TX. Information provided on November 4, 2022. Used with permission.
15. Goldrick-Rab and Kendall, "The Real Price."
16. Goldrick-Rab and Kendall, "The Real Price."
17. Goldrick-Rab and Kendall, "The Real Price."
18. Goldrick-Rab and Kendall, "The Real Price."
19. *See* the Meal Plan report at https://fsapartners.ed.gov/knowledge-center/library/dear-colleague-letters/2022-11-03/fafsar-simplification-act-changes-implementation-2023-24.

Chapter 6: I Could Never Qualify for Grants or Scholarships

1. *See* Mark Kantrowitz, "Millions of Students Still Fail to File the FAFSA Each Year," September 17, 2018, at https://www.savingforcollege.com/article/millions-of-students-still-fail-to-file-the-fafsa-each-year. This article from 2018 identifies the core issue that, although funding is available, students fail to submit the FAFSA and therefore do not qualify for the funding. Specifically, "despite increases in the percentage of undergraduate students filing the Free Application for Federal Student Aid (FAFSA) each year, millions of students who would have qualified for college grants still fail to file the FAFSA." Sadly, "more than two million students would have qualified for the Federal Pell Grant in 2015–2016, if they had only filed the FAFSA. Of them, 1.2 million would have qualified for the maximum Federal Pell Grant." Sadder still, "of the students who did not file the FAFSA, more than a third would have qualified for the Federal Pell Grant." Bottom line: file the FAFSA.

2. Students can become "million-dollar scholars" by applying for admission to many different colleges and summing up the financial aid offers from the various schools to reach the $1 million total. Unfortunately, the student would be unable to use all the scholarships because they are generally college specific. Still, it is a noteworthy achievement that shows industriousness, initiative, and determination to gain an education. In a similar vein, there have been a few outstanding students who have won several prestigious scholarships concurrently, such as Gates, Dell, Coca-Cola, etc. In those cases, the scholarship organizations often worked together to allow the highly qualified student to benefit from all of the awards (e.g., by deferring one award by a year, letting the student use another for graduate school). Aspiring college students with a strong work ethic and competitive statistics can learn from both these approaches. Information provided by Mark Kantrowitz, December 15, 2022.
3. Free Application for Federal Student Aid (FAFSA), US Department of Education, https://studentaid.gov/h/apply-for-aid/fafsa.
4. The Sunnyside Foundation provides financial assistance to practicing Christian Scientists who reside in the state of Texas. *See* https://sunnysidetexas.org/.
5. *See* Kiwanis Scholarships at https://www.kiwanis.org/childrens-fund/grants/scholarship-opportunities.
6. *See* Rotary International scholarships at https://www.rotary.org/en/our-programs/scholarships..
7. Will Geiger and Kayla Korzekwinski, "Top College Merit Based Scholarships," Scholarships 360, October 27, 2022, https://scholarships360.org/scholarships/great-merit-scholarships/.
8. Geiger and Korzekwinski, "Top College Merit Based Scholarships."
9. Casey Gendason, owner of Casey Gendason Guidance, Dallas, TX. Information provided on November 4, 2022. Used with permission.
10. Be aware that many academic scholarships are only in the $500 to $1,000 range. But also note that some 300 colleges award academic scholarships for at least half tuition, so it is worth the time to investigate if your target college does so. Information provided by Mark Kantrowitz, December 15, 2022. Used with permission.
11. Casey Gendason, "Information."
12. Start with free scholarship databases with excellent coverage of available scholarships such as Fastweb.com at https://www.fastweb.com/registration/step_1 and the College Board's Big Future at https://bigfuture.collegeboard.org/

pay-for-college/scholarship-search. Then check out MyScholly, "16 Insider Facts about College Scholarships and Financial Aid," September 16, 2020, at https://myscholly.com/16-insider-facts-about-college-scholarships-and-financial-aid/. Note: the myscholly.com website requires a fee to search their database.

13. There are over 400 Promise or free tuition scholarships, and they all have locality restrictions that typically limit eligibility to residents of the city or state. If, perhaps, parents are willing to move to a different location to take advantage of the generous financial aid, be aware that this often entails residency requirements. Frequently, the move must occur at least a year, and sometimes a full calendar year, before enrolling in college. You may also have to graduate from an in-state high school and comply with the requirements for in-state tuition. *See* state residency requirements at https://www.savingforcollege.com/article/state-residency-requirements-for-in-state-tuition.

14. *See* NCES scholarship data at https://nces.ed.gov/fastfacts/display.asp?id=31.

15. *See* NCES scholarship data at https://nces.ed.gov/fastfacts/display.asp?id=31.

16. *See* College Board's Big Future at https://bigfuture.collegeboard.org/pay-for-college/scholarship-search.

17. Ann Carrns, "Thousands of Students Missing Out on College Grants, Study Finds," *New York Times*, February 4, 2022. "Roughly 1.7 million high school graduates didn't file the Free Application for Federal Student Aid in the 2020–21 school year. And just under half of them—about 813,000 students—were eligible for federal Pell Grants aimed at low income students."

18. Nicole Pelletiere, "Teen Awarded over $1 Million in Scholarships from 18 Colleges," *Good Morning America*, March 2, 2021, https://www.goodmorningamerica.com/living/story/teen-awarded-million-scholarships-18-colleges-76186041. Before concluding that these awards made the student an overnight millionaire, it is useful to note some relevant facts. First, she would only be able to use about $60,000 annually because scholarships would generally be restricted to just one college. Second, she likely applied to many colleges to get the competitive financial aid offers that contributed to the million dollar total. Third, the average institutional grant at a private nonprofit four-year college is $16,505 for one year. Fourth, the cost of attendance at such private nonprofit colleges averages $38,124 according to data in the 2015–16 NPSAS. In sum, she did a superb job of applying for scholarships, which other students can emulate, but she did not become a millionaire.

19. Pelletiere, "Teen Awarded."

20. Pelletiere, "Teen Awarded."

21. Steve Jobs, "Commencement Address," transcript of speech at Stanford University, Stanford, CA, June 12, 2005, https://news.stanford.edu/2005/06/14/jobs-061505/.
22. Steve Jobs, "Commencement Address."
23. Kathryn Flynn, "4 Ways a Work-Study Job Can Pay Off," *Discover*, updated March 3, 2021, https://www.discover.com/student-loans/college-planning/how-to-pay/financial-aid/work-study-job-pay-off.
24. Sara Goldrick-Rab and Nancy Kendall, "The Real Price of College," The Century Foundation, March 3, 2016, https://tcf.org/content/report/the-real-price-of-college/?agreed=1.
25. *See* "How Long Will It Take to Fill out the FAFSA?" on the FAFSA Help Page, United States Department of Education, at https://studentaid.gov/help/how-long. Find actual FAFSA completion time data reported in the Student Aid.gov website at https://studentaid.gov/sites/default/files/fsawg/datacenter/library/2020-2021-application-demographics.xls.
26. Goldrick-Rab and Kendall, "The Real Price."
27. Goldrick-Rab and Kendall, "The Real Price."
28. Goldrick-Rab and Kendall, "The Real Price."
29. Also be alert to a catch-22 involving prior year income calculations for two-year community colleges. When a student quits their job to go to school full time, the college financial aid administrator can and should use professional judgment (PJ) to disregard the earned income from that prior job. However, many community colleges don't actually apply professional judgment to make this adjustment. Since the FAFSA is based on prior-year income, this means it takes *two* years before the student can qualify for a Pell Grant. An associate's degree is a two-year degree and a certificate is a one-year degree so the student could miss out on an otherwise available grant. Information provided by Mark Kantrowitz, December 15, 2022.

Chapter 7: I Can Get an Athletic Scholarship

1. NCAA, Chart, "Estimated Probability of Competing in College Athletics," updated April 8, 2020, https://www.ncaa.org/sports/2015/3/2/estimated-probability-of-competing-in-college-athletics.aspx.
2. NCAA, "Estimated Probability."
3. Anemona Hartocollis, "Rick Singer, Mastermind of Varsity Blues Scandal, Is Sentenced to 3½ Years in Prison," *New York Times*, January 4, 2023, at

https://www.nytimes.com/2023/01/04/us/rick-singer-sentenced-college-admissions-scandal.html.

4. Hartocollis, "Rick Singer."

5. *See* NCAA Chart at https://ncaaorg.s3.amazonaws.com/research/pro_beyond/2020RES_ProbabilityBeyondHSFiguresMethod.pdf.

6. NCAA, "Estimated Probability."

7. NCAA, "Estimated Probability."

8. Athnet Sports Recruiting, "Head Count versus Equivalency Scholarships," https://www.athleticscholarships.net/sports-scholarships/head-count-versus-equivalency-scholarships.htm. "The difference between Head Count scholarships and Equivalency scholarships can best be understood as sports that are guaranteed full-ride scholarships (Head Count) versus sports that divide the scholarships as partial scholarships (Equivalency)."

9. Athnet Sports Recruiting, "Head Count."

10. Athnet Sports Recruiting, "Head Count."

11. Athnet Sports Recruiting, "Head Count."

12. ScholarshipStats.com, "Scholarship Limits 2020–21," accessed June 4, 2022, https://scholarshipstats.com/ncaalimits.

13. ScholarshipStats.com, "Scholarship Limits 2020–21."

14. Daniel Wilco, "FCS Championship: Everything you need to know," NCAA, January 13, 2020, at https://www.ncaa.com/news/football/article/2020-01-11/fcs-championship-everything-you-need-know. "Unlike in all other NCAA sports, NCAA Division I football is split into two divisions." In 2006, the higher level, formerly known as "Division 1-A, became the Football Bowl Subdivision (FBS) and the lower level, Division 1-AA, became the Football Championship Subdivision (FCS)."

15. Wilco, "FCS Championship."

16. NCAA reports only on athletic scholarships awarded by the colleges. But if we include private athletic scholarships, the total percentage increases slightly. As of 2011, less than 2 percent of college students received athletic scholarships. *See* http://www.studentaidpolicy.com/fa/20110505athleticscholarships.pdf. Based on analysis of more recent data from the 2015–16 National Postsecondary Student Aid Study (NPSAS), that 2 percent figure had declined to 1.3 percent of undergraduate students receiving athletic scholarships, with an average scholarship of $10,631. Student athletes should also be aware that an athletic scholarship may replace the institutional aid they would otherwise have

received based on financial need. Information provided by Mark Kantrowitz, December 15, 2022.

17. ScholarshipStats.com, "Scholarship Limits 2020–21."
18. ScholarshipStats.com, "Scholarship Limits 2020–21."
19. NCAA, "Estimated Probability."
20. NCAA, "Estimated Probability."
21. NCAA, "Estimated Probability."
22. NCAA, "Estimated Probability."
23. NCAA, "Estimated Probability."
24. Muhammad Ali's memorable comment regarding his title bout with Joe Frazier on March 8, 1971, was featured in Muhammad Ali quotes on www.quotefancy.com.
25. John Brodhead Jr., MD, Executive Vice Chairman, Department of Medicine, at the Keck School of Medicine of the University of Southern California (USC), former team physician for USC Athletics, and director of Athletic Medicine. Interview on September 14, 2022. Used with permission.
26. Oyez, *National Collegiate Athletic Association v. Alston*, accessed January 26, 2022, https://www.oyez.org/cases/2020/20-512, citing *National Collegiate Athletic Association et al v. Alston*, 141 S. ct. 2141 (2021), https://www.supremecourt.gov/opinions/20pdf/20-512_gfbh.pdf.
27. *National Collegiate Athletic Association v. Alston*, No. 20-512, slip op. at 4 (US June 21, 2021).
28. *Nebraska Quarterly*, "Fall 2022 Issue," Vol 118, No. 3, p 34.
29. Nebraska Athletic Communications, "NIL Update from Nebraska Athletics," January 12, 2023, https://huskers.com/news/2023/1/12/nil-update-from-nebraska-athletics.aspx.
30. Jo Craven McGinty, "March Madness Is a Moneymaker. Most Schools Still Operate in Red," *Wall Street Journal*, March 12, 2021, https://www.wsj.com/articles/march-madness-is-a-moneymaker-most-schools-still-operate-in-red-11615545002.
31. McGinty, "March Madness."
32. McGinty, "March Madness."

Chapter 8: I Need Networking in College for Career Success

1. Genevieve Carlton, "A History of the Ivy League," *Best Colleges* (blog), September 30, 2021, https://www.bestcolleges.com/blog/history-of-ivy-league/.
2. The Handshake Network is billed as the largest network of students, universities, and recruiters. *See* https://joinhandshake.com/network-trends/ for a recent survey revealing six things to know about the 2023 cohort of college job seekers.
3. Information provided by Mark Kantrowitz, December 15, 2022. Used with permission.
4. "The Importance of Networking in College," The Haven at College, July 26, 2019, https://thehavenatcollege.com/networking-in-college/.
5. The Haven, "Networking in College."
6. The Haven, "Networking in College."
7. The Haven, "Networking in College."
8. The Haven, "Networking in College."
9. The Haven, "Networking in College."
10. *See* the National Society of Professional Engineers that offers free student memberships at https://www.nspe.org/membership/types-membership.
11. Peggy Noonan, "The Old New York Won't Come Back," *Wall Street Journal*, February 25, 2021, https://www.wsj.com/articles/the-old-new-york-wont-come-back-11614296201.
12. Noonan, "The Old New York."
13. Douglas Belkin, "College Students Demand Coronavirus Refunds," *Wall Street Journal*, April 10, 2020, https://www.wsj.com/articles/college-students-demand-refunds-after-coronavirus-forces-classes-online-11586512803.
14. Belkin, "College Students Demand Refunds."
15. Anjelica Cappellino, J.D., "More Than 70 Universities Sued for Refunds Following COVID-19 Campus Closures," Expert Institute, April 27, 2022, https://www.expertinstitute.com/resources/insights/universities-sued-for-covid-19-refunds-following-campus-closures/.
16. Douglas Belkin and Melissa Korn, "To Fight Coronavirus, Colleges Sent Students Home. Now Will They Refund Tuition?" *Wall Street Journal*, March 19, 2020, https://www.wsj.com/articles/to-fight-coronavirus-colleges-sent-students-home-now-will-they-refund-tuition-11584625536.

17. Belkin and Korn, "To Fight Coronavirus."
18. Belkin and Korn, "To Fight Coronavirus."
19. Belkin and Korn, "To Fight Coronavirus."
20. Belkin and Korn, "To Fight Coronavirus."
21. Belkin and Korn, "To Fight Coronavirus."
22. Zig Ziglar quoted in Goodreads.com. Mr. Ziglar added some zing to a maxim by the Roman philosopher Seneca, ca. 60 CE, that "luck is what happens when preparation meets opportunity." Zig's quote is easier to remember, but you'll impress your new boss if you quote Seneca. Your call.

Chapter 9: Going to College Is a Risk-Free Endeavor

1. Salary data can be found at https://www.bls.gov/ooh/.
2. Melissa Korn, "Some 43% of College Grads Are Underemployed in First Job," *Wall Street Journal*, October 26, 2018, https://www.wsj.com/articles/study-offers-new-hope-for-english-majors-1540546200.
3. Korn, "College Grads Are Underemployed."
4. Korn, "College Grads Are Underemployed."
5. Korn, "College Grads Are Underemployed."
6. Korn, "College Grads Are Underemployed."
7. Jeffrey Selingo and Matt Sigelman, "The Crisis of Unemployed College Graduates," *Wall Street Journal*, February 4, 2021, https://www.wsj.com/articles/the-crisis-of-unemployed-college-graduates-11612454124.
8. Selingo and Sigelman, "Unemployed College Graduates."
9. Selingo and Sigelman, "Unemployed College Graduates."
10. *See* NCES graduation rates at https://nces.ed.gov/fastfacts/display.asp?id=40.
11. Tamara Hiler, Lanae Erickson Hatalsky, and Megan John, "Failing Our Kids," *Dallas Morning News*, July 10, 2016.
12. Specifically, based on the 2015–16 NPSAS, Pell Grant recipients in bachelor's degree programs are one-third more likely to borrow to pay for their education (84 percent vs. 51 percent), and therefore graduate with thousands more dollars of debt ($41,182 vs. $26,715). Among students in associate's degree programs, Pell Grant recipients are twice as likely to borrow (59.3 percent vs. 29.8 percent) and therefore graduate with substantially more debt ($19,847 vs. $14,171) than non–Pell Grant recipients. *See* NPSAS report at https://nces.ed.gov/pubs2018/2018466.pdf.

13. Hiler, Hatalsky, and John, "Failing Our Kids."
14. Hiler, Hatalsky, and John, "Failing Our Kids."
15. Hiler, Hatalsky, and John, "Failing Our Kids."
16. Hiler, Hatalsky, and John, "Failing Our Kids."
17. Hiler, Hatalsky, and John, "Failing Our Kids."
18. Hiler, Hatalsky, and John, "Failing Our Kids."
19. Hiler, Hatalsky, and John, "Failing Our Kids."
20. Hiler, Hatalsky, and John, "Failing Our Kids."
21. *See* the table of Federal Pell Grant Recipient rates at highly selective colleges at https://thecollegeinvestor.com/38195/what-is-undermatching/.
22. Hiler, Hatalsky, and John, "Failing Our Kids."
23. Hiler, Hatalsky, and John, "Failing Our Kids."
24. "Education and Socioeconomic Status," American Psychological Association, July 2017, https://www.apa.org/pi/ses/resources/publications/education.
25. *See* Mark Kantrowitz, *Who Graduates From College? Who Doesn't*, (Cerebly, Inc., 2021). The first chapter presents "Startling Statistics" that detail several key predictors.
26. Douglas Belkin, "Recent Grads Doubt College's Worth," *Wall Street Journal*, September 29, 2015, https://www.wsj.com/articles/recent-grads-doubt-colleges-worth-1443499440.
27. Belkin, "Recent Grads."
28. *See* National Postsecondary Student Aid Study (NPSAS) 2015–16 at https://nces.ed.gov/pubs2018/2018466.pdf.
29. Belkin, "Recent Grads."
30. Belkin, "Recent Grads."
31. Belkin, "Recent Grads."
32. The term "heavily indebted" requires further explanation. An objective definition of excessive debt would be "when the borrower's debt-service-to-income ratio—the percentage of monthly gross income devoted to repaying student loan debt—is 10 percent or more under a standard 10-year repayment plan." *See* http://www.studentaidpolicy.com/excessive-debt/Excessive-Debt-at-Graduation.pdf. For delays in achieving financial goals caused by student debt, *see* https://www.savingforcollege.com/article/student-loan-debt-causes-delays-in-achieving-major-financial-goals. "When student loan debt exceeds annual

income after graduation, college graduates are twice as likely to delay getting married, having children, and buying a home." Both articles are by Mark Kantrowitz. Used with permission.

33. Preston Cooper, "Is College Worth the Cost? That Depends," *Wall Street Journal*, November 5, 2021, https://www.wsj.com/articles/college-worth-cost-debt-major-computer-science-11636142138.
34. Cooper, "Is College Worth the Cost?"
35. Cooper, "Is College Worth the Cost?"
36. Cooper, "Is College Worth the Cost?" The opportunity cost analysis of "lost revenue while enrolled" rarely considers living expenses as offsetting the revenue that could have been earned. Without this element, the results can be exaggerated. To avoid that exaggeration, students can offset the figure with normal living expenses.
37. Cooper, "Is College Worth the Cost?"
38. Cooper, "Is College Worth the Cost?"
39. Cooper, "Is College Worth the Cost?"
40. Jon Marcus, "Will That College Degree Pay Off? A Look at Some of the Numbers," *Washington Post*, November 1, 2021, https://www.washingtonpost.com/education/2021/11/01/college-degree-value-major. The College Scorecard data is powerful, but it has some limitations owing to its minimum cell size of 30 for NCES data. Information provided by Mark Kantrowitz, December 15, 2022. Used with permission.
41. Marcus, "Will That College Degree Pay Off?"
42. *See* College Scorecard at https://collegescorecard.ed.gov. Click on the site, pull up the "Find the Right Fit" menu, and answer some intuitive questions to help you research and compare colleges based on their fields of study, costs, admissions, and results.
43. Marcus, "Will That College Degree Pay Off?"

Chapter 10: I'll Get a Job in My Field That Will Cover My Debt

1. This rule of thumb is elegant because it requires only a simple comparison of two figures, rather than a difficult calculation of speculative numbers. Mark Kantrowitz originated the rule at http://www.studentaidpolicy.com/excessive-debt/.

2. Lisa Bannon and Andrea Fuller, "USC Pushed a $115,000 Online Degree. Graduates Got Low Salaries, Huge Debts," *Wall Street Journal*, November 9, 2021, https://www.wsj.com/articles/usc-online-social-work-masters-11636435900.
3. Bannon and Fuller, "$115,000 Online Degree."
4. Information provided by Mark Kantrowitz, December 15, 2022. Used with permission.
5. Bannon and Fuller, "$115,000 Online Degree."
6. "Median Annual Earnings of US College Graduates from 1990 to 2020," Statista, https://www.statista.com/statistics/642041/average-wages-of-us-college-graduates/.
7. Indeed Editorial Team, "Average Salary for College Graduates," Indeed, February 22, 2021, https://www.indeed.com/career-advice/pay-salary/average-salary-for-college-graduates.
8. Indeed, "Average Salary."
9. Indeed, "Average Salary." The Indeed listing inexplicably omits Nursing, which has a starting salary in the $70,000 range as would be expected after the pandemic.
10. Note that the Education career field qualifies for Public Service Loan Forgiveness (PSLF) that forgives the remaining debt after 10 years (120 payments) in an Income-Driven Repayment plan.
11. Andrew Van Dam, "The Most Regretted (and Lowest-Paying) College Majors, " *Washington Post*, September 2, 2022, https://www.realcleareducation.com/2022/09/07/the_most-regretted_and_lowest-paying_college_majors_51823.html.
12. Andrew Van Dam, "College Majors with the Highest Unemployment Rates, and Other Reader Questions! " *Washington Post*, September 16, 2022, https://www.washingtonpost.com/business/2022/09/16/jobs-for-dropouts/.
13. Rebecca Smith and Andrea Fuller, "Some Professional Degrees Leave Students with High Debt but without High Salaries," *Wall Street Journal*, December 1, 2021, https://www.wsj.com/articles/some-professional-degrees-leave-students-with-high-debt-but-without-high-salaries-11638354602.
14. Smith and Fuller, "Professional Degrees."
15. Smith and Fuller, "Professional Degrees."

16. Smith and Fuller, "Professional Degrees."
17. Smith and Fuller, "Professional Degrees." Note that if the student used federal loans and repaid using Income-Driven Repayment, the remaining debt would be forgiven after 20 or 25 years of payments.
18. Richard Vedder and Justin Strehle, "The Diminishing Returns of a College Degree," *Wall Street Journal*, June 4, 2017, https://www.wsj.com/articles/the-diminishing-returns-of-a-college-degree-1496605241.
19. Vedder and Strehle, "Diminishing Returns."
20. Vedder and Strehle, "Diminishing Returns."
21. Vedder and Strehle, "Diminishing Returns." Payscale.com also publishes the College Return on Investment (ROI) report at https://www.payscale.com/college-roi, with breakout by college major at https://www.payscale.com/college-roi/major. For an excellent analysis of return on investment for private versus public schools, *see* "What It's Like Attending Stanford University?" on the Financial Samurai website at https://www.financialsamurai.com/what-its-like-attending-stanford-university/.
22. Vedder and Strehle, "Diminishing Returns." Be somewhat cautious with this sort of analysis, however, because the distribution of students by academic major can vary considerably. This becomes apparent when comparing liberal arts colleges on the highest average income after graduation. A school that is disproportionately focused on STEM would show a higher average income after graduation.
23. Vedder and Strehle, "Diminishing Returns."
24. Vedder and Strehle, "Diminishing Returns."
25. Vedder and Strehle, "Diminishing Returns."
26. Vedder and Strehle, "Diminishing Returns."
27. Vedder and Strehle, "Diminishing Returns."
28. Chuck McGee, "Evaluating Today's Expensive College Degree," *Wall Street Journal*, June 14, 2017, https://www.wsj.com/articles/SB1243084852605996448840458320573005154807.
29. McGee, "Today's Expensive College Degree."
30. Melissa Korn, "Some 43% of College Grads Are Underemployed in First Job," *Wall Street Journal*, October 26, 2018, https://www.wsj.com/articles/study-offers-new-hope-for-english-majors-1540546200.
31. Korn, "College Grads Are Underemployed."
32. Korn, "College Grads Are Underemployed."

Chapter 11: I Can Get a Loan without Collateral

1. The term "education–industrial complex" was first used in a 2012 article titled "Exploring the Dangers of the Education–Industrial Complex," based on an interview with Dr. Anthony Picciano regarding "for-profit" educational corporations published in *EvoLLLution* (sic), October 10, 2012, https://evolllution.com/opinions/audio-exploring-the-dangers-of-the-education-industrial-complex.
2. *Borrowed Future: How Student Loans Are Killing the American Dream*, directed by David DiCicco (Franklin, TN, Ramsey Solutions, 2021).
3. Anthony ONeal, *Debt-Free Degree: The Step-by-Step Guide to Getting Your Kid through College without Student Loans* (Franklin, TN: Ramsey Group, 2019).
4. DiCicco, *Borrowed Future.* The notions of "good debt" and "bad debt" as applied to college loans need to be carefully considered. Student debt serves a useful societal purpose, so in that sense it's "good debt." But nobody wants to be saddled with 20 years of debt repayment, so in that sense it's "bad debt." As discussed in the previous chapter, the rule of thumb is to acquire no more student debt than your first-year salary. That amount of debt could qualify as good debt, because it produced the degree to earn the salary to pay off the debt.
5. DiCicco, *Borrowed Future.*
6. DiCicco, *Borrowed Future.*
7. National Defense Education Act, 20 U.S.C. §§ 401-589, 1958.
8. Infoplease, "Educational Attainment by Race and Hispanic Origin, 1940–2014," https://www.infoplease.com/us/education/educational-attainment-race-and-hispanic-origin.
9. DiCicco, *Borrowed Future.*
10. Information provided by Mark Kantrowitz, December 15, 2022. Used with permission.
11. The Bankruptcy Abuse Prevention and Consumer Protection Act of 2005 (BAPCPA) (11 USC 101, et. seq, Pub. L. 109–8, 119 Stat. 23, enacted April 20, 2005) made several changes to the United States Bankruptcy Code. *See* next endnote.
12. The BAPCPA 2005 dealt with a number of technical issues. Student loans had already been non-dischargeable in bankruptcy for many years before the BAPCPA in 2005. But prior to the 2005 law, private loans had to be associated with a 501(c)(3) nonprofit for the lender to be protected from a bankruptcy discharge. One well known nonprofit that operated in this capacity was

the San Diego-based Training, Education, and Resource Institute (TERI). So BAPCPA eliminated the need for lenders of private student loans to be associated with a nonprofit organization to be protected from discharge in bankruptcy. The Bankruptcy Abuse Prevention and Consumer Protection Act of 2005 (BAPCPA) (11 USC 101, et. seq, Pub. L. 109–8, 119 Stat. 23, enacted April 20, 2005). Information provided by Mark Kantrowitz, December 15, 2022. Used with permission.

13. Sallie Mae split into two companies in 2014, one called Sallie Mae and one called Navient. Sallie Mae got the private student loan business while Navient got the business servicing federal student loans in the Direct Loan Program. Navient also retained Sallie Mae's Federal Family Education Loan (FFEL) Program that covered loans issued by private and state lenders but guaranteed by the federal government. Navient later bought Earnest, a lender of private student loans, in 2017. The agreement allowed Navient to make private student loans in its own name starting in 2019. Navient stopped servicing federal student loans in the Direct Loan Program in 2022. Their Direct Loan servicing portfolio was transferred to Aidvantage, a division of Maximus. Navient continues to own FFEL Program loans. Information provided by Mark Kantrowitz, December 15, 2022. Used with permission.

14. For a list of Direct Loan service providers *see* https://studentaid.gov/manage-loans/repayment/servicers.

15. Alex Mitchell, "College Is Broken: Reflections and Predictions," HackerNoon, Medium, April 10, 2019, https://medium.com/hackernoon/the-state-of-college-today-reflections-and-predictions-468600ccbd96.

16. Mitchell, "College Is Broken."

17. Mitchell, "College Is Broken."

18. Rebecca Ballhaus and Andrea Fuller, "Why Washington Won't Fix Student Debt Plans that Overload Families," *Wall Street Journal*, December 8, 2021, https://www.wsj.com/articles/college-university-student-debt-parent-grad-plus-loans-congress-school-borrowing-11638930489. There was bipartisan agreement on the new loan limits in the recent Congress, including capping the amount of PLUS loan borrowing for the first time. The legislation got stalled when a problem arose over Title IX between Democrats and Republicans on reauthorization of the Higher Education Act.

19. Ballhaus and Fuller, "Washington Won't Fix Student Debt."

20. Ballhaus and Fuller, "Washington Won't Fix Student Debt."

21. Ballhaus and Fuller, "Washington Won't Fix Student Debt."

22. Ballhaus and Fuller, "Washington Won't Fix Student Debt."

23. Ballhaus and Fuller, "Washington Won't Fix Student Debt."

24. Ballhaus and Fuller, "Washington Won't Fix Student Debt."

25. Melanie Hanson, "Student Loan Debt vs. Other Debts," Education Data Initiative, updated October 12, 2021, https://educationdata.org/student-loan-debt-vs-other-debts.

26. Ballhaus and Fuller, "Washington Won't Fix Student Debt."

27. *See* https://fsapartners.ed.gov/knowledge-center/library/electronic-announcements/2022-12-07/federal-student-aid-posts-quarterly-portfolio-reports-fsa-data-center. *See also* "Student Loan Default Has Serious Financial Consequences," Pew Charitable Trusts, April 7, 2020, https://www.pewtrusts.org/en/research-and-analysis/fact-sheets/2020/04/student-loan-default-has-serious-financial-consequences.

28. Ryan Lane, "Class of 2019 Borrowed Less, Report Finds," NerdWallet, October 12, 2020, https://www.sfgate.com/business/personalfinance/article/Class-of-2019-Borrowed-Less-Report-Finds-15640982.php.

29. Meredith Kolodner, "Stuck in It until I Die: Parents Get Buried by College Debt Too," The Hechinger Report, November 19, 2020, https://hechingerreport.org/parent-plus-loan-stuck-in-it-until-i-die-parents-get-buried-by-college-debt-too.

30. Danielle Douglas-Gabriel and John D. Harden, "The Faces of Student Debt," *Washington Post*, April 6, 2021, https://www.washingtonpost.com/education/2021/04/06/who-owes-student-debt.

31. Tawnell D. Hobbs and Andrea Fuller, "How Baylor Steered Lower-Income Parents to Debt They Couldn't Afford," *Wall Street Journal*, October 13, 2021, https://www.wsj.com/articles/baylor-university-college-debt-parent-plus-loans-11634138239.

32. It's not just Parent PLUS loans that are causing headaches in people over 50. It is also loans borrowed for their own education, whether for undergraduate school or graduate school. When a borrower goes into default, the loans persist, often into retirement. The effect is cumulative, often ending only when the borrower dies. Information provided by Mark Kantrowitz, December 15, 2022. Used with permission.

33. Hobbs and Fuller, "Debt They Couldn't Afford."

34. Hobbs and Fuller, "Debt They Couldn't Afford."

35. According to the GAO report, about a third of borrowers 65 and older are in default, while about half of borrowers 75 and older are in default. *See* https://www.gao.gov/assets/gao-17-45-highlights.pdf.

36. Hua Hsu, "Student Debt Is Transforming the American Family," *New Yorker*, September 2, 2019, https://www.newyorker.com/magazine/2019/09/09/student-debt-is-transforming-the-american-family. The article cites Caitlin Zaloom's book *Indebted: How Families Make College Work at Any Cost* (Princeton University Press, May 4, 2021).

37. Hsu, "Student Debt."

38. Hsu, "Student Debt."

39. Hsu, "Student Debt."

40. Hsu, "Student Debt."

41. Hsu, "Student Debt."

42. Hsu, "Student Debt."

Chapter 12: I Can Discharge My College Debt in Bankruptcy

1. *See* the Bankruptcy Code relating to discharge of student debt at 11 U.S.C. § 523(a)(8). The Bankruptcy Abuse Prevention and Consumer Protection Act of 2005 was a refinement on existing bankruptcy law as discussed in chapter 11. *See also* http://www.studentaidpolicy.com/fa/20070814pslFICOdistribution.pdf.

2. Richard Pallardy, "History of Student Loans: Bankruptcy Discharge," Saving for College Website, March 18, 2021, https://www.savingforcollege.com/article/history-of-student-loans-bankruptcy-discharge. This excellent article summarizes the evolution of the bankruptcy code and the forces that formed it.

3. Pallardy, "History of Student Loans."

4. *See* GAO Report at https://www.gao.gov/assets/hrd-77-83.pdf.

5. *See* Education Amendments of 1976 at https://www.govinfo.gov/content/pkg/STATUTE-90/pdf/STATUTE-90-Pg2081.pdf.

6. Pallardy, "History of Student Loans."

7. *See* https://www.govinfo.gov/content/pkg/STATUTE-92/pdf/STATUTE-92-Pg2549.pdf.

8. Mark Kantrowitz, "How to Bankrupt Your Student Loans," *Forbes*, November 24, 2020, https://www.forbes.com/sites/markkantrowitz/2020/11/24/how-to-bankrupt-your-student-loans/?sh=745fd6bc5960.

9. Kantrowitz, "How to Bankrupt Your Student Loans."

10. In addition to the statutes discussed in the text, several legislative steps were involved in the march toward eliminating the bankruptcy option for student debt:

    In 1979, an amendment clarified that the five-year limit applied to loans backed " . . . in whole or in part by a governmental unit or a nonprofit institution of higher education." *See* https://www.govinfo.gov/content/pkg/STATUTE-93/pdf/STATUTE-93-Pg387.pdf.

    In 1984, a set of bankruptcy amendments further tightened the rules on bankruptcy discharge by dropping "of higher education" from the wording of the legislation. *See* Bankruptcy Amendments and Federal Judgeship Act of 1984 at https://www.govinfo.gov/content/pkg/STATUTE-98/pdf/STATUTE-98-Pg333.pdf. This increased the restrictions on bankruptcy discharge of student loans to now include private loans backed by nonprofit institutions, rather than just government loans.

    In 1990, the Crime Control Act extended the period before which bankruptcy proceedings could commence to seven years after repayment began. *See* https://www.congress.gov/bill/101st-congress/senate-bill/3266. *See also* Richard Pallardy, "History of Student Loans: Bankruptcy Discharge," Saving for College Website, March 18, 2021, https://www.savingforcollege.com/article/history-of-student-loans-bankruptcy-discharge.

11. Wolf Richter, "Taxpayers Face $435 Billion in Student-Loan Losses, Already Baked in: Leaked Education-Department Study," Wolfstreet.com, November 22, 2020, https://wolfstreet.com/2020/11/22/taxpayers-face-435-billion-in-student-loan-losses-already-baked-in-department-of-education-study/.

12. Kantrowitz, "How to Bankrupt Your Student Loans."

13. The Brunner test was first articulated in the case of *Brunner v. New York State Higher Education Services Corp.*, 831 F.2d 395 (1987) decided by the Second Circuit of the United States Court of Appeals in Albany, NY. The court applied a three-prong test to determine if a college debt should be discharged in bankruptcy. Other courts use the totality of circumstances test, which is similar to the Brunner test, but omits the third prong. The totality of circumstances test has been adopted by the 8th Circuit, while the Brunner test has been adopted by the 2nd, 3rd, 4th, 5th, 6th, 7th, 9th, 10th, and 11th Circuits. *See* https://www.forbes.com/sites/markkantrowitz/2020/11/24/how-to-bankrupt-your-student-loans/.

14. Michon, Kathleen, “Student Loans in Bankruptcy: The Brunner Test,” The Bankruptcy Site, Nolo, accessed February 3, 2022, https://www.thebankruptcysite.org/resources/bankruptcy/debt-relief/student-loans-bankruptcy-the-brunner-test.

15. Preston Mueller, “The Non-Dischargeability of Private Student Loans: A Looming Financial Crisis?” *Emory Bankr. Dev. J.* 229 (2015), available at https://scholarlycommons.law.emory.edu/ebdj/vol32/iss1/11.

16. Mueller, “The Non-Dischargeability of Private Student Loans.”

17. Mueller, “The Non-Dischargeability of Private Student Loans.”

18. Mueller, “The Non-Dischargeability of Private Student Loans.”

19. *See* the College Board’s “Trends in Student Aid” data, row 29 of Table 2 at https://research.collegeboard.org/media/xlsx/trends-student-aid-excel-data-2022.xlsx. The allocation of dollars among federal and private student loan programs bears discussion. Of the $1.6345 trillion in *federal* student loans outstanding, only $207.8 billion is in the Family Federal Education Loan program (FFELP). Of that, $78.3 billion is held by the US Department of Education in so-called ECASLA loans (Ensuring Continued Access to Student Loans Act) which provided DOE new authority to purchase FFELP loans. So, the commercially held FFELP loans total only about $129.5 billion, or 7.9 percent of the total. Information provided by Mark Kantrowitz, December 15, 2022. Used with permission.

20. Elan Amir, Jared Teslow, and Christopher Borders, “The MeasureOne Private Student Loan Report,” MeasureOne, December 21, 2021, https://f.hubspotusercontent00.net/hubfs/6171800/assets/downloads/MeasureOne%20Private%20Student%20Loan%20Report%20Q1%202021.pdf.

21. Amir, Teslow, and Borders, “The MeasureOne Private Student Loan Report.”

22. The offset of income tax refunds is through the Treasury Offset Program (TOP). *See* https://fiscal.treasury.gov/top/.

23. “Social Security Offsets: Improvements to Program Design Could Better Assist Older Student Borrowers with Obtaining Permitted Relief,” US Government Accountability Office, December 19, 2016, https://www.gao.gov/products/gao-17-45.

24. Robert E. Nugent, “Think Twice before Taking Large Student Loans,” *Wall Street Journal*, December 14, 2021, https://www.wsj.com/articles/college-loans-student-debt-parents-university-11639433330.

25. Nugent, "Think Twice."
26. Nugent, "Think Twice."
27. Josh Mitchell, "The US Makes It Easy for Parents to Get College Loans—Repaying Them Is Another Story," *Wall Street Journal*, April 24, 2017, https://www.wsj.com/articles/the-u-s-makes-it-easy-for-parents-to-get-college-loansrepaying-them-is-another-story-1493047388.
28. Mitchell, "The US Makes It Easy."
29. Mitchell, "The US Makes It Easy."
30. Credit scores were obtained for federal loans after the fact in the FFEL Program when the lenders sought to securitize the loans. At this point in their careers, most students have a thin or nonexistent credit history. Information provided by Mark Kantrowitz, December 15, 2022. Used with permission.
31. Mitchell, "The US Makes It Easy."
32. Mitchell, "The US Makes It Easy."
33. Mitchell, "The US Makes It Easy."
34. Mitchell, "The US Makes It Easy."
35. Mitchell, "The US Makes It Easy."
36. Rebecca Safier, "Can Student Loan Debt Eat up Your Social Security Benefits?," Student Loan Hero, January 25, 2021, https://studentloanhero.com/featured/social-security-payments-for-student-loans.
37. Congressional Budget Office, Publication 58494, "Costs of Suspending Student Loan Payments and Cancelling Debt," September 22, 2022, https://www.cbo.gov/publication/58494.
38. The new Income-Driven Repayment (IDR) plan will be implemented through a US Department of Education regulatory change, which will make it less likely to be successfully challenged in court than the president's proposed student loan forgiveness of $10,000. Opponents know that it will survive court challenge if the Biden administration follows proper procedures for regulatory change under the Administrative Procedures Act, and that it can't be blocked under the Congressional Review Act because there is split control of Congress. Accordingly, the new Income-Driven Repayment plan has a good chance to survive scrutiny and be implemented. Information provided by Mark Kantrowitz, December 15, 2022. Used with permission.
39. For a comprehensive list of other student loan forgiveness programs, *see* https://studentaid.gov/manage-loans/forgiveness-cancellation.

40. Some are concerned that negative effects of the IDR proposal will arise because student borrowers will be asked to repay only a fraction of their debt amount while the remainder will be treated like a grant. A grant on such a massive scale could have a number of unforeseen consequences. For a discussion of possible adverse policy ramifications from this new IDR program including budget cost, tuition inflation, and potential for abuse, *see* a thought-provoking Brookings article by Adam Looney, titled "Biden's Income-Driven Repayment Plan Would Turn Student Loans into Untargeted Grants," September 15, 2022, at https://www.brookings.edu/opinions/bidens-income-driven-repayment-plan-would-turn-student-loans-into-untargeted-grants/.
41. Looney, "Biden's Income-Driven Repayment Plan."

Conclusion

1. Josh Mitchell, "A Crimson Tide of Debt," *The Atlantic*, August 1, 2021, https://www.theatlantic.com/ideas/archive/2021/08/public-universities-debt/619546.
2. Alex Mitchell, "College Is Broken: Reflections and Predictions," HackerNoon, Medium, April 10, 2019, https://medium.com/hackernoon/the-state-of-college-today-reflections-and-predictions-468600ccbd96.
3. Mitchell, "College Is Broken."
4. Mitchell, "College Is Broken."
5. Mitchell, "College Is Broken."
6. Mitchell, "College Is Broken." However, a recent ruling by the Consumer Financial Protection Bureau (CFPB) and another by the US Department of Education found that ISAs are simply another form of debt. Since Truth in Lending Act (TILA) disclosures apply, ISAs won't have any special privileges and marketers can no longer claim they aren't loans. They will have a role to play, but be wary of the hype that they are the end of student loans. Information provided by Mark Kantrowitz, December 15, 2022. Used with permission.
7. Mitchell, "College Is Broken."
8. In the short term, however, contrary to this prediction, enrollment at community colleges shrank more than any other type of college during the pandemic. *See* https://nscresearchcenter.org/current-term-enrollment-estimates/. With the pandemic winding down, it will be interesting to see if enrollment at community colleges will rise again.
9. Mitchell, "College Is Broken."

10. Mitchell, "College Is Broken."

11. Mitchell, "College Is Broken."

12. Mitchell, "College Is Broken."

13. Doug Lederman, "The Number of Colleges Continues to Shrink," Inside Higher Ed, August 2, 2021, https://www.insidehighered.com/news/2021/08/02/number-colleges-shrinks-again-including-publics-and-private-nonprofits.

14. Lederman, "The Number of Colleges Continues to Shrink."

15. Scott L. Wyatt and Allen C. Guelzo, "College Doesn't Need to Take Four Years," *Wall Street Journal*, February 3, 2023, https://www.wsj.com/articles/college-doesnt-need-to-take-four-year-higher-educaion-credentials-university-degree-training-credits-students-116675370630.

16. Lauren Day, "Big Island Man Pays Off $50k in Student Loan Debt in One Year," Khon2, updated December 16, 2020, https://www.khon2.com/coronavirus/big-island-man-pays-off-50k-in-student-loan-debt-in-one-year.

17. Day, "Big Island Man Pays Off $50k."

18. Day, "Big Island Man Pays Off $50k."

19. Author's recollection from a 2012 Appalachian Trail hike. The hiker referred to herself by her trail name of "Happy Feet."

Resources for Further Reading

1. Malcolm Gladwell, "Lord of the Rankings," *Revisionist History* podcast, July 1, 2021, https://www.pushkin.fm/podcasts/revisionist-history/lord-of-the-rankings.

2. Christopher L. Eisgruber, "I Lead America's Top-ranked University. Here's Why These Rankings Are a Problem," *Washington Post*, October 21, 2021, https://www.washingtonpost.com/opinions/2021/10/21/i-lead-americas-top-ranked-university-heres-why-these-rankings-are-problem/.

3. Eisgruber, "I Lead America's Top-Ranked University."

4. Josh Zumbrun, "Rebellion Over College Rankings Seems Likely to Fail," *Wall Street Journal*, January 28–29, 2023, p. A2, https://www.wsj.com/articles/rebellion-over-college-rankings-seems-likely-to-fail-11674794247.

5. Zumbrun, "Rebellion Over College Rankings Seems Likely to Fail."

6. Eisgruber, "I Lead America's Top-Ranked University."

7. Colin Driver interview by Jeff Selingo, "When Podunk U. Ranked No. 1," LinkedIn NEXT newsletter, September 18, 2022, https://www.linkedin.com/pulse/when-podunk-u-ranked-1-jeff-selingo/?trk=pulse-article. For another thought-provoking article by Jeff Selingo on trends in education, *see* "What's Next for Higher Ed in 2023," on LinkedIn, January 6, 2023.

Credits

Continued from the copyright page

National Collegiate Athletic Association (NCAA). Graphic entitled: "Estimated Probability of Competing in College Athletics" located at: https://www.ncaa.org/sports/2015/3/2/estimated-probability-of-competing-in-college-athletics.aspx. Copyright © 2015. Reproduced by permission of National Collegiate Athletic Association.

Scholarship Stats. Athletic Scholarship Charts from Scholarship Stats. https://scholarshipstats.com/ncaalimits. Copyright © 2022. All rights reserved. Reproduced by permission.

Sara Goldrick-Rab. From "The Real Price of College" by Sara Goldrick-Rab and Nancy Kendall. Copyright © 2016 by Sara Goldrick-Rab and Nancy Kendall. Reproduced by permission.

The Wall Street Journal. From "Some 43% of. College Grads Are Underemployed in First Job" by Melissa Korn. Reprinted with permission of *The Wall Street Journal.* Copyright © 2018. Dow Jones & Company, Inc. All Rights Reserved Worldwide. License number 5421491439474.

The Wall Street Journal. From "Recent Grads Doubt College's Worth" by Douglas Belkin. Reprinted with permission of *The Wall Street Journal.* Copyright © 2015. Dow Jones & Company, Inc. All Rights Reserved. Worldwide. License number 5421500462237.

The Wall Street Journal. From "The U.S. Makes It Easy for Parents to Get College Loans" by Josh Mitchell. Reprinted with permission of *The Wall Street Journal.* Copyright © 2017. Dow Jones & Company, Inc. All Rights Reserved. Worldwide. License number 5421501111689.

The Wall Street Journal. From "Is College Worth the Cost?" by Preston Cooper. Reprinted with permission of *The Wall Street Journal.* Copyright © 2021. Dow Jones & Company, Inc. All Rights Reserved. Worldwide. License number 5421510323093.

The Wall Street Journal. From "The Diminishing Returns of a College Degree" by Richard Vedder and Justin Strebble. Reprinted with permission of *The Wall Street Journal.* Copyright © 2017. Dow Jones & Company, Inc. All Rights Reserved. Worldwide. License number 5421511314868.

The Wall Street Journal. From "Five Reasons Why Congress Won't Tackle Student Debt" by Rebecca Ballhaus and Andrea Fuller. Reprinted with permission of *The Wall Street Journal.* Copyright © 2021 Dow Jones & Company, Inc. All Rights Reserved. Worldwide. License number 5421510991938.

About the Author

DAVID F. SHUTLER has had careers in the military, business, and law. Graduating with a bachelor's degree in English from Duke, a juris doctor from Penn State Dickinson Law, and a master of business administration from University of Nebraska, he served as a lawyer in the US Air Force before retiring as a colonel in 1999. After retiring, he worked as a business developer for a large corporation, ran a private law practice, and founded a construction company focused on saving energy. Over his career, he has launched a data analytics company, a candy manufacturing company, and a commercial real estate venture. Dave's three sons live with their families on the East and West coasts. He lives a plane ride away in Dallas with his wife, Katie.